Set Sail and Sing

NATIONAL ASSOCIATION OF
TEACHERS
of **SINGING**
———★★★———

NATIONAL ASSOCIATION OF TEACHERS OF SINGING BOOKS

The National Association of Teachers of Singing (NATS) publishes high-quality books for singers, teachers, and other voice professionals. NATS books provide valuable and trusted resources that enhance singing pedagogy and support the important work of all singing professionals.
NATS is the leading professional organization devoted to the science and art of singing.

ABOUT THE NATIONAL ASSOCIATION OF TEACHERS OF SINGING

Founded in 1944, the National Association of Teachers of Singing (NATS) is the world's largest professional association of voice teachers and collaborative pianists with more than seven thousand members in the United States, Canada, and more than thirty-five other countries. Whether working in independent studios, community schools, elementary and secondary schools, higher education, or the medical field, NATS members represent the diversity of today's music landscape, teaching in all musical styles. For more information, visit NATS.org.

RECENTLY PUBLISHED NATS BOOKS

Practical Vocal Acoustics: Pedagogic Applications for Teachers and Singers by *Kenneth W. Bozeman*

The Functional Unity of the Singing Voice, Second Edition Expanded by *Barbara M. Doscher*

Trauma and the Voice: A Guide for Singers, Teachers, and Other Practitioners edited by *Emily Jaworski Koriath*

The Singing Book, Fourth Edition by Cynthia Vaughn and Meribeth Dayme edited by *Matthew Hoch*

Unlocking Meaning in Art Song: A Singer's Guide to Practical Analysis Using Schubert Songs by *Beverly Stein*

Student-Centered Voice Pedagogy: Working with Students toward Developing Artistry, Authenticity, and Autonomy edited by *Jeanne Goffi-Fynn and Matthew Hoch*

Voices of Influence: Exploring the Journey of a Teacher and Student in the Voice Studio by *Brian Manternach*

Practical Vocal Acoustics: Pedagogic Applications for Teachers and Singers, Second Edition by *Kenneth W. Bozeman*

Everyday Voice Care: The Wellness Guide for Singers, Actors, and Talkers, Second Edition by *Joanna Cazden*

Set Sail and Sing: A Singer's Guide to Cruise Ship Careers and Performance by *Tanya C. Roberts*

Set Sail and Sing

A Singer's Guide to Cruise Ship Careers and Performance

Tanya C. Roberts

BLOOMSBURY ACADEMIC
NEW YORK • LONDON • OXFORD • NEW DELHI • SYDNEY

BLOOMSBURY ACADEMIC
Bloomsbury Publishing Inc, 1359 Broadway, New York, NY 10018, USA
Bloomsbury Publishing Plc, 50 Bedford Square, London, WC1B 3DP, UK
Bloomsbury Publishing Ireland, 29 Earlsfort Terrace, Dublin 2, D02 AY28, Ireland

BLOOMSBURY, BLOOMSBURY ACADEMIC, and the Diana logo are
trademarks of Bloomsbury Publishing Plc.

First published in the United States of America 2026.

A catalog record for this book is available from the Library of Congress.

ISBN: HB: 979-8-216-36850-2
         PB: 979-8-216-36851-9
       ePDF: 979-8-216-36852-6
      eBook: 979-8-216-36853-3

Series: National Association of Teachers of Singing Books

Typeset by Integra Software Services Pvt. Ltd.
Printed and bound in the United States of America.

For product-safety-related questions, contact productsafety@bloomsbury.com.

To find out more about our authors and books, visit www.bloomsbury.com
and sign up for our newsletters.

For the crew.

CONTENTS

LIST OF FIGURES

LIST OF TABLES

ACKNOWLEDGMENTS

First off, thank *you* for even reading this page. I've been guilty of skipping over acknowledgments in books myself, so the fact that you're here means a great deal.

This book was born out of a desire to share something that I wish I had known much earlier in my career: that ships could provide full-time singing careers as well as meaningful ways to see the world. Performing at sea was an option that I didn't discover until I was ten years into my career as a singer—and there was no single place to find all the information I needed. If you want to sing at sea, the path can feel so opaque, piecemealed across tips from a friend, snippets on social media, secondhand stories from another singer, and the occasional buried blog. This book exists to change that, to make the opportunities visible, and to help singers consider this path early in their professional lives.

Along the way, I've had extraordinary support. My husband, Ned Hanlon, has been my anchor through it all—a constant source of encouragement, stability, and love.

Over a glass of wine in Los Angeles, Daniel Neer casually suggested I pitch this book to NATS instead of quietly self-publishing. That conversation became the ripple that grew into a wave.

I owe my cruise ship career to Graham Fandrei, who selected me as the sole soprano for the inaugural Opera on the High Seas cast—and who graciously tolerated the 100-page cast manual I wrote and my well-intentioned refusal of letting any new hires sign their contracts until after they'd read them. Eric De Gray, my first cruise director, taught me what it truly means to work at sea, while Cruise Director Ernest Marchain championed my transition into the administrative side of ships. I'm also grateful to Signe Bjorndal, retired director of entertainment for Azamara, who believed in my ability to move up from cast vocalist to cruise director amid a raging pandemic.

I'm deeply grateful to my interviewees—Amanda Poulson, Branden James, James Clark, and Carl Wishneusky—for speaking so openly about their lives and careers.

My early readers—Emily Hanlon, Stoyan Dobrev, and Ned—offered invaluable insight with the perfect mix of encouragement and honest critique.

This book also carries the imprints of all the places I wrote it. The idea first sparked in an Alfama apartment in Lisbon. The original proposal and early chapters took shape on the Azamara *Onward* while sailing in Oceania. A good portion was drafted while gazing out over the Black Sea from a villa in Bulgaria—with heartfelt thanks to Stoyan for hosting me and offering endless support. Many pages came to life at my kitchen table in my beloved Upper West Side apartment. Creative momentum was fueled in coworking spaces—shout-out to Wollow in Varna and Beahive in Beacon for the comfy chairs and strong coffee. And to the opera professionals around the globe who welcomed me to speak to their singers about shipboard careers while this book was in motion—Stefan Gordon at the Tokyo Opera Studio, Kalin Tchonev at Varna International, and James Marvel at Florida State University—your enthusiasm reinforced my belief that singers are hungry for this information.

To the publishing team who brought this book into being: Matthew Hoch at NATS, for taking a chance on a completely unknown first-time author; Michael Tan at Bloomsbury, for being so kind and making the process far less daunting than I imagined; Anne Hunt, for expertly overseeing the page proofs process with clarity and precision; and Erica Tape, for treating my baby with such care in editing.

Finally, this is for all singers—whether they stand on a stage, in a booth, or in the corner of a lounge—who follow the call of their art. A career in music takes courage, and what a privilege it is to do what you love, to give voice to your soul, and to carry your song into the world. May you always find an audience—somewhere, anywhere—ready to listen, whether on land or at sea.

Introduction: Why Singers Should Consider Cruise Ships

For singers looking to build a dynamic and rewarding career, the high seas offer a world of opportunity. Cruise ship entertainment has become a major part of modern-day travel, creating a demand for skilled vocalists who can captivate audiences night after night. Whether you're a classically trained opera singer, a powerhouse belter, a contemporary pop force, or a jazz maven, you'll find cruise ships provide a unique stage where artistry and adventure intersect.

I didn't set out to build a career at sea, but once I did, it changed my entire life. Over the past seven years, I've performed hundreds of shows at sea, sailed to all seven continents, and worked in every major singing capacity onboard, from production cast vocalist to guest entertainer, while developing a deep understanding of cruise ship entertainment. I've served as a cruise director and entertainment manager, worked behind the scenes in casting and show development, and coached countless performers on how to launch sustainable careers at sea. I wrote this book because so much of this world has gone undocumented, and because I believe cruise ships offer a uniquely rewarding path for singers of all backgrounds and training.

In recent decades, the cruise industry has grown exponentially, transforming from an exclusive experience for the elite into an accessible and diverse industry, catering to tens of millions of passengers annually. This growth has fueled the demand for high-quality entertainment, making cruise ships an expanding career path for singers. According to industry body Cruise Lines International Association, entertainment is one of the most utilized features on cruises, with 70 percent of cruise ship passengers reporting that they attend at least one entertainment offering while onboard.[1]

The expansion of the cruise industry has been remarkable. In 1970, only about 500,000 passengers set sail on cruise vacations.[2] By 2023, that number had skyrocketed to over 31 million.[3] Major cruise lines such as Royal Caribbean, Carnival, and Norwegian have continuously introduced larger and larger ships with increasingly elaborate entertainment options.[4] Meanwhile, luxury and expedition lines like Azamara and Viking have carved out their own niche, emphasizing enrichment and destination-based experiences in which entertainment is curated to align with cultural and thematic elements of each voyage.[5]

The surge in popularity has been driven by several factors. Advances in shipbuilding technology have allowed for the creation of vessels that rival world-class hotels, featuring expansive theaters, sophisticated sound and lighting systems, and immersive entertainment venues.[6] Additionally, the growing accessibility of cruising—through competitive pricing, global itineraries, and a broader range of onboard experiences—has attracted a wider demographic of travelers, all of whom demand live entertainment as part of their voyage.[7]

With this growth comes an ever-expanding array of opportunities for vocalists. Cruise lines employ singers in a variety of roles, from mainstage production cast members to solo lounge performers to specialty guest entertainers to cruise directors. The demand for live instrumental music has also increased, with bands, jazz trios, and classical ensembles becoming standard offerings across many fleets.[8]

Beyond frequent performance opportunities, a career at sea offers numerous advantages. Singers can travel the world while living alongside diverse and multicultural crews, providing significant opportunities for personal growth and cultural awareness. The structured nature of cruise contracts provides financial stability, including accommodations, meals, and health care, allowing performers to save money while building their careers.[9] Furthermore, working on a cruise ship can foster connections with fellow performers, musicians, and industry professionals, opening doors to future opportunities both on land and at sea.

However, while the lifestyle can be exciting and fulfilling, it is not without its challenges. Long contracts, time away from friends and family, and the unique demands of performing at sea require adaptability, professionalism, and stamina. These challenges will be discussed later in this chapter and throughout the book.

Shifting Traditional Performance Paths for Singers

While the cruise industry has experienced substantial growth, most traditional performance avenues for singers in the United States have stagnated or seen contraction due to economic pressures, changing audience habits, and shifts in the entertainment landscape. Both nonprofit and for-profit theaters, concert halls, and independent live music venues have faced significant challenges, leading to fewer opportunities for professional singers.

The nonprofit performing arts sector has struggled financially in recent decades. The financial pressures on opera houses and symphony orchestras have led to significant retrenchment with cuts to the number of performances and production sizes. Sadly, many companies have shuttered entirely. Between 2023 and 2024 alone, nearly ten opera companies in the United States either closed or significantly reduced their programming due to declining ticket sales, shrinking donor support, and diminishing government support.[10] In 2013, the New York City Opera, long considered the people's opera, declared bankruptcy after seventy years.[11] Even the venerable Metropolitan Opera has faced financial instability, relying on millions of dollars of emergency funding from its own endowment to survive recent seasons.[12]

Nonprofit regional theaters have also been impacted, citing declining attendance and funding. According to *The New York Times*, a survey of seventy-two regional theaters revealed a 20 percent decrease in the number of productions in upcoming seasons compared to pre-pandemic levels, with two to three organizations closing their doors on a monthly basis.[13] Increased difficulty in finding funding from public and private sources has exacerbated issues caused by the concerning trend of declining audience numbers. When adjusted for inflation, the budget of the National Endowment for the Arts was more than twice the size in 1992 than it was in 2019.[14]

Live music venues, from jazz clubs to cabarets, have also been affected. The rise of digital streaming has reshaped how audiences consume music, reducing the demand for in-person performances. Small and midsize venues, crucial to emerging artists, have faced closures due to rising rent costs and changing entertainment preferences. In contrast, larger concert tours and major festivals have thrived, but these opportunities are often limited to established artists with significant industry backing.[15]

While many land-based performing arts organizations are still facing serious economic fallout in the wake of the COVID-19 pandemic, the cruise industry has demonstrated a robust post-pandemic recovery, creating a surge in opportunities for performers at sea. In 2028, global cruise passenger volume is projected to reach 41.9 million, representing a 21.1 percent increase over 2024 and a 41.1 percent increase over 2019.[16] This resurgence is driven by pent-up consumer demand and enhanced health and safety protocols leading cruise lines to expand their entertainment offerings and, consequently, their need for skilled performers.

One of the key reasons cruise ships remain a stable employment option is their continual need to provide live entertainment across their fleets. Unlike regional

Figure I.1 Author at a White Night deck party in the Norwegian fjords. Photograph by Ned Hanlon.

theaters or concert venues that may struggle with fluctuating ticket sales, cruise ships operate on a fixed revenue model, meaning that entertainment budgets are built into their business structure.[17] This provides greater job security for performers compared to other live performance industries, which can be heavily influenced by seasonal demand or economic downturns.

Cruise lines seek to differentiate themselves from competitors through various means, including price points, itineraries, onboard atmospheres, and target guest demographics. Vessels tailor their entertainment options to their needs, leading to increased variety and scope of entertainment. From full-scale musical productions to intimate lounge performances, ships' programming is constantly developing, requiring a steady influx of talented singers. This consistent demand means that vocalists can find work, often with opportunities for contract renewals or promotions within a company.[18] As long as the cruise industry continues to thrive, singers who embrace the unique challenges of life at sea can benefit from a stable career path that allows them to perform regularly while enjoying the perks of travel and financial stability.

This book is drawn from my firsthand experience and the insights of colleagues I've worked with around the world. While cruise ship entertainment is an international industry, this book is written from a primarily North American perspective—as I am a Canadian-American author, my frame of reference reflects the structure and culture of cruise lines headquartered in the United States, many of which have set the global standard for onboard entertainment. Since cruise ship entertainment has been underrepresented in published scholarship until now, many details do not have formal citations simply because they've never been documented.

Who This Book Is For

This book serves as a comprehensive guide for singers considering anything from short-term work to a lifelong career in the cruise industry. It is designed for aspiring performers who are curious about working at sea, seasoned professionals looking for new opportunities, and educators or mentors looking for information to help guide singers in their career paths. If you are a vocalist who loves to perform, desires financial stability, and dreams of traveling the world while doing what you love, this book is for you. As you will learn, the varied musical styles found on cruise ships provide opportunities for singers of all kinds. Throughout the book, we will explore performances of all kinds, ranging from pop and rock to jazz, opera, and musical theater. There are places for singers of all musical genres at sea.

Many young performers fresh out of college or conservatory find themselves wondering how to turn their training into a sustainable career. Cruise ship contracts offer a potential launchpad, providing steady compensation, performance experience, networking opportunities, and a chance to develop real-world professionalism in a structured environment. Those who have already spent years in the entertainment industry may also find new possibilities on cruise ships, where they can apply their skills in a unique setting while benefiting from stable employment and travel opportunities.

For freelance singers who are accustomed to piecing together gigs to make ends meet, cruise ship work offers stability that can be difficult to find on land. The financial benefits of working at sea—including paid accommodations, meals, and health care—allow performers to save money while avoiding working second or even third jobs to make ends meet. Singers who have performed in theme parks, touring productions, or corporate entertainment will find that cruise ships present many of the same benefits, but with the added appeal of global travel.

Educators, vocal coaches, and mentors who work with young singers will also benefit from this book, gaining insights into a career path that is often overlooked in traditional music education. By understanding the opportunities and challenges of singing at sea, they can better guide their students toward careers that align with students' talents and aspirations.

As you read this book, it is important to note that the nature of cruise ship work will not appeal to everyone. The lifestyle can be demanding, and some find that the structured environment impedes their desire for independence and freedom. Cruise ship singers must adhere to strict schedules, follow company policies based on nautical hierarchy, and sometimes perform multiple shows per night, all while adjusting to life in a confined space with limited personal privacy. Nonetheless, for many, the adventure, performance opportunities, and exposure to a wealth of international people and cultures can make performing at sea a singularly rewarding experience unlike any other in the entertainment industry.

How to Read This Book

Throughout this book, I've aimed to give you a clear, systematic guide to everything you need to know in order to sing at sea. The chapters follow a natural progression, starting with an introduction to the cruise entertainment landscape (seascape?), then exploring how to learn more about it, moving on to how to prepare for it, and finally guiding you through what it's like to be part of it. As you'll see, there are several career tracks you can follow as a cruise ship singer, and in each chapter, I'll outline how the information applies to each path. While these tracks differ, there's also a fair amount of overlap, so you may notice some repetition. Think of it as reinforcement rather than redundancy; it's all in service of giving you the most complete picture possible.

The most effective way to read this book is straight through, from cover to cover. But if you'd rather focus on a particular type of cruise ship entertainment, you can jump to the sections that are most relevant to you. For example, if you're curious about being a guest entertainer, you'll find a dedicated section in each chapter with targeted information. So, feel free to skip what doesn't apply to your interests—I won't be the least bit offended. After all, I wrote this book for you!

In the chapters ahead, we will explore the realities of singing at sea, the challenges and rewards of various positions, the skills required to succeed, and the steps needed to secure a contract. But first, let's take a closer look at how cruise ship entertainment differs from land-based gigs.

Notes

1   Rebecca Gibson, "Millennials Leading the Charge for Luxury Cruising, Says CLIA," *Cruise & Ferry*, January 29, 2018, https://www.cruiseandferry.net/articles/millennials-leading-the-charge-for-luxury-cruising-says-clia.

2   Tamara Hardingham-Gill, "'The Love Boat': How a TV Show Transformed the Cruise Industry," *CNN*, February 14, 2025, https://edition.cnn.com/travel/the-love-boat-how-a-tv-show-transformed-cruise-industry/index.html.

3   Cruise Lines International Association, "State of the Cruise Industry Report," April 9, 2024, https://cruising.org/sites/default/files/2025-03/2024%20State%20of%20the%20Cruise%20Industry%20Report_updated%20050824_Web.pdf.

4   Brittany Chang, "I've Sailed on Royal Caribbean, Carnival, and Norwegian Ships. Here's Which Was My Favorite—and How to Choose the Right Cruise for You," *Business Insider*, November 16, 2024, https://www.businessinsider.com/royal-caribbean-vs-carnival-norwegian-cruises-compared-review-2024-11.

5   Alissa Grisler, "Best Luxury Cruise Lines," *U.S. News & World Report*, updated November 18, 2024, https://travel.usnews.com/cruises/best-cruise-lines.

6   Jill Sayles, "Discover the World's Most Beautiful Cruise Ships That Rival Five-Star Hotels," *MSN*, accessed February 21, 2025, https://www.msn.com/en-us/travel/tripideas/discover-the-world-s-most-beautiful-cruise-ships-that-rival-five-star-hotels/ss-AA1oK8Xy.

7   Cruise Lines International Association, "2022 Global Market Report," accessed August 15, 2025, https://cruising.org/sites/default/files/2025-03/2022%201R%20CLIA%20001%20Overview%20Global%20FINAL.pdf

8   Charlotte Cullinan, "Must-Watch Cruise Ship Shows: The Best Live Acts This Year," *Love Exploring*, July 10, 2022, https://www.loveexploring.com/galleries/amp/141637/mustwatch-cruise-ship-shows-the-best-live-acts-this-year.

9   Carnival Entertainment, "Why Carnival?" accessed August 15, 2025, https://www.carnivalentertainment.com/about/why-carnival.

10 David Walsh, "Syracuse Opera Files for Bankruptcy, One of Numerous Smaller Companies in the US in Trouble or Simply Closing Down," *World Socialist Web Site*, December 26, 2024, https://www.wsws.org/en/articles/2024/12/27/rqfc-d27.html.

11 Michael Cooper, "New York City Opera Files for Bankruptcy," *New York Times*, October 3, 2013, https://www.nytimes.com/2013/10/04/arts/music/new-york-city-opera-files-for-bankruptcy.html?smid=nytcore-ios-share&referringSource=articleShare.

12 Javier C. Hernández, "Met Opera Taps Its Endowment Again to Weather Downturn," *New York Times*, January 25, 2024, https://www.nytimes.com/2024/01/25/arts/music/met-opera-endowment-finances.html?smid=nytcore-ios-share&referringSource=articleShare.

13 Michael Paulson, "A Crisis in America's Theaters Leaves Prestigious Stages Dark," *New York Times*, updated July 25, 2023, https://www.nytimes.com/2023/07/23/theater/regional-theater-crisis.html?smid=nytcore-ios-share&referringSource=articleShare.

14 Randy Cohen, "NEA Budget Losses," Americans for the Arts, accessed February 22, 2025, https://www.americansforthearts.org/sites/default/files/5.%202018%20NEA%20Discretionary%20Spending.pdf.

15 Cathy Applefeld Olsen, "Live Music's Tale of Two Recoveries: Indie Venues Still Struggle Despite 'Golden' Return of Touring," *Forbes*, March 18, 2024, https://www.forbes.com/sites/cathyolson/2024/03/18/live-musics-tale-of-two-recoveries-indie-venues-still-struggle-despite-golden-return-of-touring.

16 Cruise Lines International Association, "State of the Cruise Industry Report 2025," May 22, 2025, https://cruising.org/sites/default/files/2025-07/State%20of%20the%20Cruise%20Industry%20Report%202025.pdf.

17 Zachary Crockett, "The Economics of Cruise Ships," *Hustle*, updated June 24, 2024, https://thehustle.co/the-economics-of-cruise-ships.

18 Warshaw Entertainment, "Top 5 Reasons to Work on a Cruise Ship as a Musician, Vocalist or Performer," accessed February 22, 2025, https://www.warshawentertainment.com/blog/top-5-reasons-to-work-on-a-cruise-ship-as-a-musician-vocalist-or-performer.

1 Understanding Cruise Ship Entertainment

Cruise ship entertainment is a vibrant and dynamic industry that provides performers with steady work, enthusiastic audiences, and unparalleled travel experiences. However, it differs significantly from land-based performance opportunities, requiring singers to adapt to unique challenges, expectations, and professional structures. While the insights in this chapter are broadly applicable, many of the examples and generalized experiences described are drawn from roles that involve longer contracts, such as production cast vocalists, lounge entertainers, and cruise administrators, which come with responsibilities beyond performance alone and represent the majority of job opportunities available to singers at sea. In contrast, short-term roles like guest or step-on entertainers involve a different set of commitments, often limited to headline performances or port-day engagements. This chapter will explore the key differences between cruise ship and land-based gigs, provide an overview of major cruise lines and their entertainment structures, and highlight the importance of versatility and adaptability for building a career at sea.

How Cruise Ship Entertainment Differs from Land-Based Gigs

Performing on a cruise ship differs significantly from traditional land-based gigs in both the variety of entertainment offered and a gig's impact on the performer. These differences affect everything from job stability and audience engagement to logistical considerations and daily life. Understanding these distinctions is crucial for singers considering careers at sea.

Variety of Entertainment Offered

Cruise ship entertainment encompasses a broad range of performance types designed to appeal to diverse passengers. Unlike a land-based performance setting, where artists often specialize in one genre or venue, cruise ship performers must be prepared for multiple performance formats.

- **Production Shows:** Large-scale productions similar to Broadway or West End performances. These shows incorporate elaborate sets, lighting, and choreography and often require singers to perform in multiple roles within a single contract.
- **Themed Revues and Cabarets:** Musical showcases that highlight various genres, including jazz, rock, pop, and classical. These revues are typically presented in smaller, more intimate entertainment venues, such as small theaters or lounges. Performers may be required to have solo cabarets and be able to shift between genres within a single night.
- **Guest Entertainers:** Headliners for limited engagements, often featuring tribute acts, comedy, or specialty acts that cater to specific audience demographics and provide contrast to the resident onboard entertainment.
- **Step-On Entertainers:** Local performers who come aboard only while the ship is docked. These entertainers typically offer performances that reflect the port region's cultural or artistic heritage, providing guests with authentic experiences that complement their time ashore.
- **Lounge Entertainment:** Music in lounges, atriums, or dining areas requiring a flexible approach to performing in settings that are interactive and less formal.
- **Interactive and Themed Experiences:** Immersive entertainment, such as interactive murder mysteries, sing-alongs, and game show performances in which entertainers must engage directly with passengers.

While not all entertainers are expected to perform in all of these formats, the range of ship entertainment clearly benefits performers who are versatile and adaptable, comfortable performing different styles in various settings and multiple times per day throughout a contract.

Impact on the Performer

Beyond the diversity of entertainment offerings, working as a cruise ship performer has a profound impact on the artist's daily life, career trajectory, and professional development. Several key factors differentiate cruise ship contracts from land-based gigs.

- **Job Stability and Contract Length:** Unlike freelance or short-term gigs on land, cruise contracts for production cast vocalists, lounge entertainers, and cruise administrators generally last four to six months, providing steady employment but also requiring performers to commit

Figure 1.1 Cruise ship atrium configured for live music performance.
Courtesy Holger Wulschlaeger/Shutterstock.

to extended periods at sea. While this stability is beneficial for financial security, it can be challenging for those accustomed to more flexible, independent performance schedules.

- **Adapting to a Rotating Audience:** Unlike theater productions in which performers typically encounter a consistent audience demographic, cruise ship entertainers perform for fluctuating guests on a weekly basis on average. Depending on where the ship is in the world, the nationality breakdown of the guests will shift, bringing with it new cultural understandings and expectations for the entertainment onboard. This requires performers to continuously refine their audience-engagement skills and adjust their delivery based on passengers' preferences and expectations.

- **Performance Frequency and Repertoire Flexibility:** When working on a ship, there are no set days off during a contract, regardless of position. That said, it is not uncommon for cruise performers to end up with at least one day off each week, but it is never guaranteed. A strenuous schedule and the potential for multiple shows per night demands strong vocal endurance and adaptability to changes in set lists or performance conditions. Unlike land-based singers who may spend months preparing for a single role, cruise singers must master and maintain a diverse repertoire and may be asked to learn new music onboard very quickly.

- **Technical and Logistical Adaptations:** Performing on a moving vessel presents unique physical challenges, including maintaining balance, stability, and overall wellness onstage while the ship is in motion. Additionally, onboard technical teams often have limited setup and rehearsal time between shows, requiring performers to adjust quickly to changing technical conditions.

- **Self-Sufficiency in Costumes, Hair, and Makeup:** Unlike large-scale productions on land where performers have dedicated wardrobe, hair, and makeup teams, cruise ship entertainers are responsible for their own styling. Singers typically apply stage makeup, style their hair, and maintain their costumes without external assistance. This level of self-sufficiency can be an adjustment for those used to backstage support but is a crucial skill for thriving in the cruise entertainment industry.

- **Crew Responsibilities and Ship Life:** Unlike land-based performers who leave the venue after a show, cruise performers live where they work. This means adhering to shipboard regulations, participating in mandatory safety drills, and engaging with passengers beyond performances. The close-knit community onboard also fosters strong professional and personal relationships but requires a high degree of adaptability to communal living and limited personal space.

- **Opportunities for Growth:** Many cruise lines offer pathways for career progression, including opportunities to extend and renew contracts, take on managerial roles, transition into cruise administration, or work as guest entertainers.

Understanding how cruise ship entertainment differs from land-based gigs is critical for any performer considering a career at sea. The next section will explore

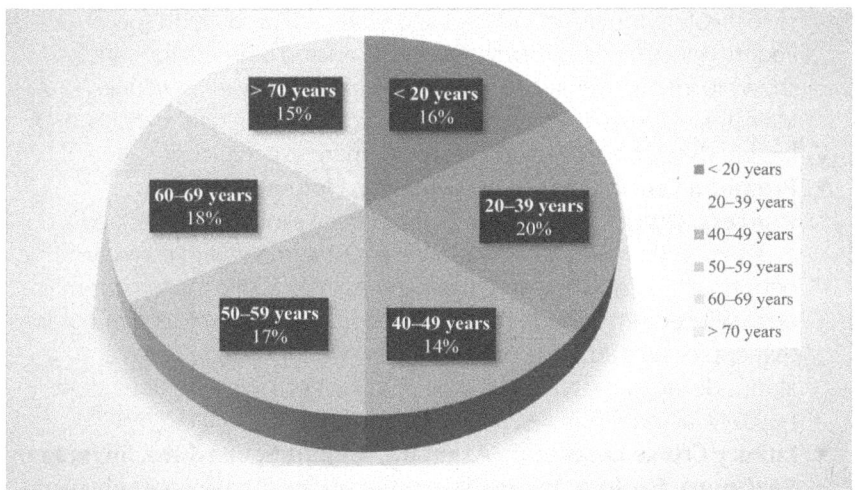

Figure 1.2 Percentage of cruise passengers by age group.
Source: Cruise Lines International Association (2025).

the structure of cruise lines and how they organize their entertainment offerings, giving insight into the industry's professional landscape.

Overview of Cruise Lines and Their Entertainment Structure

The cruise industry is diverse, with different companies catering to various demographics, budgets, and expectations. These differences extend to the way entertainment is structured, the types of performances offered, and the opportunities available for singers. This section will examine the major categories of cruise lines, their entertainment structures, and the roles singers can expect to fulfill.

Types of Cruise Lines and Their Entertainment Offerings

Cruise lines can generally be divided into four categories: mainstream, premium, luxury, and expedition. Each offers a unique entertainment experience based on passenger demographics, brand identity, and vessel size.

- **Mainstream Cruise Lines (e.g., Royal Caribbean, Carnival, Norwegian, MSC, etc.):** These cruise lines cater to mass-market travelers, offering large-scale entertainment. Their ships are large, typically boasting 2,500 to 6,000 passengers, and often equipped with Broadway-style theaters, multilevel lounges, and high-tech production spaces. Performances range from full-scale musicals and high-energy variety shows to interactive game shows and live music in various venues. Mainstream cruise lines rely heavily on production singers, dancers, and live bands to create a dynamic entertainment experience.

- **Premium Cruise Lines (e.g., Celebrity, Holland America, Princess, Disney, etc.):** These brands offer a slightly more refined experience, blending Broadway-style entertainment with classical music performances, jazz trios, and guest entertainers. While the focus remains on quality entertainment, these lines often cater to an older demographic that appreciates intimate performances in lounges and cabarets alongside larger theater productions, as well as a smaller guest count typically ranging from 1,500 to 2,500 passengers.
- **Luxury Cruise Lines (e.g., Azamara, Regent Seven Seas, Silversea, Seabourn, Explora, Viking, Windstar, etc.):** Entertainment on luxury lines is curated to reflect the upscale atmosphere and smaller vessel size, typically hosting 500 to 1,500 guests. Performances include jazz ensembles, classical quartets, cabaret singers, and local guest acts. The focus is on sophistication and cultural enrichment, with themed performances that align with destinations.
- **Expedition Cruise Lines (e.g., Lindblad, Ponant, Hurtigruten, etc.):** Expedition lines prioritize education and enrichment over traditional entertainment. Instead of large production shows, these ships host guest

Figure 1.3 Premium cruise ship docked in St. Thomas, US Virgin Islands. Courtesy eskystudio/Shutterstock.

lectures, cultural performances, and smaller musical acts that enhance the exploration experience. Singers on these lines may perform in intimate settings or as part of enrichment programs for typically fewer than 500 guests.

The Structure of Cruise Ship Entertainment Departments

The entertainment department onboard a cruise ship is a well-organized hierarchy designed to efficiently run multiple performance venues as well as guest activity and enrichment programs. Unlike a land-based theater, which typically has a director, stage managers, and a production team focused on a single venue, cruise ship entertainment must span multiple performance areas and activities. The department structure is more consistent with nautical hierarchy and varies depending on the size of the ship and the cruise line's operational model. The smaller the vessel, the more proverbial hats one can expect to wear; nonetheless, most lines operate with a version of the following positions:

1 **Cruise Director (CD):** This person is the head of the entire entertainment operation onboard. The cruise director oversees all entertainment programming, guest activities, and enrichment. This person is the face of the entertainment department and works closely with the hotel director, the senior officer who oversees all hospitality concerns on a cruise ship, to ensure entertainment aligns with the ship itinerary, food and beverage operations, shore excursions, and guest expectations. The cruise director is always a front-facing position, and on smaller vessels, this person frequently performs as well, with appearances that range from variety shows, deck parties, formal ceremonies, and at least one solo show.

2 **Assistant Cruise Director (ACD):** The assistant cruise director supports the CD by managing the daily entertainment and activities schedule, supervising activity staff and performers, and hosting events. This person often carries the weight of the administrative work within the department, such as ensuring that safety training is up to date for everyone and communicating all pertinent information to guest entertainers and enrichment personnel. Similar to the CD, the ACD may also be required to perform in shows, at parties, and as a solo headliner.

3 **Entertainment Manager (EM):** Some cruise lines have an entertainment manager who handles logistics, schedules, and administrative tasks, allowing the CD and the ACD to focus on guest engagement. This role is usually found on larger vessels. The EM works largely behind the scenes and is not required to perform.

4 Production Manager (PM): The production manager is responsible for the technical aspects of onboard productions, including sound, lighting, and stage effects. The PM ensures all performances run smoothly and coordinates rehearsals, set changes, and A/V adjustments. On smaller vessels, this position is frequently covered by the A/V team.

5 Bandmaster (BM): The bandmaster (or musical director) is responsible for overseeing all musicians onboard. This person ensures that musicians are prepared for their scheduled performances, liaises with the CD and the EM on musical programming, and manages rehearsals. The bandmaster also plays a key role in coordinating live music performances for themed events and special occasions.

6 A/V and Technical Team: This team includes lighting technicians, sound engineers, and stagehands who handle the execution of all technical aspects of entertainment. Unlike a land-based theater, where technicians may be assigned to one show, cruise ship tech teams must support multiple performances in different venues each night.

7 Broadcast Team: This team oversees the ship's in-house television production, ensuring that daily programs, announcements, and entertainment schedules are broadcasted to guest cabins and public areas. The broadcast team manages filming, editing, and live streaming of ship events.

8 Production Cast (Singers and Dancers): These are resident performers contracted for several months to perform in production shows. Singers and dancers work together to deliver Broadway-style performances, themed musical revues, and variety acts. Production cast members must be versatile, as they often perform in multiple shows and participate in interactive events with guests. It is not uncommon for a lead production cast vocalist to also perform in a headlining solo show.

9 Company Manager: This is a member of the production cast who oversees the day-to-day operations of the singers and dancers. This person is responsible for maintaining show quality, implementing artistic notes from shoreside producers, supporting cast welfare, occasionally managing rehearsal schedules, preparing voyage reports, and serving as a liaison between performers and onboard leadership. While the company manager may report to the CD or the EM, this person focuses on the artistic and logistical needs of the cast rather than guest-facing programming.

10 Wardrobe Supervisor: The wardrobe supervisor oversees the maintenance, repair, and organization of costumes for production shows and themed events. This person coordinates with performers, dressers, and the entertainment management team to ensure all wardrobe items are performance ready. On smaller ships, this role is commonly held by a production cast member, while on larger ships with extensive entertainment offerings, this is frequently a separate position that reports to the EM.

11 **Lounge Entertainers:** These are solo vocalist-instrumentalists and duo or trio acts who perform in more intimate settings such as lounges, atriums, and bars. Lounge entertainers engage directly with guests, often taking song requests and adjusting their performances to fit the atmosphere of the venue on a given night.

12 **Musicians:** Cruise ships employ musicians in two primary capacities: those who play in production shows and those who perform in party bands. Production musicians are skilled sight-readers who accompany live performances in the ship's theater, playing alongside the production cast singers and dancers. Party-band musicians are typically hired within a preformed band unit and perform a range of music, from laid-back lounge sets to high-energy deck parties, creating an engaging and frequently lively atmosphere for guests.

13 **DJ:** A dedicated DJ is often onboard to provide music for themed parties, nightclub venues, and special events. The DJ plays a crucial role in setting the energy of social spaces and is responsible for curating music that suits the onboard atmosphere and passenger demographics under the guidance of the CD.

14 **Cruise Staff:** Also referred to as activity staff, people in these roles are responsible for hosting trivia, karaoke, deck parties, and social games. Unlike in a land-based theater, where front-of-house staff assist only before and after a performance, cruise staff actively engage with guests through their cruise experiences. On smaller vessels, the production cast often doubles as cruise staff, while on larger vessels, the roles are separate.

15 **Youth Program Team:** These are staff responsible for planning and running onboard activities for children and teens, including games, arts and crafts, education programs, and themed events. These roles are typically found on larger family-friendly ships with dedicated kids' clubs or teen spaces.

16 **Guest Entertainers:** Guest entertainers are external performers, such as comedians, magicians, and tribute artists, who are contracted for shorter engagements. They typically perform one or two headline acts per voyage and do not participate in the day-to-day onboard operations.

17 **Step-On Entertainers:** These are local performers who board the ship temporarily while it is docked in port. They typically present a short cultural

performance that reflects the traditions of the region through music, dance, and song. Step-on entertainers are onboard for only a few hours and do not participate in shipboard life or entertainment operations beyond their scheduled shows.

18 Enrichment Personnel: These externally contracted individuals provide specialized programming to enhance the guest experience. Enrichment personnel typically embark for one or two cruises at a time, and may include special-interest or destination speakers, clergy, and instructors of games and hobbies. They offer guests opportunities for learning and personal enrichment while at sea.

Contrasting Small-Ship and Large-Ship Entertainment Departments

On larger ships (e.g., Royal Caribbean, Norwegian, and MSC), entertainment departments function like full-scale production companies with large casts, high-tech theaters, and multiple entertainment venues operating simultaneously. These ships have larger A/V teams, more elaborate productions, and specialized positions such as ice-skating show producers, aerial rigging technicians, and orchestra leaders.

On smaller ships (e.g., Azamara, Seabourn, and Viking), the entertainment department is leaner, with fewer cast members and simplified show formats. While these ships may include Broadway-style productions, shows tend to be more limited in scale, and intimate cabarets, classical music, or solo performances play a larger role in the entertainment plan. The cruise director and the director's assistant often play a more hands-on role, frequently performing alongside the entertainment team.

How Entertainment Fits into Hotel Operations

Unlike in a land-based theater, where entertainment exists as a standalone entity, cruise ship entertainment is fully integrated into the hotel department. The cruise director reports to the hotel director, who oversees all guest-facing operations, including dining, housekeeping, guest services, and excursions. Entertainment is designed to complement the overall guest experience rather than being the sole focus of operations.

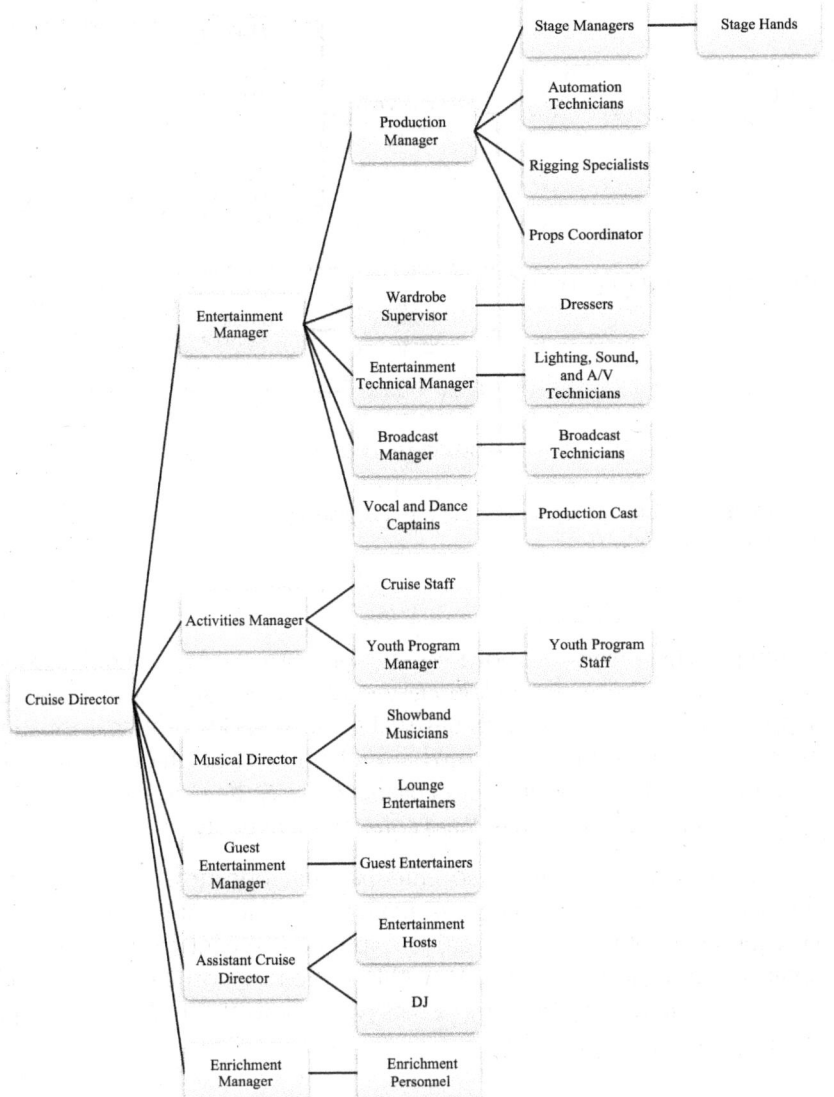

Figure 1.4 Example of a large entertainment department organizational chart. Author made.

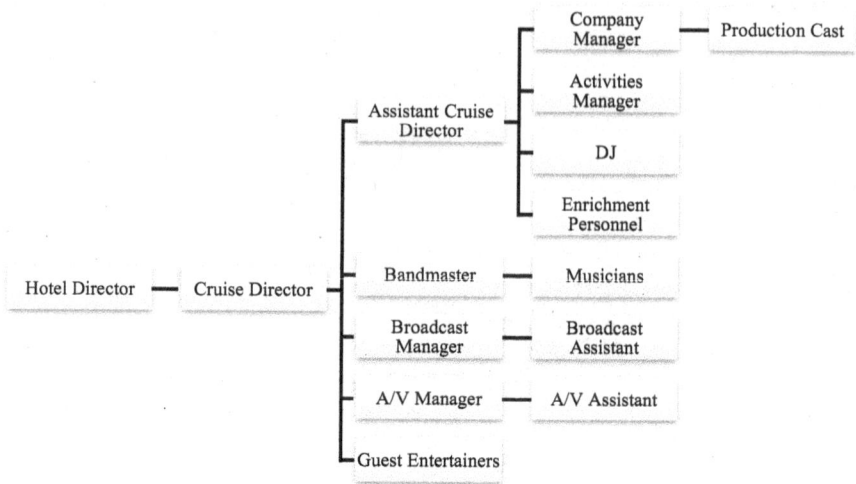

Figure 1.5 Example of a small entertainment department organizational chart. Author made.

For example, the timing of shows must align with dining schedules, shore excursions, and special events. Additionally, entertainment staff may be required to support other hotel-related activities, such as hosting VIP events, participating in guest drills, and assisting with crowd control. This level of integration requires performers to be highly flexible and collaborative, as they are part of a larger hospitality team rather than an isolated entertainment entity.

Understanding the structure of an entertainment department is crucial for performers considering a career at sea. From the hierarchy of leadership to the integration with hotel operations, cruise ship entertainment requires flexibility, adaptability, and the ability to work within a broader hospitality framework. The next section will explore why versatility is key to thriving in this unique performance environment.

The Importance of Versatility and Adaptability

One of the most essential traits for a successful cruise ship performer is versatility. Unlike land-based performers who may specialize in a single genre or performance style, cruise ship entertainers must be prepared to perform in diverse settings and under varying conditions that may change at the last minute. Adaptability is equally critical, as life at sea presents unique challenges that require performers to be flexible, professional, and resilient.

Versatility as a Performer

Performers at sea must be comfortable with a wide range of musical styles and performance formats. Singers are expected to have extensive repertoires to accommodate different themed nights, guest requests, and venue changes.

- **Multiple Show Formats:** Cruise ship entertainers often participate in multiple shows per voyage. A singer might perform in a Broadway-style revue one night, lead a jazz set in a lounge the next, and participate in a themed deck party by the end of the cruise.
- **Audience Adaptation:** Because guests onboard generally change with each voyage, performers must be skilled at reading their audiences. What worked for one sailing may not resonate with the next, requiring quick adjustments in song selection, energy levels, and engagement techniques, such as bantering with the audience during a cabaret.
- **Collaboration across Departments:** Singers may be asked to perform alongside musicians, from jazz trios to full orchestras, or even provide vocals for interactive guest experiences like game shows or trivia. They may be asked to provide music for special events hosted by the food and beverage department, such as destination-themed dinners. The ability to collaborate with various crew members and adapt to different arrangements is a key to success.

Adaptability to Cruise Life

Beyond performance skills, adaptability to the lifestyle and work environment onboard is essential. Cruise ship contracts come with unique living conditions, work expectations, and personal adjustments that require flexibility.

- **Living in Close Quarters:** Unlike working in a theater where performers go home after a show, cruise entertainers typically live onboard for months at a time. We will discuss the living situations of different performance tracks later, but cabins are often shared with another crew member, personal space is limited, and performers must adjust to life in a communal setting.
- **Changing Schedules:** Cruise ship entertainment schedules are fluid, often dictated by port schedules, weather conditions, and guest demographics. Performers must be prepared for last-minute show changes, unexpected cancellations, or adjusted performance times.
- **Ship Motion and Performance Challenges:** Singing and dancing on a moving vessel is vastly different from performing on a stable stage. Performers must develop strong core balance and learn how to adjust

their movements and vocal control to accommodate the motion of the ship. It is also important to note that ships are rarely docked in the evening, as they are usually underway to the next port. This is exactly the time frame in which most shows are programmed due to the guests all being onboard, so most performances will take place while at sea.

- **Compliance with Ship Regulations:** Cruise ship entertainers (with the exception of guest and step-on entertainers) are also considered crew members. This means they must participate in safety drills, adhere to ship protocols, and engage with guests beyond the stage.

Professional Growth through Versatility

Cruise ship entertainment provides a valuable opportunity for performers to expand their skill sets and become more well-rounded artists. Many entertainers leave their contracts with improved musicianship, greater stage confidence, and a stronger work ethic. Some key areas of growth include these:

- **Vocal and Physical Endurance:** Performing on a near-daily basis builds stamina and vocal resilience, skills that are beneficial for any long-term performance career.
- **Networking and Career Expansion:** Cruise contracts introduce performers to international colleagues, opening doors to future opportunities in theater, touring, and event entertainment.
- **Improvisation and Quick Thinking:** The need to adapt to last-minute changes fosters strong improvisational skills, making performers more capable of handling unpredictable situations on and off stage.
- **Dislocation from Land:** While ships provide opportunities for advancement, the length of contracts can make it difficult to maintain relationships with contacts on land, such as with agents and casting directors. Proactive communication is necessary to maintain and grow these relationships while working at sea.

Entertainment as Part of the Larger Cruise Ship Ecosystem

While entertainment plays an important role in the guest experience, it is essential for performers to understand that the entertainment department is not a stand-alone entity. Instead, it is one of many interconnected departments that contribute to the overall success of cruise operations. A cruise ship functions as a floating city, and entertainment is just one element of the guest experience.

Food and beverage, accommodations, excursions, or onboard activities may take precedence, with entertainment forced to align with these large operational priorities.

The Ship as the Destination: Large-Ship Operations

On larger cruise ships, particularly those operated by mainstream lines such as Royal Caribbean, Carnival, and Norwegian, the ship itself is often the primary attraction. These massive vessels feature sprawling amenities such as water parks, indoor malls, go-kart tracks, zip lines, and luxury spas. Entertainment exists alongside numerous activity options, competing for the attention of passengers; however, it is important to note that these ships often sail itineraries focused on well-traveled, high-volume destinations in the Caribbean and Florida, so the ports themselves are not necessarily the highlight of the trip. Guests spend more time engaging with onboard attractions, including but certainly not limited to entertainment, than exploring ashore.

The Ports as the Destination: Small-Ship Operations

On smaller cruise ships, such as those operated by Azamara, Seabourn, and Viking, the emphasis is less on the ship itself and more on the destinations. These vessels cater to travelers who seek less touristy, more historically or geographically significant ports that do not have the infrastructure to accommodate larger vessels. As a result, entertainment plays a more subdued role in the overall cruise experience, with the focus instead being on exploration, dining, and enrichment programming.

Many guests on smaller ships choose to retire early after long days of exploring ports or engaging in immersive shore excursions. Unlike on large ships, where entertainment is designed to energize and engage guests late into the night, smaller-ship entertainment serves as a quiet coda to the day, often consisting of relaxed performances, such as piano bar sessions, jazz trios, and classical quartets.

Understanding the Bigger Picture

As a performer, it is crucial to recognize that while entertainment is important, it is just one component of the broader cruise experience. The cruise industry is built on hospitality and guest satisfaction, and every team—whether it be a front-of-house department such as entertainment, food and beverage, housekeeping, or shore excursions, or a back-of-house department such as deck or engine—must work together to create a seamless and enjoyable experience for the passengers. Entertainers who understand their role within this larger ecosystem are more likely to succeed in the industry and develop positive working relationships with crew members from other departments.

While entertainment is an exciting and dynamic part of the cruise experience, it exists within a larger hospitality framework that prioritizes the holistic guest experience above all else. For singers interested in pursuing this career path, the next step is determining which role best suits their skills and ambitions. In the next chapter, we will explore the five primary career tracks available to singers at sea, breaking down the specific opportunities, expectations, and requirements of each.

2 The Five Career Tracks for Singers at Sea

Cruise ship entertainment is far from one-size-fits-all. Singers who choose to perform at sea will find a variety of roles available to suit different skills, temperaments, and career goals. Whether you thrive as part of a high-energy cast, prefer the independence of a solo act, or see yourself stepping into a leadership role, there's a place for you in the maritime entertainment world.

In this chapter, we'll explore five primary career tracks for singers at sea. Each of these paths offers unique advantages and presents its own set of challenges. In the previous chapter we focused mainly on roles that involve long-term contracts with the cruise line and deep integration into the shipboard team, but now we'll get into more detail about those and others with short-term or even one-off engagements. Understanding the distinctions between these roles is crucial to finding the one that aligns best with your voice, your values, and your vision for the future.

From the collaborative and physically demanding life of a production cast vocalist to the creative flexibility of a lounge entertainer, to the autonomy of a guest entertainer, the short-term engagements of a step-on entertainer, or the leadership responsibilities of a cruise administrator, this chapter will guide you through the nuts and bolts of each option. Each path is presented in the form of a professional job profile to help you gain a clear sense of what's expected, how to prepare, and how each role fits into the larger cruise-ship ecosystem.

Path 1: Production Cast Vocalist

Job Overview

Production cast vocalists are singers who are part of a ship's resident production cast, performing in typically large-scale, high-energy shows produced by the cruise line. These singers are featured in full-scale musical productions that may include Broadway-style revues, tribute shows, themed musical extravaganzas, and original productions.

This role is commonly found on major cruise lines, including Royal Caribbean, Norwegian, Carnival, Princess, Holland America, Celebrity, and Disney. Luxury brands like Cunard and Azamara may also employ production vocalists for smaller-scale productions.

In addition to performing, production vocalists are typically required to do their own show-ready hair, wigs, and makeup, following design guidelines provided during rehearsals. They must also attend all mandatory onboard trainings. Before embarking, all cast members must successfully complete and pass a comprehensive preemployment medical examination to be cleared for shipboard work.

Primary Responsibilities

- Perform multiple production shows per cruise, often in large theaters with advanced staging and special effects.
- Rehearse as needed to maintain a high performance standard throughout the contract.
- Perform additional duties such as theme night appearances, cast meet-and-greets, or participation in enrichment activities.
- Maintain personal and group choreography, staging, and blocking as set by the cruise line's entertainment department.
- Participate in emergency drills, adhere to safety regulations as a crew member, and attend additional trainings as required.

Required Skills and Qualifications

- Strong vocal ability in a variety of styles, including pop, rock, jazz, musical theater, contemporary, and occasionally classical.
- Professional performance experience, preferably in musical theater, commercial music, or live productions.
- Ability to harmonize and blend well with other singers in a group setting.
- Strong stage presence and the ability to engage an audience.
- Strong dance or movement ability is helpful, though extensive dance training is typically not necessary.
- Sight-reading and the ability to learn music quickly is a plus, as is experience working with live bands or backing tracks.

Performance and Rehearsal Schedule

- Singers perform in 2–5 major shows per cruise, depending on the ship itinerary. Shows are usually 45 minutes in duration and performed twice per evening.
- Rehearsal periods vary; most cast members rehearse for 4–8 weeks on land before embarking on a contract, with a 1–2-week installation period onboard for new productions and/or new casts.
- Rehearsals continue onboard to maintain show quality and adjust to technical or cast changes.
- Sound checks, costume fittings, and tech rehearsals are frequently required on performance days.

Challenges and Expectations

- Long contracts (typically 6–9 months) requiring consistent vocal performance and endurance.
- Often living in shared crew accommodations, most frequently with fellow cast members.
- Adjusting to ship life, including safety protocols and limited personal space and freedom.
- Performing in a variety of conditions, including rough seas that may affect balance and stage movement.
- Adapting to cast changes, as replacements may be introduced mid-contract.
- Maintaining vocal health while performing in different climates and conditions.
- Responsiblity for doing hair, wigs, and makeup to show-ready standards as per company design.
- Attendance at all mandatory safety trainings, crew inductions, and onboard drills.
- Mandatory preemployment medical examination to be cleared for duty.
- With some production companies that cast performers on behalf of cruise lines, paying a financial penalty for voluntarily leaving contracts early.

Career Progression and Opportunities

- Production vocalists can advance to vocal captain, overseeing harmonies and vocal quality within the cast, and/or company manager, acting as a liaison between the cast and the cruise director.

- Some transition into guest or step-on entertainer roles, developing their own headline acts and performing as independent contractors.
- Others move into cruise administration, such as becoming an entertainment manager or cruise director.
- Many singers use their cruise experience as a stepping stone to theater, television, recording careers, or performance opportunities on land in theme parks, corporate entertainment, or touring productions.

Compensation

- Production cast vocalists typically earn between US$4,000 and US$6,000 per month, depending on the cruise line, experience level, and complexity of the role.
- Contracts usually include airfare, accommodations, meals, laundry service, crew recreational areas and activities, and access to medical care onboard.
- During the rehearsal period on land, performers are generally provided with airfare to the rehearsal site, accommodations, and a weekly per diem or stipend.
- Some production companies casting on behalf of the cruise line may offer contract-completion bonuses or stipends for travel days.

Figure 2.1 Large-capacity ship theater for production shows and headline acts. Courtesy gbautista87/Shutterstock.

- Perks may include guest-status privileges, free shore excursions in exchange for escorting guests, or passenger-cabin upgrades for more elite vocalist positions.

Path 2: Lounge Entertainer

Job Overview

Lounge entertainers perform regularly in onboard venues such as piano bars, cocktail lounges, poolside stages, and other intimate performance spaces. Being in a category that includes solo vocalists, piano-bar entertainers, singer-instrumentalists, duos, trios, and full party-band vocalists, they bring ambience and energy to the ship, contributing to the relaxed, social atmosphere that many guests seek during their cruise.

Lounge-entertainer roles are available across almost all cruise line, but depending on the cruise line, the entertainment may be geared toward dance music, jazz, classical crossover, pop covers, or easy listening.

Lounge entertainers may be contracted directly by cruise lines or through third-party entertainment agencies. They typically perform independently of production casts, though collaboration may occur for special events or theme nights.

Primary Responsibilities

- Perform multiple 45-minute sets per day or per evening in rotating venues such as lounges, atriums, pool decks, and dining areas. Most contracts stipulate that a lounge entertainer can be scheduled for a maximum of 5 sets per day.
- Create a welcoming and engaging environment for guests, encouraging sing-alongs, requests, or dancing as appropriate to the venue.
- Adjust setlists and musical style based on the time of day, audience energy, cruise itinerary, and guest requests.
- Set up and break down personal or group gear as needed.
- Interact with guests both on and off stage, maintaining a high level of professionalism and approachability.
- Attend mandatory safety trainings and drills as required for crew members.

Required Skills and Qualifications

- Strong vocal ability and musicianship in a variety of genres including pop, rock, jazz, soul, Motown, adult contemporary, and international hits.

- Ability to engage a crowd and create a vibrant, inclusive experience for guests.
- Experience performing live in casual or upscale venues, such as hotels, restaurants, piano bars, or corporate events.
- For party-band singers, the ability to front a band, move comfortably around a stage, and lead high-energy sets.
- For solo or duo performers, skills in self-accompaniment; live looping is a plus.

Performance and Rehearsal Schedule

- Singers perform 6 days per week, with 3 to a maximum of 5 sets per day depending on the ship's schedule.
- Rehearsals are generally self-scheduled and self-directed, with minimal onboard tech or staging rehearsal unless the set is tied to a special event.
- Performers are expected to arrive with performance-ready setlists.

Challenges and Expectations

- Contracts range from 3 to 6 months, with some flexibility depending on the role and itinerary.
- Lounge entertainers live in crew accommodations and are considered part of the ship's crew, subject to safety drills, inspections, and codes of conduct.
- The casual and guest-facing nature of the role means artists must be "on" even outside performance hours, as they may frequently encounter guests in social settings.
- Vocal stamina and adaptability are critical, as performers sing nightly in various environments, including outdoor venues.
- Most lounge entertainers are responsible for providing, shipping, transporting, and maintaining their own instruments and gear. Sound equipment is typically provided by the cruise line.

Career Progression and Opportunities

- Lounge entertainers can elevate their profiles by cultivating a strong guest following, which can lead to repeat contracts or transitioning to guest-entertainer status.
- Musicians may also shift into bandmaster roles, overseeing the musical direction of all musicians onboard.

- Entertainers who specialize in unique or crossover genres may find opportunities to brand themselves beyond cruise work for land-based gigs, private events, or even recording opportunities.

Compensation

- Lounge entertainers typically earn between US$2,500 and US$4,000 per month as soloists or in duos, and around US$1,500–$3,000 per month as band singers, depending on the cruise line and experience.
- Contracts usually include airfare, accommodations, meals, laundry service, crew recreational areas and activities, and access to medical care onboard.
- Perks may include guest-status privileges, free shore excursions in exchange for escorting guests, or passenger-cabin upgrades for higher-tier lounge acts.

Figure 2.2 Pianist-vocalist Carl Wishneusky.
Photograph by Carl Wishneusky.

Carl Wishneusky: Keys across the Seas

www.carlspiano.com | @carls_piano

Carl Wishneusky never set out to become one of the cruise industry's most in-demand pianist-vocalists, but the seed was planted long before his first contract. "I'd done a number of cruises as a passenger to get away from the New England winters," he recalls. "I'd be on the ships, and I'd look at the musicians and be like, *Hey, I could do that. That looks like a fun way to make some money and get away from the wintertime.*"

Nervous but determined, he found an agency in Montreal called Proship and followed their instructions to the letter—perhaps too literally. "I went overboard," he laughs.

> I spent months putting this portfolio together—it was a trifold color brochure with panache and style and repertoire . . . and there were three discs: one was an audio CD of me playing classical music. One was an audio CD of me playing lounge music. And the other was a DVD of me performing in a piano bar. I spent so much time and money putting this whole thing together.... I mailed it off to Proship and they received it on a Friday. They called me right away: "We got your portfolio.... Can you leave on Wednesday?"

His first gig, at age 23, was on Princess Cruise Line's *Island Princess*, running between San Juan and Acapulco through the Panama Canal. "I played in a lounge for two hours a night before a jazz trio.... That was the gig—so easy."

With a background in classical piano, vocal performance, and composition, Carl had spent years performing on land. But shipboard work offered unique differences—some obvious, others surprising. "My favorite difference is not having to lug shit everywhere," he says. "Of course, you have a captive audience when you're on a ship.... People didn't necessarily come because they wanted to hear you. They're there because they've got nowhere else to go."

Reading the room is key: "Age is a big part of that.... One of my little secrets is if you play music for someone that was popular when they were 15 years old, they'll be happy."

If you're entertaining as a pianist-vocalist, Carl believes,

> you should have at least 500 songs, minimum. And you have to be cool with doing the songs that you might not like. People are going to want to hear "Sweet Caroline" and "Piano Man" and depending on the age group, you've got to learn some Rihanna and Taylor Swift nowadays. And less and less, you have to know some Rat Pack stuff.... That's waning like crazy.... You have to have all the big ones completely done, memorized, and ready. But what will set you apart from everyone else is the ability to have a bunch that will surprise people.

Carl's own repertoire has grown to over 2,000 songs.

I'm actually finding that some songs that are always in my mind, I go to play them, and bits are missing, which is a bit worrying. But when you realize there's several thousand songs and you haven't played some for 15 years, it shouldn't be too surprising that every chord change or every lyric doesn't come to mind. Luckily, I can make stuff up and have fun by improvising when that happens. People, in my experience, love it when I start changing the words to things.

A lounge entertainer's day is largely self-directed.

Your day is essentially free.... That can be divided between exercise, going ashore, practicing, eating, drinking, meeting up with people.... Most [sets] start around eight at night, maybe nine.... You're going to have three or four 45-minute sets. I find that when it comes to breaks, it makes way more sense not to take planned breaks, but to really feel the room. If you've got great energy, just keep going and take a longer break afterward.

Audience involvement is part of the fun. "If it's a good singer, I'm going to use them because it gives my voice a rest and it makes it different for the audience.... Sometimes it's even great when they're terrible because it's kind of funny.... The comedic aspect of any performance is very important."

Success in this role requires certain personality traits and work styles.

I think what's going to give someone the best chance of success is, even if you're not naturally so, to be outgoing. Many entertainers, we're actually introverts, but we are extremely well-trained extroverts.... A lot of musicians falter because they care so much about their music, but people just want to turn their brains off and hear songs that they've heard before.... Find the balance between making yourself happy and making others happy.

His advice for newcomers?

Record yourself; watch and listen to yourself. As hard as that may be to do, the number-one best way to improve is to take yourself out of your head and be an audience member to yourself. It's great when people say you're wonderful, but you're going to hear things in yourself that you can improve.... It's hard, it's embarrassing, and it's weird, but boy, is it important to listen to yourself.

Carl has been performing at sea for 18 years, yet the novelty hasn't worn off.

I recall the very first contract—I met a lot of musicians who laughed at me and said, "You silly boy, you're going to hate it. Within a year, you're going to realize it's just another job." But it never happened to me.... I like making people happy. I like playing music, I like singing, I like traveling, I like being in the sun. And even when the people I meet are boring, and a lot of times they are, maybe I'm making their day a little bit better.

He does stress the importance of going in with clear-eyed expectations.

It's probably not a way to get rich. It's not going to be the perfect audience every night. Any respectable musician might feel a little let down compared to land gigs. But keep a good, open mind, commit to performing well, and it can be really fun and gratifying. If you're also clever, it can be a lucrative experience. Look at me— I'm building my house on 21 acres of land, and that's all I've ever done for work.

"I'm just a happy guy when I'm out there," he says. "Just enjoy it. It's been 18 years now, and I'm still having fun when I go out there."

Path 3: Guest Entertainer

Job Overview

Guest entertainers are headlining performers contracted for short-term engagements. These acts are typically self-contained acts, such as vocalists, comedians, magicians, instrumentalists, tribute artists, or musical groups, that perform one or two feature shows in the main theater during a cruise. Guest entertainers are not considered part of the ship's resident cast or crew and usually travel with access to passenger amenities.

This role is common across most cruise lines, which often rotate guest entertainers weekly, giving guests fresh headliner acts for each week of their voyage.

Guest entertainers bring at least two polished shows, typically 45 minutes in length, and are expected to be self-sufficient, professional, and experienced performers who can reliably deliver high-impact shows with minimal technical support and rehearsal time. This path typically requires working with an entertainment agent or agency that serves as a liaison between the performer and the cruise line, production company, or entertainment director, without which it is very difficult to secure guest-entertainer bookings.

Primary Responsibilities

- Perform one or two 45-minute headlining shows per cruise, each typically performed twice in one evening, usually in the ship's main theater.
- Provide complete, self-contained shows with all charts and tracks ready for rehearsal with the ship's band or audio system.

- Participate in a rehearsal for all musical and technical aspects with onboard technicians and musicians, typically the same day as the show.
- Provide all video and visual content used in the show, such as animated or still backgrounds, formatted in advance for use by the ship's A/V team on rear and/or side stage screens.
- Engage with guests in a professional and friendly manner; some lines may ask for optional meet-and-greets, Q&A sessions, or hosting of dining tables.
- Maintain a high level of performance quality with minimal rehearsal time.

Required Skills and Qualifications

- A fully developed act with professional performance experience in theaters, cabarets, corporate events, or previous cruise contracts.
- Strong vocal and/or musical skills and stage presence, and the ability to hold the attention of an audience.
- Professional-quality promotional materials, including videos, headshots, tech riders, and bios.
- Ability to adapt the show as needed for different audiences or performance lengths.
- Experience working with live musicians or using backing tracks; charts and click tracks must be professionally prepared.
- Familiarity with formatting and delivering video for seamless integration with shipboard A/V systems.

Performance and Rehearsal Schedule

- Guest entertainers have one to two performance nights per cruise.
- Rehearsals are limited to a single sound check or run-through, often with the ship's show band on the day of the performance.

Challenges and Expectations

- Contracts are short term, often ranging from 3 days to 2 weeks, with one week being most common; some acts are booked for back-to-back sailings.
- Guest entertainers must arrive fully self-sufficient, with all necessary equipment, costumes, and show materials, prepared to perform on the same day they travel to the ship. Although those responsible for onboard scheduling typically try to avoid this, it can and does happen.

- Travel can be demanding, with air travel to the port city and land transportation to the ship arranged by the cruise line or agency.
- Technical flexibility is key, as performance conditions, musician skill, and A/V support may vary between ships.
- Guest entertainers, particularly vocalists, are featured acts on a cruise, expected to offer something distinct from the entertainment already provided onboard. As a result, many cruise lines give booking preference to non-vocalist guest entertainers or novelty acts.
- Guest entertainers can experience a disconnection onboard. Though listed on the guest manifest and enjoying guest-level privileges, they are onboard to work and are not fully treated as passengers. At the same time, they are not considered crew and typically do not have access to crew-only areas beyond the backstage and dressing rooms. The transient nature of this role means they are constantly meeting new crew and guests only to say goodbye days later, making it difficult to build a lasting sense of community.

Career Progression and Opportunities

- Successful guest entertainers often build long-term relationships with cruise lines, resulting in repeat bookings, referrals, and expansion into land-based touring and corporate events.
- Guest entertainers may branch into cruise-ship consulting or directing, or producing shows for other performers.
- For singers, this track can provide more flexibility and artistic control than other sea-based opportunities, especially later in a career.

Compensation

- Guest entertainers typically start at US$3,500 per week with greater earning potential based on the performer's experience, demand, and reputation.
- Contracts include airfare, accommodations in guest cabins, meals in guest dining venues, and luggage allowances.
- A hotel stay the night before boarding is customary, especially when international travel is involved, but it is not guaranteed. Accommodations may vary depending on the itinerary and scheduling.
- An agent commission of 15 percent is standard and should be factored into overall earnings.
- Travel days and rehearsal time may also be compensated, depending on the cruise line.

Figure 2.3 Guest entertainer duo Branden & James.
Photograph by Curtis Brown Photography.

Branden & James: Redefining Guest Entertaining

www.brandenjames.com | @brandenjmusic

Branden & James, the duo of American tenor Branden James (known for *America's Got Talent*) and Australian cellist James Clark (a former music educator), have built an international performance career spanning more than 60 countries and countless cruise contracts. Their signature blend of classical crossover vocals, virtuosic cello playing, and lush pop arrangements has made them a standout act in the world of guest entertainers. As a married couple and musical team, they bring authenticity, intimacy, and artistic integrity to their shows—qualities that consistently captivate cruise audiences.

"We both love travel. We love the concept of adventure," says James. "Cruising is not our preferred method of travel … although we do talk about how easy it is to unpack once and be taken to a bunch of different places." Still, he adds, "There are parts of the world that we've seen because of cruising that we wouldn't have seen otherwise."

Branden first considered cruise work after his time on *America's Got Talent*. "I was 36 at the time and feeling especially old for trying to potentially break into a solo career…. I'd always known that maybe the cruise industry is something you can age well into." Through a friend's industry contacts, he received advice that stuck: "She said, 'You really need to show bookers what you can do. You need a show on a ship that's filmed.' That first hurdle is kind of insane, because if you've never been on a ship, how do you get on a ship to shoot?"

As a duo, they discovered that pitching themselves as both soloists and a team doubled their value to cruise lines, many of which could contract them for multiple shows while providing only one cabin. "They called us *Four Shows, One Cabin* in the office," James says. Branden adds, "Sometimes we'd only perform one or two duo shows and not even touch the solo shows ... and then get the [same] fee."

Despite the artistic opportunities, they quickly learned that life at sea has its quirks. "It's the only gig I think I've ever done where you show up the week of and you don't know until you get on board when you're performing," says Branden. "We guest entertainers exist in a very gray area where you're not full passengers and you're not full crew," adds James. "We fall in the cracks constantly."

That ambiguity often extends to basic logistics. "There was no soap in the shower to wash your hands," Branden recalls of one of their early cruises. "We went up to guest services and said, 'There's no soap in our cabin.' They said, 'Oh yeah, we don't provide soap for guest entertainers.'" James laughs, "The gentleman helping us gave us some Irish Spring from his own cabin."

Artistically, the cruise environment has been liberating. "Producing a show on a cruise ship is kind of like a blank canvas," Branden says. "It's more of a safe space to try something out than in a concert where you're selling hard tickets.... Cruise guests want to get to know you.... The storytelling between songs became just as important as the music itself."

Their visibility doesn't end when they leave the stage. "Once you do your show, then you're kind of famous on board for the week," Branden explains. "That might mean fielding a lot of questions, hosting dinners.... You can't just go into your room and hide because you're very visible." Even in port, guests often stop them to chat or take photos. It's all part of the unique rhythm of ship life—one that blends performance, hospitality, and constant engagement.

Their sound—blending classical, pop, and Broadway—emerged during a long stint playing piano-bar gigs in Santa Fe. "People would come in and want to hear an aria or something ... or 'Hotel California,' and then the next breath, some Broadway show," James recalls. They also gave the cello a lyrical role in their arrangements: "It really helped inform our sound."

To refine their stagecraft and identity as a true duo, Branden & James worked with cruise performer-turned-director Michael Ziegfeld. "We kind of were constantly refining ways to get the cello out of just accompanying land and into more duetting.... We wanted him to shine just as much," Branden explains. Ziegfeld also helped them elevate the overall theatricality of their show. "He knew all the words to say—like 'gobo.' I didn't know what a gobo was," James laughs. "He gave full-on lighting cues and where to put blackouts and restores and how long they should be. Stuff that we had no idea about." Even smaller choices—like how often to walk to pick up a water cup—became intentional elements of the performance.

Audience connection remains central to their performance style. "Transitions between your songs can be a great opportunity to get to know you," James says. "They love when things go wrong.… They want to see how you respond, like real and authentically." Branden adds, "Our ship shows are a little more up-tempo than we might play on land.… And the pitfall is when people program far too many ballads in a row."

Their shows now include a mix of live performance and carefully chosen tracks. "We have three quite tricky things in our main show … that make life a lot easier if we put them to tracks," James explains. "But 75 percent of our show is live." On larger ships, they enjoy full bands and production; on smaller luxury ships, they adapt to a more intimate lounge setting, often performing self-accompanied.

Though married, they don't make their relationship a focal point of their show. "We don't feel like the cruise environment is necessarily the right place for us to profess our love for one another," Branden says. "We just don't include that part of our story." Still, guests often notice. "Perceptive people … they'll ask us, 'Are you guys a couple?' They'll notice the rings.… They'll say, 'I see the way you guys are looking at each other onstage.'" In the early days, the reactions weren't always welcoming. "People wanted to return their CDs at one point," James admits. "I haven't had any of that since the pandemic."

When asked what advice they'd give to aspiring guest entertainers, Branden is clear: "One giant misconception is that everyone who sings on a cruise ship is a talentless hack.… There's incredible talent when you get out at sea." James adds, "Don't be a diva. Do be patient. Do be kind to everyone.… You're not going to get the red carpet rolled out for you, probably ever."

They're also mindful of shipboard conduct and brand alignment. "There are codes of things that you can say or not say," James explains. Branden adds, "Cruise lines these days are really paying attention to people's social media presence.… They want a well rounded person who's not controversial.… Cruise lines are very neutral environments."

Still, the rewards have been immense. "We've been to Russia before the war … tons of Asia, Israel … parts of Africa that I wouldn't have been to … the Panama Canal, the Suez Canal," James reflects. "Things I would never have been able to do … or afford to do all of that in one lifetime."

"It's also made me realize that as you get older, life doesn't necessarily get easier," Branden says, "but you are much more equipped to deal with things and let things roll off your back." And perhaps most of all, they've learned to adapt. "Roll with the punches," James says. "That's what works well in that environment." It's a lesson that's served them not just at sea but also in life, and one that continues to carry their music, and their partnership, to new and unexpected horizons.

Path 4: Step-On Entertainer

Job Overview

Step-on entertainers are local performers who come aboard a cruise ship while it is docked in port to offer culturally relevant, destination-focused entertainment. Unlike in other entertainment roles, step-on entertainers are not part of the ship's crew or guest manifest and do not live onboard. Instead, they board the ship temporarily—often for just a few hours—to deliver a single performance or program before disembarking.

The purpose of this role is to deepen the guests' understanding of the destination by offering cultural content that complements the itinerary. These roles are especially common on smaller lines such as Azamara, Viking, Seabourn, and Oceania, which prioritize location-based experiences. Step-on entertainers might include opera singers in Italy, flamenco dancers in Spain, steelpan players in the Caribbean, or traditional folk musicians in Greece, and their sets often involve storytelling or speaking about local culture, history, and traditions.

Step-on entertainers are usually hired through local talent or destination management agencies that have existing relationships with cruise lines. However, it is not uncommon for cruise directors or entertainment managers to work directly with performers or groups, especially if there is an established relationship or strong guest feedback from a prior engagement.

Primary Responsibilities

- Provide one or more 45-to-60-minute performances tied to the destination or cultural context of the cruise port.
- Arrive at the ship with all required materials, instruments, costumes, and visual aids.
- Coordinate with the ship's entertainment team to manage access, timing, and logistics.
- Depart the ship upon completion of the event.

Required Skills and Qualifications

- Professional experience as a performer.
- Deep knowledge of the local culture and the ability to communicate it effectively and respectfully.
- Ability to present in the operational language of the cruise ship (or with translation support) for guests.
- Self-sufficiency and excellent time management, as embarkation, performance, and disembarkation typically happen within the same day.

Performance and Rehearsal Schedule

- Step-on entertainers typically perform once or twice per ship visit, often in the late afternoon or early evening, depending on the ship's scheduled departure time.
- There is generally very little rehearsal time with onboard technicians; entertainers must arrive prepared to perform.
- Sound and lighting checks are minimal and usually occur just prior to the performance.

Challenges and Expectations

- Entertainers must work quickly and efficiently with ships' teams to set up and deliver high-impact presentations.
- Schedules are tight, and any delay in port operations or ship arrival can compress or alter the performance timeline.
- Entertainers must be flexible and able to adapt to unexpected technical or logistical issues.
- There is limited opportunity for audience interaction or postshow feedback, as the entertainer disembarks shortly after the performance.

Career Progression and Opportunities

- Step-on entertainers may be invited back regularly by cruise lines that return to the same ports.
- Entertainers may also be recommended by port agents, local entertainment agencies, or tourism boards.
- For performers with strong feedback and professionalism, this path can lead to more frequent engagements across multiple cruise lines.
- Some entertainers evolve their offerings into full guest-entertainer acts for longer-term cruise contracts.

Compensation

- Step-on entertainers are typically paid per engagement. There is a tremendous range in fees, from US$200 to US$25,000, depending on the size and prestige of the act, cruise line, and location. The average pay typically ranges from US$3,000 to US$4,000 per step-on act.
- Cruise lines often arrange for port access, escort onto the ship, and basic hospitality such as meals while onboard.
- Accommodations and travel to the port are usually the responsibility of the performer.

Path 5: Cruise Administrator

Job Overview

Cruise administrators are members of a ship's entertainment management team—typically cruise directors, assistant cruise directors, or activity managers—who are also performers. These hybrid roles combine entertainment leadership and guest-facing administrative duties with regular performance responsibilities. While not hired primarily for their singing, many individuals in these positions contribute vocally during welcome shows, sail-away parties, production shows, special events, and destination programming.

These roles exist on nearly every cruise line and are essential to the day-to-day operations of onboard entertainment. On smaller ships or enrichment-focused lines like Azamara, Seabourn, and Oceania, it's especially common for cruise directors or assistant cruise directors to sing headlining shows as part of their programming. Larger cruise lines may feature vocal performances by administrative staff less frequently, depending on the ship's structure and entertainment roster.

This path is ideal for experienced performers who also have strong organizational, communication, and leadership skills and are interested in expanding their careers into cruise operations and guest programming.

Primary Responsibilities

- Serve as a key leader in the entertainment department, managing events, supervising staff, and representing the department in daily operations.
- Host major events such as welcome-aboard shows, game shows, trivia, sail-aways, and special theme nights.

- Perform vocally during official ship functions—this might include singing at embarkation events, port celebrations, destination lectures, private events such as weddings or burials at sea, or mainstage productions.
- Write, schedule, and execute daily entertainment programming, ensuring smooth coordination between departments.
- Act as a spokesperson for the ship, providing announcements and introducing performances.
- Provide guest services, often fielding questions, handling special requests, and troubleshooting onboard issues.

Required Skills and Qualifications

- Strong leadership and interpersonal skills; previous experience as a team leader, event host, or customer service representative is a plus.
- Performance ability, especially in vocal music, public speaking, or stage hosting.
- Knowledge of onboard entertainment logistics and guest demographics.
- Comfort with multitasking and managing logistics under pressure.
- Ability to work long hours, maintain high energy, and represent the brand under all circumstances.
- Previous cruise experience is often required; many administrators are promoted from within.

Performance and Rehearsal Schedule

- Cruise administrators may sing or perform several times per cruise, depending on the ship's programming needs and the administrator's vocal ability.
- Performance responsibilities are typically layered on top of a full-time schedule of administrative duties.
- Rehearsals for musical numbers or special events are often brief and squeezed between meetings and operational tasks.
- Singing may be part of cohosted acts or featured appearances during official programming.

Challenges and Expectations

- Cruise administrators are "on" nearly all day, balancing operational duties, guest engagement, and performance expectations.

- Because performance is not their sole focus, administrators must maintain vocal health and readiness while juggling an intense workload.
- Unlike cast, administrators are often not given time or resources to rehearse extensively.
- Ten- to fourteen-hour days and high guest visibility mean minimal downtime and high standards of appearance and energy.
- The dual nature of this role requires flexibility and the ability to shift quickly between managerial and performance mindsets.
- Contracts for cruise administrators vary but typically require four months on with two months off.

Career Progression and Opportunities

- Many cruise directors begin their careers as production cast vocalists, lounge entertainers, or activity staff.
- Advancement can lead to hotel-director onboard or shoreside corporate roles.
- Some performer-administrators transition into guest-entertainer work later in their careers.
- Other cruise administrators leverage the leadership and hospitality experience into land-based jobs in event management, arts administration, or tourism.

Compensation

- Cruise administrator salaries vary widely by cruise line and rank. Most typically, activity managers may earn US$2,000–$4,000 per month, assistant cruise directors earn US$4,000–$6,000 per month, and cruise directors earn US$5,000–$15,000 or more per month, depending on experience, bonus structure, and ship class.
- Contracts typically include crew accommodations, meals, laundry, and health-care access, as well as round-trip airfare and frequently a hotel stay the night prior to embarkation for a contract.
- Administrators may also receive ratings or revenue-based bonuses and perks like guest dining privileges, single cabins, or discounts on shore excursions and spa treatments, depending on rank and the ship offerings.

Amanda Poulson: A Career Spanning Every Singing Role at Sea

www.amandapoulson.com | @theamandapoulson

Figure 2.4 Cruise director Amanda Poulson.
Photograph by Kanstantsin Karatysheuski.

Amanda Poulson began her musical journey early, debuting as a child extra in opera productions at age 10 and touring internationally as a featured dancer by 14. A graduate of the University of Wisconsin–Madison with a bachelor of music in vocal performance, she has performed everything from radio jingles and rock vocals to opera, musical theater, and Broadway blockbusters. Amanda's cruise ship career is just as diverse: She has sailed as a production cast vocalist, assistant cruise director, cruise director, and guest entertainer, performing across all seven continents. Notably, she portrayed Tanya in *Mamma Mia!* aboard *Allure of the Seas* and suspended forty feet in the air as the lead vocalist in *Blue Planet*. Her solo guest entertainer shows continue to earn standing ovations for their eclectic mix of Broadway, opera, and popular music.

In the cruise industry, Amanda's trajectory has mirrored the artistic growth many singers aspire to: starting in the ensemble, evolving into leadership, and finally stepping out solo. Her experience provides rare insight into how each role shapes a singer differently: "Once you get to guest entertainer, it's more fun because you get to choose what you sing," she says.

In a lot of the other roles, especially production cast, you have to fit the role—singing styles that you're not necessarily the most comfortable with. And maybe the song isn't in the key that would be perfect for you.... But as you start building your own material ... putting your own show together, you have an ownership over it that is special and thrilling and much more fulfilling.

She didn't jump directly to headliner status—it was a gradual build:"If I had tried to do a guest [entertainer] show without having done production shows, I wouldn't know what audiences responded to," Amanda explains. "Once I'd done cast for a while, I started doing little sets, and once I'd done little sets, I started building my thirty minutes, and then my thirty minutes turned into an hour with tracks. And then a cruise director said, 'You're ready. Get it charted.' It all built organically."

That kind of progression is typical for singers who grow within the cruise world. But Amanda also made a lateral shift into cruise administrator roles, where she eventually became cruise director—a career path that offers visibility, stability, and leadership, but greater challenges: "The biggest one for me was the vocal fatigue," she recalls. "I was not used to talking all day. As the cruise director, that's what you do—talking in meetings, chatting with guests, going to dinners. There's no sick track for your show. If you're sick ... you either don't go on or you push like hell.... There is no vocal rest."

While singers often imagine life as a cruise director to be glamorous or authoritative, Amanda warns that the job is demanding, especially when you still have to perform: "I would get to 5:00 p.m., look at my schedule, and be like, 'Oh, I have a tech run. I have a show tonight,'" she says. "On the one hand, it became so comfortable that I could put my fake ponytail on and go out and do my show standing on my head ... but the vocal fatigue was really challenging."

She laughs now at her own lack of vocal discipline: "I drank too much coffee. I tried to stay hydrated.... I wish I had some beautiful health regime—I don't. I'm a bad girl. I drank too much coffee and ate pizza." But she also learned hard lessons, like when her hotel director sent her home mid-party because she was too sick to be dancing, even if she wasn't singing.

That combination of overextension and resilience defines much of Amanda's path. In ensemble work, she found joy in teamwork: "When you're in the cast, you're working with a team.... You know who's going to have your back. Someone's going to hold your zipper together.... That teamwork onstage is special."

As a soloist, she's learned to rely on herself. "You sink or swim by yourself on that stage. While that is magical and wonderful, it can get lonely ... but all the pressure is on you, which is also thrilling." Some singers thrive in casts; others are made for solo stardom. Amanda values both. "I'm lucky—I liked both. But now, at my age, I would much rather just do my own thing."

Her shows now feature a mix of musical theater, opera, pop, and storytelling and have taken her across all seven continents. But not without some drama: "There was one show—I *think* I hear the captain say, 'Bravo, bravo, bravo!' I'm standing onstage thinking to myself as I sing, 'Did he just say "bravo"?'... Also, I'm the voice of the ship. And on 'bravo', I need to go to the bridge. And here I am standing in my sparkly dress!" (In cruise-ship parlance, "bravo" isn't a form of praise—it's the emergency code for fire, a call for crew to immediately activate their emergency duties.) She paused the show, called the bridge, confirmed everything was under control, and walked back onstage to finish her song. "And then the captain came on: 'Ladies and gentlemen, terribly sorry. I was watching on the monitor to make sure Amanda had finished her number, as I know I had rudely interrupted her. I wanted to reassure you that everything is okay.'"

It wasn't the first memorable mishap—she once vomited from seasickness in the wings twice mid-show, and on another contract, she fell off the front of the stage into the audience during *We Will Rock You*—but she always got back up. Literally.

Table 2.1 Common Cruise Ship Vocal Ranges by Role

Role	Typical Range	Style Notes
Female Production Vocalist (Soprano)	G3 to C6	Strong legit/mix; occasional belt to F5
Female Production Vocalist (Belt/Mezzo)	G3 to F5	Strong belt/mix; pop/rock emphasis
Male Production Vocalist (Tenor)	C3 to B4	Strong mix/belt; occasional extension to D5
Male Production Vocalist (Bari-Tenor)	A2 to B4	Belt/mix with strong low register; pop/rock and MT
Male Production Vocalist (Baritone)	A2 to G4	Rick lower register; strong pop and MT ballads
Lounge Entertainer (Any Gender)	Flexible	Must adapt to wide variety of genres
Guest Entertainer (Any Gender)	Flexible	Must sustain full-length solo show
Step-On Entertainer (Any Gender)	Flexible	Short-format, high-impact act with cultural significance
Cruise Administrator (Any Gender)	Flexible	Must sustain full-length show after hosting all day; vocal stamina is key

Which Cruise Ship Singing Path Is Right for You?

A decision flowchart for aspiring seafarers of song

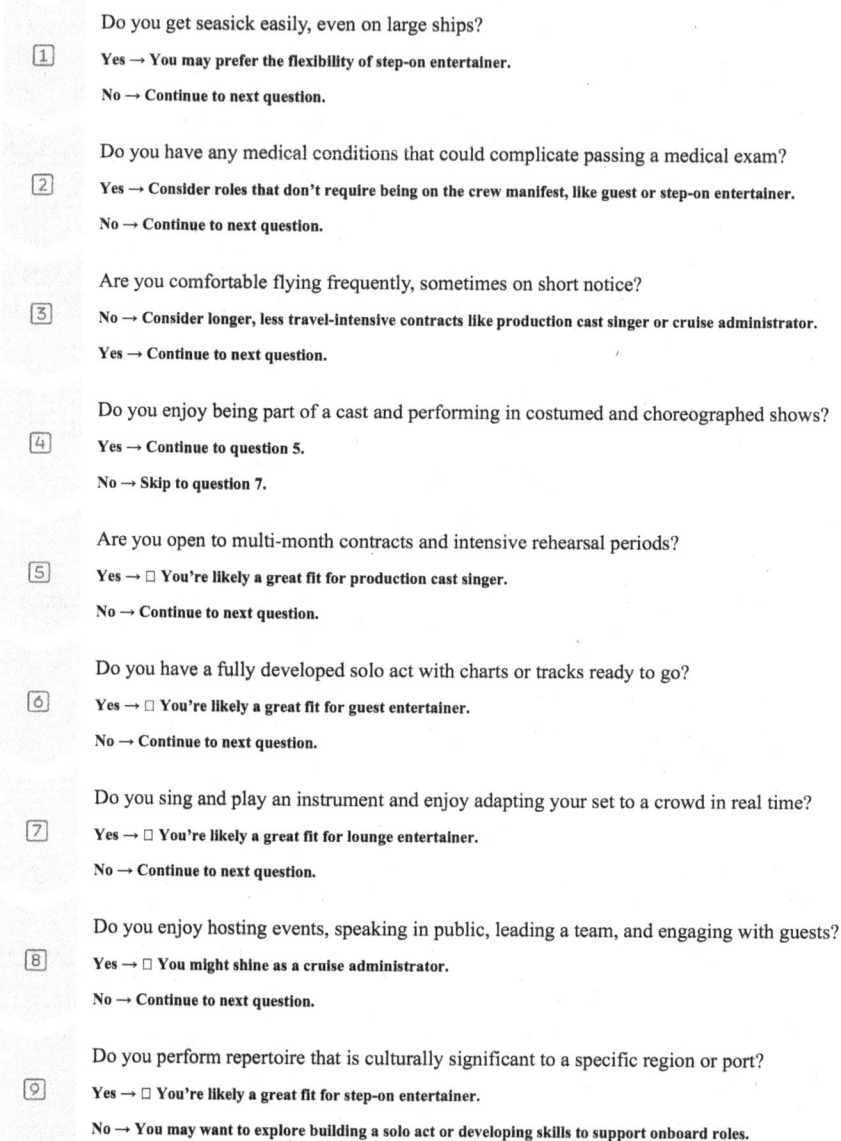

1 Do you get seasick easily, even on large ships?

Yes → You may prefer the flexibility of step-on entertainer.

No → Continue to next question.

2 Do you have any medical conditions that could complicate passing a medical exam?

Yes → Consider roles that don't require being on the crew manifest, like guest or step-on entertainer.

No → Continue to next question.

3 Are you comfortable flying frequently, sometimes on short notice?

No → Consider longer, less travel-intensive contracts like production cast singer or cruise administrator.

Yes → Continue to next question.

4 Do you enjoy being part of a cast and performing in costumed and choreographed shows?

Yes → Continue to question 5.

No → Skip to question 7.

5 Are you open to multi-month contracts and intensive rehearsal periods?

Yes → ☐ You're likely a great fit for production cast singer.

No → Continue to next question.

6 Do you have a fully developed solo act with charts or tracks ready to go?

Yes → ☐ You're likely a great fit for guest entertainer.

No → Continue to next question.

7 Do you sing and play an instrument and enjoy adapting your set to a crowd in real time?

Yes → ☐ You're likely a great fit for lounge entertainer.

No → Continue to next question.

8 Do you enjoy hosting events, speaking in public, leading a team, and engaging with guests?

Yes → ☐ You might shine as a cruise administrator.

No → Continue to next question.

9 Do you perform repertoire that is culturally significant to a specific region or port?

Yes → ☐ You're likely a great fit for step-on entertainer.

No → You may want to explore building a solo act or developing skills to support onboard roles.

Figure 2.5 Decision flowchart to help singers determine their cruise ship path. Author made.

For Amanda, cruise ships didn't just provide a career. They shaped her identity as a singer, a leader, and a human being: "It all evolved for me as naturally and as perfectly as it possibly could have," she says. She found her voice in more ways than one—by testing it in different settings, by building stamina in tough roles, and by creating shows that reflected her full artistic self. Ships gave her the space to fail, to grow, to laugh, and to step into her spotlight.

From throwing up in the wings to fielding bravo codes in rhinestones, Amanda Poulson proves that at sea, there's no such thing as a linear path—only evolution. And if you're willing to say yes to each role, each challenge, each port, and each unexpected moment, you might just find that the job changes you as much as you change the show.

Which Role Is Right for You?

The decision between pursuing mainstage production work and individual performance roles depends on your strengths, career goals, and lifestyle preferences. Production singers must enjoy structure, repetition, and collaborative artistry; individual performers must be self-starters with broad musical range, crowd awareness, and a tolerance for unpredictability.

Some singers thrive in both worlds, performing as cast members early in their cruise careers and later transitioning into guest entertainer work. Others find their niches and stay there, refining a particular brand or musical identity over many contracts.

The key is to know where you shine, where you're stretched, and how you can grow. Whether you're harmonizing in a quartet while executing choreography in front of 1,000 guests or belting solo on a deck under the stars, you'll find endless opportunities on the cruise stage for expression and connection—on your terms, and the audience's.

The cruise industry offers a wide spectrum of performance opportunities for singers, each with its own rhythm, rewards, and realities. Whether you envision yourself being part of a dazzling production cast, engaging intimately with guests as a lounge entertainer, stepping into the spotlight as a guest headliner, balancing performance and leadership as a cruise administrator, or sharing cultural heritage as a step-on entertainer, the sea has a place for you. Understanding the nuances of each path—from contract length and compensation to community dynamics and performance expectations—will help you chart a course that aligns with your talents and professional goals. No matter the route, success at sea requires not only vocal ability but also flexibility, stamina, and a willingness to embrace the ever-changing world of cruise ship life. In the next chapter, we'll explore how to prepare for and pursue these opportunities—from building your audition materials to navigating the casting process with confidence.

3 Applying, Auditioning, and Landing the Job

Getting hired to sing on a cruise ship is unlike landing a typical land-based gig. While casting calls and auditions still exist, the hiring structures and expectations vary widely depending on the type of contract. Some roles require strong musicianship, ensemble collaboration, and significant group rehearsal time prior to joining the vessel; others prize self-contained solo work, audience engagement, and self-sufficiency onboard. As a result, cruise lines rely on a range of hiring methods—some employ casting agencies or production companies, others work through music agents or talent bookers, and many roles are filled through referrals and networking. Whether you're applying as a production cast vocalist, a lounge entertainer, a cruise administrator who performs, a headlining guest entertainer, or even a one-time step-on act at a port of call, you first must understand the process. In this chapter, we'll explore the cruise ship application and audition process step by step, acknowledging the subtle differences across job types while focusing on the core elements that apply to all singers seeking work at sea.

Finding Cruise Ship Singing Jobs

Cruise-Line Direct Hiring

Some cruise lines hire singers directly through their entertainment departments. Larger companies, such as Royal Caribbean Group and Carnival Corporation, often maintain casting websites where they post open roles for production cast vocalists, lounge entertainers, and sometimes even guest entertainers. Applying directly through these portals typically requires submitting a resume, a headshot, a reel, and sometimes specific audition materials tailored to the cruise line's branding and show style.

Cruise administrators—such as cruise directors, assistant cruise directors, and activity managers—are also often hired directly by the cruise line's human resources and entertainment departments. Unlike performers who are hired through internal production companies, cruise administrators typically apply through the main corporate career portal of the cruise line.

Entertainment Agencies and Production Companies

Many cruise lines outsource the casting, staffing, and even production of their entertainment offerings to specialized agencies. These companies act as intermediaries, holding auditions, creating show concepts, producing full-scale performances, curating talent pools, and recommending performers to the cruise lines they represent. Some of the best-known agencies and production companies in cruise entertainment include RWS Global, Belinda King Creative Productions, and Proship Entertainment.

These agencies might cast singers into production shows, staff lounge entertainers like solo pianist-vocalists or party bands, or contract short-term guest entertainers. Each agency has its own application process, but the process typically mirrors cruise line expectations: video reels, resume and headshot submissions, and usually live callbacks. Because many of these companies are responsible for both building the shows and casting them, understanding each agency's specific brand and style is crucial when submitting materials. You can get a sense for each organization by studying its website or social media accounts.

Open Auditions and Casting Calls

From time to time, cruise lines and their partner agencies host open auditions, either virtually or in person. These are announced through platforms such as Backstage, Playbill, Casting Networks, Actors Access, and the cruise lines' official casting sites. Open auditions are common for production show performers, but lounge entertainers and guest entertainers may also find opportunities posted from time to time. Especially after the pandemic, virtual submissions have become more accepted, meaning singers from around the world can apply and be considered without necessarily attending a live audition.

Talent Scouts and Recruiters

Some singers are approached by talent scouts or cruise recruiters who specialize in sourcing entertainment talent. These individuals often scout performers at land-based shows, music festivals, or college showcases or via online platforms like YouTube, TikTok, and Instagram. While this pathway is less predictable, it is becoming more common as cruise lines expand their talent searches globally.

How I Booked My First Cruise Gig (By Breaking the Rules)

When I auditioned for my very first cruise ship contract, Azamara was casting their inaugural *Opera on the High Seas* ensemble through MCO Productions. The call was for four opera singers to perform a chamber version of *Carmen*, plus a few production shows featuring the best of opera, operetta, and golden-age musical theater.

At callbacks, I was one of many sopranos competing for a single spot. And let me tell you, standing outside the audition studio, everyone sounded like a goddess. Glorious legato lines. Shimmering high notes. Total vocal prowess. I knew I had to find a way to stand out.

So, I did exactly what you're *not* supposed to do at a classical audition: I yodeled (specifically, Gabrielle's German drinking song "Auf der Berliner Brück" from *La Vie Parisienne*, for those who are curious). Little did I know, the stage director at the casting table was a huge fan of yodeling. Going with my gut got me the gig.

The takeaway? Know your strengths. Understand the brief. And sometimes, breaking the rules (musically) is exactly what gets you hired.

Personal Recommendations and Networking

As with many industries, networking plays a critical role. A strong recommendation from a current cruise employee—especially a cruise director, musical director, or entertainment manager—can fast-track an application. Many singers land their first cruise contracts because a friend or former colleague recommended them. Maintaining strong professional relationships and being open to casual performance opportunities can open unexpected doors.

Personal recommendations are especially critical when last-minute replacements are needed. Ships often require emergency hires due to illnesses, unexpected departures, family emergencies, or travel issues. Because there is usually no time to hold full auditions in these situations, hiring managers rely heavily on trusted recommendations from within their networks to fill positions quickly and reliably.

Regional Event Agencies and Port Agents

Step-on entertainers for day-only performances while in port are usually contracted through regional agencies specializing in cultural acts, through agencies that represent local acts globally such as International Event Bookings

Table 3.1 Sample Audition Listing for a Cruise Ship Production Cast Vocalist

Casting Director	Jeremy Fitch
Project	Countess Cruise Line—January 2025 Vocalist Auditions Production Company: Countess Cruises Musical Director: Chuck Bélanger Choreographer: Donny Teeson Audition Dates: January 22–24, 2025, in NYC Callback Date: January 26, 2025, in NYC Rehearsal Start Date: February 18, 2025, in NYC Onboard Contracts: Approx. 6 months after 4–5 weeks of rehearsal Rate of Pay: Onboard salary US$1,250/week minimum (based on experience) Location: Worldwide All performers receive rehearsal pay, shared housing, and transportation for rehearsals. Vocalists receive a single exterior cabin, passenger privileges, travel privileges, and meals onboard.
Role	FEMALE-IDENTIFYING VOCALIST: 28 to 45 years old, any ethnicity, female identifying. Must have rock belt up to at least a C above middle C *and* a soprano to G5 minimum. Some shows require female-identifying vocalists to belt to an F5 and a soprano range to a C6. This performer will take on the motherly, comic-relief, or diva-type roles in our production shows. Should move well.
Audition Instructions	Initial submission via Actors Access. If invited to audition in person, please prepare 32 bars of two contrasting songs: 1) Contemporary pop, rock, or R&B song. 2) Musical theater song that shows off your range. Women must prepare a soprano song with a minimum G5. We are also seeking females who can do a sustained C6 as well—you may opt to showcase that instead of the G5. Please bring sheet music—an accompanist will be provided. Please bring your book of music. All vocalists should also bring a hard copy of their headshot and resume. IN THE ROOM: Jeremy Fitch (casting) and Erin Jodoin (accompanist)
Location	Ripley-Grier Studios, 520 8th Ave., 16th Floor, Studio 16Q, New York, NY, 10018
Contact Info	casting@countesscruises.com

(IEB), or through port agents working directly with the ship. Although port agents are not entertainment professionals, they often have relationships with local performers and can facilitate short-term bookings on behalf of the ship.

Guest Entertainer Agencies

Guest entertainers—such as headliner vocalists, magicians, comedians, tribute artists, and variety-act performers—typically follow a different hiring process from production show singers or lounge entertainers. Rather than sourcing contracts directly with the cruise line, most guest entertainers work through specialized agencies that exclusively represent acts for cruise ship bookings.

The agency's agents either book acts directly with the cruise line's entertainment department shoreside or collaborate with larger production companies that manage onboard entertainment programming on the cruise line's behalf. Guest entertainers very rarely negotiate with the ships or cruise lines themselves; representation is considered essential for accessing these short-term contracts.

Well-known agencies that specialize in representing guest entertainers for cruise ships include Blackburn International, MMEC Entertainment, Don Casino Entertainment, and Zoë Tyler International.

Each agency has a roster of acts and established relationships with cruise lines, making them the primary point of contact for securing guest entertainer contracts. Guest entertainers typically submit a two-minute reel, promotional materials, technical riders, and references to these agencies for consideration. Once accepted onto a roster, an act may be booked for anywhere from a single cruise to a season of itineraries, depending on demand.

Navigating the Submission, Audition, and Interview Process

Once you've located a potential opportunity onboard, the next step is to prepare and submit audition materials—or, depending on the role, go through an interview or agency-led vetting process. Unlike traditional auditions for land-based gigs, cruise ship auditions are often more streamlined, conducted virtually, or routed entirely through a third party such as an agency or recruiter. Understanding what's expected for each role can help you put your best foot forward.

Building a Competitive Application Package

Cruise ship casting is fast paced and competitive. Casting directors view dozens—sometimes hundreds—of submissions per week. A professional, polished package is essential not just to get noticed but also to get hired. While requirements vary by position, most audition materials can be grouped into a few core elements: visual presentation, performance documentation, and communication readiness.

Core Components for All Performer Types

Regardless of the role, most performers should have the following materials ready to go:

- **Professional headshot** (or press-quality promotional image for guest and step-on entertainer roles)
- **Performance resume** (tailored to cruise or live entertainment work for strictly singer roles and tailored to entertainment-focused experience showing leadership and guest service for cruise administration roles)
- **Demo reel** (professionally edited, no more than 2 minutes in length, with roughly 10 varied clips of 10 seconds each, plus a closing frame with contact information)
- **Clear contact information** (including representation, if applicable)
- **Availability timeline** (especially helpful for lounge, cast, administrator, and guest roles booked months out)

Your materials should be hosted on a well-organized cloud folder, personal website, or EPK (electronic press kit) that can be shared with a single link.

Production Cast Vocalists

Production shows are built around high vocal standards and ensemble cohesion. This is what casting directors look for:

- **Strong, varied reels** showing multiple styles: pop/rock, legit, musical theater, etc.
- **Dance footage** if required (some tracks are "triple threat")
- **Clear range and part** (soprano/mezzo/tenor/baritone, belt/mix/head, etc.)
- **Ability to blend and harmonize** (often tested in callbacks)

Singers auditioning for production cast roles can expect a more structured and rigorous casting process, especially if applying to a large cruise line or a production company that designs mainstage shows.

Typical steps include these:

- Submitting a headshot, resume, and performance reel

- Learning sides provided by the casting team and filming them or performing live
- Often attending a live callback, either in person or via Zoom—this may include a movement call to assess basic coordination and ability to pick up choreography
- A brief interview following the final audition—you may be asked about availability, past shipboard experience, teamwork, and guest service scenarios; they want to know if you are mature, adaptable, easy to work with, and able to live in tight quarters

Production companies may cast several months in advance and often hold auditions in major entertainment hubs like New York City, London, Toronto, or Sydney. Rehearsals typically take place on land in company studios before embarking.

Self-Tape Best Practices

A strong self-tape can set you apart. A weak one—regardless of vocal talent—can take you out of the running very quickly.

Keep these tips in mind:

- Use clean, natural lighting and quiet environments.
- Frame from mid-torso up, and ensure your eyes are visible and engaged.
- Film in front of a neutral wall or backdrop (skip virtual backdrops—they're distracting and unprofessional).
- Start with a slate: your name, height, vocal range, and song titles.
- Read the brief carefully and follow every instruction.
- Avoid overediting the recording: casting directors want clarity, not production.

Lounge Entertainers

The process for lounge entertainers—such as band singers or piano-bar performers—is usually more flexible. These performers are evaluated as much for vibe and versatility as for vocal chops. Essential submission components include the following:

- A reel showing stage presence and guest engagement—ideally filmed in front of an audience
- Repertoire list organized by genre
- If you play an instrument, multi-instrument footage for bonus points
- Information about whether you read charts or improvise

Table 3.2 Sample Audition Tracker for Cruise Ship Cast Positions

	Countess Cruises	**Cruise Line #2**
Date Applied	January 10, 2025	
Position	Female Identifying Vocalist	
Submission	Online via Actors Access	
Audition Date	January 24, 2025	
Audition Location	Ripley Grier 520 8th Ave, NYC	
Audition Rep	Requirements: • 32 bars pop, rock, or R&B • 32 bars musical theater with C6	
Audition Personnel	Jeremy Fitch (Casting Director), Erin Jodoin (Accompanist)	
Audition Notes	Bring headshot, resume and sheet music; accompanist provided	
Status	Callback invite ITR	
Callback Date	January 26, 2025	
Callback Location	Ripley Grier 520 8th Ave, NYC	
Callback Rep	Requirements: • "Defying Gravity" • "Proud Mary" • "I Could Have Danced…" • Movement combo: 4 x 8 count	
Callback Personnel	Jeremy Fitch, Chuck Belanger (Musical Director), Donny Teeson (Choreographer)	
Callback Notes	Nailed C6 in "I Could Have"; easy choreo to "Burn Baby Burn"	
Final Outcome	Contract offered! Rehearsals start February 18, 2025, in NYC	

A casual and confident tone is better than overly polished studio footage here. You're auditioning to be a crowd pleaser, not a leading man or lady. Most applications are submitted through entertainment agencies or directly to casting portals online. Live auditions are rare, though some agencies may conduct virtual interviews or live Zoom auditions to assess singers' personality and professionalism.

Guest Entertainers

Guest entertainers follow a different process entirely. They are typically not involved in auditions per se—instead, their agents submit curated promotional packages directly to cruise lines' entertainment bookers or external production companies managing guest entertainment.

This package usually includes the following:

- Two distinct 2-minute promo reels, each aligned with one of your full-length shows—ideally from live performances with audience energy and filmed within the past two years
- A tech rider with stage plots, setlists, and cue sheets for two different 45-minute shows
- A bio and show descriptions used for guest programs and marketing—your agent will inform you of the exact word count required for different cruise lines
- Optional: reviews, quotes, and social media stats

Guest entertainers do not usually audition in real time. The promotional package *is* the audition, and agents advocate on their behalf. This makes having a well-branded, high-quality promotional kit essential for securing work.

Step-On Entertainers

Like guest entertainers, step-on entertainers rely on agents or port representatives to submit pre-vetted promotional content to cruise lines or shipboard entertainment leadership. Their material is often culturally specific and may be coordinated last minute based on the itinerary. For this reason, flexibility and excellent video footage are key.

Materials include the following:

- A 2-minute performance reel showcasing cultural authenticity and quality
- A tech rider with minimal needs—simplicity is key
- A short bio in English and/or the local language or operation language of the cruise line

Step-on entertainers usually do not interact with casting or entertainment departments directly, and instead work through tourism boards, regional arts councils, or international agencies such as IEB. You may have only a few days' notice for an opportunity, so keep your materials updated and mobile accessible.

Cruise Administrators

Cruise administrators, including cruise directors, assistant cruise directors, entertainment managers, and activity managers, go through a multistep interview process rather than performance auditions.

Cruise administrators who perform should prepare the following:

- An entertainment-focused resume showing leadership and guest service—highlight things like event planning, team management, conflict resolution, revenue generation, and multilingual skills
- A professional headshot
- A 2-minute demo reel, showcasing either live performances and/or past cruise directing
- Certificates of leadership training if available and reference letters

Once a candidate applies (either through the cruise line directly or through a staffing agency such as V.Ships), the typical process includes the following:

- An initial HR screening or interview
- A second-round interview with the director of entertainment at the cruise line's corporate office; at this point, the candidate may be asked for their demo reel
- Often a third interview with the head of hotel operations, particularly if the role includes significant guest service oversight or event management
- Occasional follow-up emails or calls to references to verify onboard experience or leadership capabilities

General Tips for All Applicants

Before you apply, make sure everything is ready to go—cruise jobs can move quickly, especially when cruise lines are filling last-minute replacements. Tailor your materials to the specific role rather than relying on a one-size-fits-all approach. Keep all links current, as casting directors won't take the time to track down expired Dropbox files or broken YouTube URLs. Use clear, professional file names like "Smith_Tenor_Reel_2025" to make your materials easy to identify and access.

After submitting your materials or completing an audition or interview, it's perfectly acceptable to follow up once after 10 to 14 days. Keep your tone

Table 3.3 Sample Job Posting for a Cruise Director Position

Position	Cruise Director
Cruise Line	Countess Cruises
Contract Dates	4 months on, 2 months off; anticipated start date: fall 2025
Company Profile	At Countess Cruises, we blend luxury, adventure, and exceptional guest service to create unforgettable voyages. Our award-winning entertainment program is a cornerstone of the guest experience, offering world-class performances in intimate, elegant venues.
Position Overview	We are seeking a charismatic and experienced Cruise Director to serve as the face and voice of our onboard entertainment program. This is a dynamic role that combines leadership, public speaking, and performance. In addition to managing the entertainment team and hosting events, the Cruise Director will present a solo headliner show during each voyage, showcasing their own unique performance skills.
Key Responsibilities	• Host evening entertainment, shipboard activities and events, make daily announcements, and safety-related communication. • Oversee all entertainment programming, scheduling, and staffing in partnership with the Entertainment Manager. • Lead, mentor, and evaluate the entertainment team. • Perform a professional solo headliner show each cruise. • Liaise with other departments to ensure a seamless guest experience. • Maintain high visibility around the ship, fostering rapport with guests. • Represent us at embarkation, disembarkation, and special events.
Required Qualifications	• Minimum 2 years of experience in entertainment leadership, hospitality, or guest-facing performance roles (cruise experience preferred) • Professional-level performance ability in music, comedy, or specialty entertainment, with the ability to mount a full-length show. • Exceptional public speaking and improvisation skills. • Strong organizational and leadership abilities, with experience managing diverse teams. • Proficiency in Microsoft Office. • Fluent in English; additional languages a plus.

Compensation & Benefits	• Competitive salary, onboard accommodations, meals, and medical. • Worldwide itineraries with exciting port destinations. • Opportunity to combine travel with performance in a leadership role.
How to Apply	Submit your CV, cover letter, and performance reel via the Countess Cruises career portal: https://www.countesscruises.com/careers

Table 3.4 Most Commonly Requested Audition Songs for Production Cast Vocalists

Female Vocalists (Soprano / Mezzo / Belt)		
Song Title	**Artist / Show**	**Category**
"Edge of Glory"	Lady Gaga	Pop/Rock
"Natural Woman"	Aretha Franklin	Pop/Rock
"Make You Feel My Love"	Adele	Pop/Rock
"Proud Mary"	Tina Turner	Pop/Rock
"Rolling in the Deep"	Adele	Pop/Rock
"Someone Like You"	Adele	Pop/Rock
"The Winner Takes It All"	ABBA	Pop/Rock
"Valerie"	Amy Winehouse	Pop/Rock
"Defying Gravity"	*Wicked*	Musical Theater
"Don't Rain on My Parade"	*Funny Girl*	Musical Theater
"Good Morning Baltimore"	*Hairspray*	Musical Theater
"I Dreamed a Dream"	*Les Misérables*	Musical Theater
"Let It Go"	*Frozen*	Musical Theater
"On My Own"	*Les Misérables*	Musical Theater
"At Last"	Etta James	Jazz Standard
"Cheek to Cheek"	Irving Berlin	Jazz Standard
"Fever"	Peggy Lee	Jazz Standard
"Orange Colored Sky"	Nat King Cole	Jazz Standard
"Art is Calling for Me"	*The Enchantress*	Classical Crossover
"I Could Have Danced All Night"	*My Fair Lady*	Classical Crossover
"O mio babbino caro"	*Gianni Schicchi*	Classical Crossover
"Think of Me"	*Phantom of the Opera*	Classical Crossover

Male Vocalists (Tenor / Bari-Tenor / Baritone)		
Song Title	**Artist / Show**	**Category**
"Don't Stop Me Now"	Queen	Pop/Rock
"Faith"	George Michael	Pop/Rock
"Livin' on a Prayer"	Bon Jovi	Pop/Rock
"She's Always a Woman"	Billy Joel	Pop/Rock
"Shut Up and Dance"	Walk the Moon	Pop/Rock
"Superstition"	Stevie Wonder	Pop/Rock
"Sweet Caroline"	Neil Diamond	Pop/Rock
"Uptown Funk"	Bruno Mars	Pop/Rock
"Bring Him Home"	*Les Misérables*	Musical Theater
"I'm Alive"	*Next to Normal*	Musical Theater
"Music of the Night"	*The Phantom of the Opera*	Musical Theater
"Maria"	*West Side Story*	Musical Theater
"The Impossible Dream"	*Man of La Mancha*	Musical Theater
"This Is the Moment"	*Jekyll & Hyde*	Musical Theater
"Feeling Good"	Michael Bublé	Jazz Standard
"Fly Me to the Moon"	Frank Sinatra	Jazz Standard
"The Way You Look Tonight"	Jerome Kern	Jazz Standard
"Mack the Knife"	Kurt Weill	Jazz Standard
"Nessun dorma"	*Turandot*	Classical Crossover
"Some Enchanted Evening"	*South Pacific*	Classical Crossover
"Time to Say Goodbye"	Andrea Bocelli	Classical Crossover
"You Raise Me Up"	Josh Groban	Classical Crossover

respectful and positive—something like, "Hi [Name], just checking in regarding my submission for [role]. I'm still very interested and happy to provide anything else you might need. Thanks again for your time and consideration." Casting directors and hiring managers are used to being bombarded, but you should avoid being pushy or asking for feedback unless it was specifically offered. Plus, keep in mind that cruise casting timelines can be delayed by ship itineraries, onboard emergencies, or sudden scheduling changes, so patience and professionalism go a long way.

Red Flags and Industry Best Practices

Despite its idiosyncrasies, cruise entertainment is still part of the entertainment industry, meaning performers must stay informed, cautious, and empowered. Not every opportunity is legitimate, and not every offer is worth accepting. This section outlines key red flags to watch for, as well as the best practices that will help you protect your career and your creative work.

Red Flags to Watch For

If something feels off during the hiring process, it's worth investigating. Be wary of these:

- **Agencies that require large upfront fees** to represent you or promote you. Reputable agencies earn a commission from the contracts they secure for you—not from your pocket before you've booked a job.
- **Audition notices that are vague** or fail to name the cruise line, production company, or agency involved. If the entity behind the job isn't transparent, proceed with caution.
- **Lack of clear contracts or agreements.** Every legitimate cruise job—whether for one night or six months—should involve a written agreement outlining dates, compensation, duties, and travel arrangements.

If you're unsure about a job offer, talk to other performers, consult online forums, or seek guidance from professional organizations like NATS, AGMA, or AEA.

Best Practices for Navigating the Industry

- Research the agency, production company, or cruise line before signing any contract. A quick search can often reveal if others have had negative experiences or glowing ones.
- Keep your materials current and professional. That means having updated headshots, reels with clips filmed within the last two years, and polished resumes formatted for clarity and impact.
- Track your submissions and contacts. Whether you're applying independently or through multiple agencies, keep records of whom you've contacted, when you contacted them, what you sent, and the outcome.

You are not just an artist—you are also your own brand and business. Approach this process with both creative enthusiasm and strategic clarity.

Now it's time to take the leap and prepare for life onboard. In the next chapter, we'll dive into what to expect after you land the job: the written contract, pre-embarkation training and required documents, and what to pack for the unique lifestyle and working environment at sea.

4 Preparing for Life Onboard

Congratulations—you've gotten the gig! Whether you're about to board your first ship or you're returning to sea in a new role, you should begin every contract with preparation. Cruise ship life is unlike anything on land. Setting yourself up for success begins long before you pack your suitcase. This chapter outlines everything singers need to know—from the onboarding process to packing tips—to ensure a smooth transition from land to sea.

The Written Contract

Cruise ship contracts come in a few different formats depending on your role and who's hiring you. In all cases, read carefully before signing—these are legal documents, often issued by third-party agencies rather than the cruise lines themselves. Here's what to expect:

Production Cast Vocalists

- **Format:** Typically issued by a casting agency or production company (e.g., RWS, Belinda King, or NCLH Creative Studios) acting on behalf of the cruise line, or as an entertainment subset of the line. You'll receive a formal employment agreement or letter of intent, often as a PDF to be signed digitally (via Docusign, Adobe Sign, or a similar software).
- **What's Included:** Contract dates (including land-based rehearsals), ship assignment, weekly salary, travel terms, medical requirements, expectations around cabin sharing, costume care, and behavior clauses.
- **Key Clause:** The cruise line reserves the right to terminate the contract with little notice, usually for health, safety, or disciplinary reasons.

Lounge Entertainers

- **Format:** Usually an independent-contractor agreement or a letter of intent by an agency representing you to the cruise line. These are PDF documents signed digitally or by hand.
- **What's Included:** Performance expectations (sets per night, days off, etc.), weekly or daily rate, cabin type (often shared unless otherwise specified), visa reimbursement policy, gear responsibilities, and tech requirements.
- **Key Clause:** Contracts often include a "no replacement" policy, meaning if you break contract, the agency may not rebook you in the future.

Guest Entertainers and Step-On Entertainers

- **Format:** Usually a performance agreement or offer letter, often much simpler in scope than those for long-term roles. The contract may be directly from the cruise line or from an entertainment agency.
- **What's Included:** Embarkation and disembarkation dates, performance fee, travel and baggage reimbursement terms, number of performances, expectations for availability (e.g., meet-and-greets, safety drills, etc.), and tech specs.
- **Key Clause:** Cruise lines often reserve the right to cancel with short notice and no compensation beyond reimbursed travel.

Cruise Administrators

- **Format:** Typically a corporate employment agreement, usually through the cruise line's HR portal or via email, to be signed digitally. This may be delivered quite late in the onboarding process, sometimes only a week or two prior to signing on.
- **What's Included:** Salary and benefits, job title and duties, duration of contract, uniform policy, and rules for on- and off-duty conduct.
- **Key Clause:** Cruise lines typically retain the right to adjust your ship assignment or to extend or shorten contracts based on operational needs.

Unions and Cruise Ship Work

Cruise ship contracts occupy a unique legal space—outside the jurisdiction of most performance unions but still loosely governed by international maritime labor protections. Here's what that means in practice:

Artist Unions Don't Have Jurisdiction at Sea

If you're a member of AGMA, AEA, CAEA, ACTRA, or another artist union, cruise ship work won't violate your union status. Why?

- These unions do not have jurisdiction over cruise ship performances.
- Cruise lines operate under international flags and are not bound by land-based union agreements.
- You are typically hired as an independent contractor or foreign crew member.

The upside: You can accept cruise work without fear of penalty or loss of union membership.

The downside: You're not protected by artist union standards—no minimum rehearsal pay, overtime, pension contributions, or guaranteed days off.

Seafarer Unions and CBAs (Collective Bargaining Agreements)

If you're on the ship's crew manifest (as most production cast vocalists, lounge entertainers, and cruise administrators are), your contract technically falls under a collective bargaining agreement (CBA) negotiated by a seafarer's union.

For example:

- Azamara crew contracts are covered under a CBA negotiated by the Norwegian Seafarers' Union (NSU).
- These CBAs cover basic labor standards, including working hours, safety, medical care, repatriation rights, and more.
- The cruise line is required to provide you with a copy of the CBA prior to embarkation, typically emailed as a PDF by the cruise line or your crewing agency.
- You're automatically covered under the applicable CBA—no need to join or pay initiation fees.
- You can request union assistance in the event of serious issues (e.g., contract termination without cause, injury, or repatriation disputes).
- Enforcement may vary depending on the cruise line's flag state and the responsiveness of the union.

Practical Takeaways

- Cruise ship work is nonunion from a performer's standpoint—you're on your own when it comes to negotiating artistic conditions.
- But if you're listed as crew, you do have some legal and labor protections under maritime law, which may prove valuable if problems arise.
- Always keep a copy of your signed contract and familiarize yourself with the relevant seafarer union CBA for your cruise line.

The Onboarding Process

Once you've accepted the contract, the next step is figuring out what documents you need to provide, what training you need to complete, and how and when you'll actually join the ship. The onboarding process varies greatly depending on whether you're joining via the crew manifest or the guest manifest, and whether you've been hired through a production company or agency or directly by the cruise line. Let's walk through the process by role and manifest status.

Joining via the Crew Manifest

This is the most common onboarding route for production cast members, lounge entertainers, and cruise administrators. Signing onto the crew manifest means you'll be treated as a ship employee (as opposed to a guest) and go through official crew onboarding, safety training, and maritime protocols. Once your contract is in place, communication typically shifts to the onboarding team at the cruise line's staffing agency. They handle the logistics: collecting documents, booking flights, confirming embarkation ports, and making sure you meet all training, medical, and visa requirements.

First Points of Action

After you have accepted the offer, there are several administrative and logistical tasks you'll need to complete—some of which can take weeks or even months. Prioritize the following actions as soon as you receive your contract to avoid delays and ensure a smooth embarkation:

Apply for or check your passport.
- If you don't already have a valid passport, apply immediately, as processing can take several weeks or longer depending on your country.
- If you already have a passport, confirm that it is valid for at least 6 months beyond your contract end date—some cruise lines

recommend 9–12 months of validity to avoid issues at ports or during visa applications.

- Ensure you have at least two blank pages in your passport. Some countries may require more, so it's best to have at least six blank pages to be safe. If you don't have these, consider renewing your passport before beginning your onboarding process.

Schedule your preemployment medical exam (PEME).

- This exam must be completed at a cruise-line-approved clinic (your crewing agency will provide a list).
- Appointments can book up months in advance and results may take time to process, from a few days to a few weeks.
- Be prepared to set aside 2–3 hours for the medical appointment—it is very comprehensive and includes a general physical, a chest X-ray, a vision test, a hearing test, a drug test, blood work, and, less commonly, a gynecological examination and a dental checkup.
- You will need to provide immunization records, typically showing receipt of the following vaccinations at a minimum:
  - Measles, Mumps, and Rubella
  - Varicella
  - Tetanus
  - Yellow fever
  - Seasonal influenza
  - COVID-19
- Once approved, the medical certificate is usually valid for two years, and you are required to have the original medical paperwork and signed certificate brought with you to the ship. Digital copies or print facsimiles will not be accepted onboard.
- The cost varies around the world but expect to pay US$100–$500. Some cruise lines require you to pay out of pocket, while others will reimburse you.

Apply for a C-1/D visa (if you're not a US citizen or permanent resident).

- This visa is required for joining ships that embark from or transit through US ports.
- The application process involves completing an online DS-160 form, paying a nonrefundable fee of US$185, and attending an in-person interview at a US embassy or consulate.
- The cruise line typically provides a letter of employment or letter of guarantee to the seafarer that is submitted with the visa application.
- Processing times vary by country, but plan for about 2–3 months total from scheduling your interview to receiving your visa and passport.

Apply for a seaman's book.

- A seaman's book (also called a Seafarer's Identification and Record Book or SIRB) is usually required depending on the cruise line and the flag state of the ship you're joining.
- Your onboarding coordinator will confirm if this is needed and provide the correct application form and submission instructions.
- Processing time is typically 4–6 weeks for standard service; expedited options may be available in 5–15 business days.
- Plan on spending anywhere from US$70 to US$150, depending on the flag state and any extra expediting fees.
- Most cruise lines do not reimburse for the initial issuance of your seaman's book. They treat it like a passport—your personal responsibility. Some cruise lines will reimburse renewal costs if your book expires while you are under contract or will cover the cost if the cruise line requires you to have a seaman's book that differs from the flag state of one you already hold.

Register for required safety training.

- **Basic Safety Training (STCW):** Many cruise lines require singers to hold current STCW (Standards of Training, Certification and Watchkeeping for Seafarers) certification prior to boarding. STCW includes modules on personal survival techniques, first aid, firefighting, and personal safety and social responsibilities. Performers often need to travel to a city where the training is offered; it's not uncommon to go outside your home region to complete the training. Once completed, STCW certification is valid for 5 years and must be renewed if you continue working at sea beyond that period. The full course takes approximately 40 hours to complete and is usually conducted ashore at a certified training facility with access to a pool and firefighting zones. A typical breakdown includes this:
  - **Personal survival techniques:** 12 hours
  - **Elementary first aid:** 8 hours
  - **Fire prevention and firefighting:** 16 hours
  - **Personal safety and social responsibilities:** 4 hours
- **Security Awareness Training:** Most cruise lines also require performers to complete Maritime Security Awareness training prior to joining. This is a self-paced online course, typically taking about 4 hours to complete. It covers piracy awareness, threat identification, and the performer's responsibilities in supporting shipboard security. Unlike STCW, security-awareness training does not expire, so it usually needs to be done only once unless otherwise required by the company.
- **Crisis and Crowd Management:** If the cruise line anticipates that your safety role onboard will involve dealing directly with passengers

in the event of an emergency (which is common for singers due to their strong communication skills and comfort with commanding the attention of large groups of people), you will likely also be asked to acquire the following certificates:

- **Crisis Management and Human Behavior:**
  - This is offered at accredited maritime centers as well as online, can usually be completed in 2–4 hours, and is valid for 5 years.
  - The training covers essential topics such as crowd management, communication during emergencies, human behavior under duress, evacuation protocols, and leadership and coordination during crisis scenarios.
- **Crowd Management:**
  - This course is also offered in person and online, takes approximately 1–3 hours to complete, and is also valid for 5 years.
  - The training covers procedures for assisting passengers in emergency situations, crowd-control techniques, familiarization with emergency exits and muster stations, and communication strategies during evacuations.

Travel and Transfers

You will likely be flying internationally to join your ship. The flight will be booked by the cruise line or crewing agency, but you may not receive your flight details until one to two weeks before your embarkation date. The crewing agency will also send you a letter of guarantee (LOG), which you should carry with you. This document confirms that you are joining a vessel as crew and you may be required to show it to immigration officers at the airport. Once you arrive at your destination, you'll go through customs and immigration, collect your luggage, and look for a port representative—often holding a sign with the cruise line's or agency's name. You'll likely be grouped with other embarking crew members and transferred together to a designated hotel for an overnight stay. At check-in, hotel staff will inform you of your pickup time the next morning for transfer to the ship. Whether you have your own hotel room usually depends on the accommodations outlined in your onboard contract. If you are assigned a single cabin onboard, you'll be given a private hotel room. If you are assigned a shared cabin onboard, expect to share a hotel room with another embarking crew member. Meals and hotel expenses are usually covered but be sure to keep receipts for later reimbursement if you're instructed to pay for anything up front.

Port Check-In Process

Once you arrive at the embarkation port, you'll report to the port security at the designated terminal for check-in. You will pass through airport-like security

Table 4.1 Document Checklist for Crew

Travel Documents	Medical Documents
☐ Passport (valid for at least 6 months beyond your contract end date) ☐ C1/D Visa (if applicable) ☐ Letter of Guarantee (LOG) ☐ Flight itinerary & boarding pass	☐ Original Pre-Employment Medical Exam (PEME) and Medical Certificate ☐ Immunization Records (Measles/Mumps/Rubella, Varicella, Tetanus, Yellow Fever, Seasonal influenza, COVID-19)
Safety Certificates (STCW) ☐ Personal Survival Techniques ☐ Elementary First Aid ☐ Fire Prevention and Fire Fighting ☐ Personal Safety and Social Responsibilities ☐ Security Awareness ☐ Crisis Management & Human Behavior ☐ Crowd Management	**Additional Ship Documents** ☐ Seaman's Book ☐ Signed contract/job offer letter

either in the port terminal or onboard: Expect to have your luggage X-rayed and for you to pass through a metal detector. You'll most likely be met by the crew administrator and possibly a member of the medical team. Expect to surrender your passport (it will be held by the crew administrator for the duration of your contract), have your photo taken and receive your crew ID, complete any required COVID-19 protocols, and do drug testing (depending on cruise-line policy). You will be responsible for bringing all your luggage onboard. You'll be shown to your cabin and have a short window to settle in before being sent to collect your uniform (if applicable), begin induction training, and head to work.

Joining via the Guest Manifest

This route applies to guest entertainers—these performers are considered non-crew and board the ship as temporary passengers, though they are working.

First Points of Action

The first priority is to ensure your passport is valid for at least 6 months beyond your final disembarkation date, with at least two blank pages available. Even though as a guest entertainer your contracts are much shorter in duration than those of most crew members, the six-month passport-validity rule is a regulation that many countries require to avoid travelers overstaying their visas or becoming stranded. If you need to disembark at a different port due to unforeseen circumstances, this regulation also builds in a travel safety net. Unlike crew, you are not required to hold a seaman's book or STCW certificates, but you are personally responsible for securing any required visas. You'll need to be cleared for all countries on the itinerary, not just your embarkation and disembarkation ports, even if you don't plan to go ashore, as immigration officials may conduct in-transit inspections.

Travel and Check-In

A guest entertainer's travel process is quite similar to that of a crew member's—at least at first. You'll typically fly internationally, clear customs, and collect your luggage at the airport. In many cases, a transfer to your hotel will be arranged for you but not always, so it's essential to double-check with your agent whether you're responsible for covering the cost of transfers to the hotel and the port. If you do have to cover those expenses, be sure to save your receipts for reimbursement through your agent or booking agency. If a transfer is arranged, you'll be told at hotel check-in what time to expect your pickup the next morning, just like if you were a crew member.

However, that's where the similarities end. Once you arrive at the port, you are treated as a guest, not crew. You'll pass through security screening, either in the port terminal or onboard, but you will not undergo a drug test or crew-level clearance. A COVID-19 test may be administered, depending on current ship protocols, but this is becoming increasingly uncommon as pandemic-era policies are phased out.

Onboard Orientation

Once onboard, you'll most likely be directed to guest relations to check in, receive your key card, and make your own way to your cabin. Unlike crew, you will not need to surrender your passport, but you will be asked to put a credit card on file for any onboard expenses you incur. In most instances, a welcome letter will be waiting for you in your cabin with your rehearsal and performance details along with contact information for key figures in the entertainment department. You won't undergo any induction training, but if you arrive on the first day of a cruise, you will be required to attend the passenger muster drill. If you arrive mid-cruise, you will likely be briefed by a guest-relations officer on what to do in the event of an emergency.

Whether you're joining the crew or guest manifest, always carry hard copies of your contract, flight details, LOG, and visa confirmations and any required certificates. You may be asked to present any of these documents at any point in the process. Having printed versions ensures you're covered even if your phone dies, you lose service, or a digital file refuses to load at the worst possible moment. When it comes to boarding a ship, paper still wins the day.

What to Pack

Packing for life at sea is part art, part science, and all strategy. It's not like packing for a vacation—it's more like outfitting a tiny, floating version of your life. Whether you're joining as crew or a guest entertainer, your luggage needs to balance practicality, performance readiness, and personal comfort without exceeding airline weight limits or cabin storage space. Unlike during a land-based gig, you won't always have easy access to a drugstore or a fully stocked department store, so thinking ahead is key. What you pack (or forget to pack) can make the difference between feeling prepared and spending your first week onboard scrambling for essentials. And, of course, what you need depends heavily on the length and nature of your contract. Singers joining the ship on the crew manifest for a multi-month contract need to think long term and self-sufficiently, while guest entertainers joining for just a week or two can pack lighter but still need to cover essentials.

General Packing Approach

Before diving into the details, it's helpful to approach cruise packing with a strategy. Some international flights booked for crew include a minimum luggage allowance of 30 kilograms (66 pounds), but more often, you will be permitted two checked bags at 23 kilograms (50 pounds) each, plus one carry-on (often capped at 8 kilograms [17 pounds]) and a personal item like a backpack that can fit under the seat in front of you. Once you receive your flight details, be sure to .check your airline's specific limits, especially for carry-on size and weight. When choosing your luggage, consider collapsible options like rolling duffels or soft-sided suitcases—hard-shell luggage is difficult to store in small cabins, where space is tight and underbed storage is often your only option.

As a general rule, aim to pack at least one week's worth of clothing, assuming three outfits per day:

1 A workout outfit
2 A casual day look (think "resort casual" for onboard and comfortable streetwear for shore days—be sure to pack according to the climate of your itinerary)
3 An evening outfit, which might be cocktail attire or performance wear depending on your schedule

If you are in the production cast, assume that all performance costumes will be provided unless you are told otherwise. But if you're a lounge entertainer or cruise administrator, you'll need to bring your own performance attire. Some cruise lines host formal nights once or twice per itinerary, so check with your agent or onboarding coordinator to see if you should pack formal wear, like a tuxedo or evening gown.

Also note: If you're a singer on the crew manifest with additional hosting duties, it's not uncommon to be provided with a day uniform for nonperformance responsibilities—typically a pair of khakis or shorts and a polo shirt or button-down, with white sneakers (which you're expected to provide). Cruise administrators may be issued a similar daytime uniform. However, it's rare for entertainment staff to be given a formal evening uniform—you're usually expected to wear your own cocktail or upscale attire during evening hours so you're easily distinguishable to guests. If your contract does include a provided uniform, your onboarding team will inform you during predeparture communication.

Now that you've got the big-picture strategy in mind, let's break things down by category. Whether you're heading out for a multi-month contract or a quick guest engagement, use these lists as outlines of what to bring so you can step onboard shipshape and stress free.

Travel and Documents

All Performers (Crew and Guest)

- Passport and printed documents
- Credit card and some local currency for your arrival country
- Folder or pouch to keep all documents together
- Pen (for possible customs forms)
- Binder or folder with sheet music (digital copies are great, but hard copies are gold when tech fails)
- Printed setlists and cue sheets for the band and the A/V team (if applicable)
- Band charts—hard copies or digital (if applicable)
- Journal or notebook

Clothing and Laundry

Long-Term Contracts (Crew)

Depending on your contract, you may be responsible for laundering your personal attire, or laundry may be done for you. Plan to bring enough clothing that you will need to do laundry only once per week, if required to do so.

- Full performance wardrobe including shoes, undergarments, and accessories
- Workout attire for at least 7 days

- Resort-casual attire and streetwear for at least 7 days
- Evening attire for at least 7 days
- Formal outfit (if applicable)
- Undergarments for at least 7 days
- Swimwear and sleepwear
- Foldable hamper or laundry bag
- Laundry detergent pods and stain remover pen
- Travel garment steamer (dual voltage)
- Small clutch (for phone, ship cards, and small personal objects if pockets are not available to you in your clothing)

Short-Term Contracts (Guest)

You likely won't need to do laundry, so pack complete outfits for each day of your contract plus one spare day:

- Outfits for each scheduled show, plus one extra option
- Workout attire
- Resort-casual attire and streetwear
- Evening attire for nonperformance nights
- Formal outfit (if applicable)
- Personal undergarments
- Swimwear and sleepwear

Health and Toiletries

If you are joining the ship as crew, plan to pack enough toiletries for your first month or two onboard, especially your preferred brands. Availability onboard or in port is limited and often expensive. That said, toiletries are also very heavy, and if your luggage is overweight, you may want to consider smaller quantities of toiletries with the intention of refilling earlier in port or onboard. If you are joining as a guest, travel-size toiletries for the length of your stay will be sufficient.

- Shampoo and conditioner
- Hair-styling tools and products
- Body wash and loofah
- Hand soap and cream
- Face and body moisturizer
- Personal and stage makeup and remover
- Deodorant or antiperspirant
- Perfume or cologne
- Toothbrush, toothpaste, and dental floss
- Razor and shaving supplies
- Feminine hygiene products

- Nail file, clippers, tweezers, and small scissors
- Small first-aid kit (Band-Aids, blister pads, and antiseptic cream)
- Sunscreen and aloe vera gel (for warm-weather itineraries)
- Bug spray (for tropical destinations)
- Shower caddy (for shared bathrooms)
- Prescription medications (enough for duration of your contract) and copies of prescriptions
- Over-the-counter medications: pain reliever, cold/flu relief, and motion-sickness remedies
- Vitamins and supplements
- Glasses and/or contact lenses (if applicable)

Cabin Comfort

- Over-the-door organizer (consider the lightweight plastic variety used for shoes)
- Magnetic hooks (cabin walls are usually metal and this maximizes storage)
- Essential-oil diffuser and essential oils (also doubles as a small humidifier)
- Power strip (most cabins have a mix of North American type A and type B as well as European type C outlets; older or UK-flagged ships may also have UK type G outlets)
- Reusable water bottle

Tech and Connectivity

- Phone and charger
- Worldwide travel adapter
- Laptop or tablet
- Backing and click tracks, video backgrounds, and QLab files in cloud storage with USB backup (if applicable)
- Personal in-ear monitors and props (if applicable)
- Portable hard drive (filled with entertainment like movies, television shows, and music for times with no connectivity)
- External battery pack (helpful for charging phones on the go while in port)
- Digital reading device (preloaded with books)

What Not to Pack: Prohibited Items

- Candles and incense (open flames are not permitted onboard; if purchased in port, these items will be confiscated by security and stored until sign-off)

Staying On Top of Time Zones

Cruise ships frequently sail through multiple time zones, and when you're at sea without cell service or Wi-Fi, your phone can't reliably keep up. In fact, if your device is set to automatically detect your date and time, it may jump to the wrong time zone entirely (or not update at all), leading to missed call times, rehearsals, or even shows.

Here's what to do instead:

- Go into your phone's settings and turn off automatic time and date updates.

- When you're informed that the ship's clocks are changing (usually announced by your manager or via the daily schedule the night before), manually adjust your phone's time before going to bed.

- Choose a major city in the new time zone the ship is entering—this ensures your device stays aligned, even without a signal.

Table 4.2 Packing Checklist for Crew

Travel & Documents	Health & Toiletries
☐ 2 x collapsible checked luggage	☐ Shampoo and conditioner
☐ 1 x carry-on bag	☐ Hair styling tools & products
☐ 1 x personal item	☐ Body wash and loofah
☐ Luggage scale	☐ Hand soap and cream
☐ Travel pillow and blanket, eye mask, ear plugs	☐ Face and body moisturizer
☐ Passport & printed documents	☐ Personal and stage makeup and remover
☐ Credit card and some local currency for arrival country	☐ Deodorant or anti-perspirant
☐ A folder or pouch	☐ Perfume or cologne
☐ A pen	☐ Toothbrush, toothpaste, dental floss
☐ Sheet music, band charts, set lists, cue sheets (as applicable)	☐ Razor and shaving supplies
☐ Journal or notebook	☐ Feminine hygiene products
	☐ Nail file, clippers, tweezers, scissors
Clothing & Laundry	☐ Small first-aid kit
☐ Workout attire x 7 days	☐ Sunscreen and aloe vera gel
☐ Casual day attire x 7 days	☐ Bug spray
☐ Evening outfits x 7 days	☐ Shower caddy
☐ Formal outfit (if applicable)	☐ Vocal steamer or nebulizer
	☐ Prescription medications and copy of prescription

Clothing & Laundry	
☐ Undergarments x 7 days	☐ Over-the-counter medications
☐ Swimwear and sleepwear	☐ Vitamins and supplements
☐ Foldable hamper or laundry bag	☐ Glasses and/or contact lenses (if
☐ Laundry detergent pods and stain remover pen	applicable
☐ Travel garment steamer (dual voltage)	**Tech & Connectivity**
☐ Small clutch	☐ Backing and click tracks, video backgrounds, Q-Lab files (if applicable)
Cabin Comfort	☐ Personal in-ear monitor and props (if
☐ Over-the-door organizer	applicable)
☐ Magnetic hooks	☐ Portable hard drive
☐ Essential oil diffuser and essential oils	☐ External battery pack
☐ Power strip	☐ Digital reading device
☐ Reuseable water bottle	

- Firearms, ammunition, or any weapons
- Cooking appliances
- Large sports equipment
- Anything flammable or explosive
- Hazardous chemicals
- Alcohol or recreational drugs (although most cruise lines permit crew to bring on one sealed bottle of wine or spirits or a six-pack of beer per port after embarkation)

One final word of advice: Always pack your essential items in your carry-on. This includes all prescription medications, your passport and documents, and any performance-critical items like band charts, USBs with tracks, essential toiletries, and at least one performance outfit. Luggage can be delayed or lost in transit, and it's not uncommon to be asked to perform on embarkation day, so make sure you're ready to go even if your checked bags don't arrive when you do.

With your bags packed and your documents in hand, you're ready to board. But getting on the ship is only the beginning. In the next chapter, we'll explore how to navigate ship life—from daily routines and unspoken rules to crew hierarchies, social dynamics, and what it really means to live, work, and play at sea.

5 Navigating Ship Life

Whether you're joining a ship for six weeks or six months, life onboard is unlike anything on land. Cruise ships are self-contained, floating communities with their own social rules, hierarchies, and cultural rhythms. As a singer, you'll live where you work, share space with colleagues from dozens of nationalities, and navigate both the glamour of guest-facing performance and the realities of crew life below deck. This chapter explores what it means to live and work at sea—not just the logistics of cabin life, crew messes, and limited internet, but also the soft skills required to thrive in a tight-knit, multicultural, and often intense environment. Learning to adapt, communicate across cultures, and maintain a strong sense of self are just as essential as vocal technique. Welcome to ship life—unpredictable, exhilarating, and profoundly transformative.

What to Expect Onboard

Living on a cruise ship as crew means embracing a lifestyle that's part dormitory, part workplace, and part backstage greenroom—all at once. While guests enjoy spacious suites and endless buffets, your day-to-day will be shaped by the rhythms and realities of crew life below deck.

Cabin Life

Crew cabins vary depending on your role and rank. Production cast vocalists and cruise administrators usually receive larger single accommodations, while lounge entertainers may share smaller crew cabins with a roommate. Guest entertainers almost always receive guest cabins. Most crew cabins include a compact en suite bathroom, twin beds or bunks, a small desk or vanity, limited storage, and, if you're lucky, a porthole. Space is tight, so smart organization and mutual respect (if you have a roommate) go a long way.

It's important to remember that your cabin is company property, not personal property. You're expected to keep it clean, report any damages promptly, and treat it with care. You are not permitted to make permanent modifications or

Figure 5.1 Example of a crew corridor with a staircase and watertight doors. Courtesy MaleeS/Shutterstock.

decorate with any items that pose a fire hazard, such as string lights, candles, or incense. That said, many singers find creative ways to personalize their spaces. Walls are typically magnetic, so you can hang lightweight souvenirs, photos, or organizational tools using magnetic hooks and clips. A little ingenuity goes a long way in making a small space feel like home—without breaking any rules.

Cooking appliances and irons are also not allowed in cabins due to fire risk, though hair tools like curling irons, flat irons, and travel-sized garment steamers are usually acceptable. Always check your line's specific policies to be safe.

Figure 5.2 Example of a senior officer's cabin and bathroom on a luxury vessel. Photograph by the author.

Bringing food into your cabin can be tempting, especially after a long day. However, perishable food is typically not permitted, as it can attract pests. Nonperishable snacks—such as granola bars, instant noodles, or sealed nuts—are generally allowed and can make for handy between-show sustenance.

To ensure health and safety standards are maintained, weekly cabin inspections are carried out by officers onboard—typically right after crew drill. Inspectors check for cleanliness, adherence to safety regulations, and any unauthorized items. Failing inspection can lead to written warnings or the loss of certain privileges, so it's wise to keep your space tidy and rule compliant.

Meals and the Mess

Meals are typically served buffet-style in the crew mess or staff mess, and in most cases, any crew member can dine in either. The difference is less about rank and more about culinary preference. The crew mess often reflects the dominant nationalities among the crew—commonly Indonesian, Filipino, and Indian—so expect flavorful curries, rich dishes, noodles, and spiced meats. The staff mess, on the other hand, tends to offer more Western or Eurocentric options, aligning with the tastes of officers and senior staff. You might find pasta, roast meats, salads, and simpler, less spiced fare there.

Food quality and variety can differ from ship to ship and port to port. While some crew grow tired of mess offerings quickly, others find it manageable with a bit of creativity or enjoy the opportunity to expand their palettes. Some singers—particularly production cast vocalists, guest entertainers, and cruise administrators—may have guest-area dining privileges for some meals, but this varies widely across cruise lines and contracts.

If you have dietary restrictions, it's important to communicate them to your manager, who can liaise with the mess attendants or the food-and-beverage manager on your behalf. Vegetarian and pork-free options are often available by default, but more specific needs—such as gluten intolerance, nut allergies, or religious dietary rules—may require special requests. Where there is a serious medical condition, such as celiac disease, the ship may grant permission for you to collect your meals directly from the galley, bypassing the buffet to avoid cross contamination.

Internet and Communication

Ship internet has come a long way, but it's still often slower and more expensive than what you're used to on land. Most cruise lines offer discounted crew Wi-Fi packages or daily data allowances. WhatsApp is the go-to app of most seafarers for keeping in touch with one another and loved ones abroad. Expect to adapt your communication habits and plan ahead for port days if you need to upload large files or make important calls.

Receiving Mail Onboard

Getting physical mail while you're working on a cruise ship is possible, but it's not as straightforward as having something sent to a street address. Because ships move constantly, mail is usually routed through one of three main channels:

1   Port Agents
Cruise lines often have port agents in the ports they visit. These agents can receive mail and packages sent ahead for both crew and passengers and then deliver them to the ship when it arrives. If you're using a port agent, you'll need the correct address format (usually your name and ID number, your department, the ship name, and the agent's contact information). Your crew office or HR department can provide the most up-to-date details.

2   Crew Centers
Many home ports have crew centers that handle mail and packages specifically for crew members. These centers often also have services like wire transfers, snacks, and internet access. Crew members can have their mail sent to the crew center's address in the home port and pick it up when the ship is docked there. This can be one of the most reliable options, especially for regular deliveries.

3 Company Addresses

Some cruise lines maintain PO boxes or other centralized addresses for mail delivery. Mail sent to these addresses is then forwarded to the appropriate ship or port. While convenient for friends and family, this method can be less reliable due to potential delays and handling by multiple personnel along the way.

Port Days and IPM

Port days are a highlight of ship life. If you're not scheduled to work, you can disembark and explore, restock your toiletries, or simply enjoy some sunshine. However, not all contracts offer equal freedom. Singers on the crew manifest should expect to have safety drills, rehearsals, and hosting responsibilities, while singers on the guest manifest usually have more opportunity to explore. That said, managing your time well can allow you to enjoy remarkable destinations while fulfilling your duties onboard.

It's also important to be aware of IPM (In Port Manning), a rotating safety requirement that ensures a percentage of the crew remains onboard in case of emergency while the ship is docked. IPM is usually organized by a color-coded system: Each crew member is assigned a color group, and each port day is assigned a color. If your color is up that day, you must stay onboard, regardless of your work schedule.

Most cruise lines allow you to swap IPM with another crew member if needed, as long as both parties share the same emergency duties and follow the proper process. This typically involves submitting a form signed by both crew members and approved by your manager and the safety officer. IPM responsibilities are generally once per week, depending on how often the ship is in port, and, of course, there is no IPM on sea days, since all crew are onboard.

Depending on your nationality and the local immigration laws, you may need to carry your passport, a shore pass, or both when going ashore. In some ports, additional documentation is required, and in rare cases, crew may not be permitted ashore at all, either due to their nationalities or because of heightened security levels in the port. If documentation is needed, the crew administrator will communicate the collection and return process. Always follow these procedures carefully to avoid immigration issues or being denied shore leave.

Rules and Routines

There are rules unique to ship life, like wearing your name tag in guest areas, avoiding guest elevators and certain venues, and always washing your hands upon entering the mess. Each cruise line has its own code of conduct, and it's important to familiarize yourself quickly. Things like curfews, alcohol limits, and

What Happens During a Charter Cruise?

Every so often, your entire cruise contract will take an unexpected turn—when the ship is fully chartered by an outside company, organization, or special-interest group. In these cases, the normal cruise itinerary may stay the same, but the entire onboard experience is customized to suit the charter client.

There are typically three types of charter experiences from the perspective of the entertainment team:

Full Integration: The charter client wants all the ship's built-in entertainment. You perform as usual, possibly with minor tweaks to content or scheduling.

Full Replacement: The client brings their own performers, speakers, or entertainment program and doesn't use any of the ship's existing entertainment team. In this case, you may find yourself with unexpected, but paid, time off.

Hybrid Model: The client uses a mix of their own and the ship's entertainment. For example, you may still perform one show but not the others, or you may be asked to join in a welcome party or theme night outside your usual duties.

If you are not required to perform during a charter and want to take advantage of the time off, you may apply for permission to temporarily disembark the ship. This is called applying for shore leave. The request usually requires approval by these people:

Your division head (typically the cruise director or entertainment manager)

Your department head (usually the hotel director or general manager)

The HR manager (a corporate representative onboard)

If approved, this time can be used to rest, travel, or explore. However:

Any travel expenses incurred during shore leave are the sole responsibility of the crew member.

Shore leave is not paid.

That said, if you choose to remain onboard—even if you're not performing—you will still be paid, as you are still considered "on contract" and are present for safety duties. In other words, unless formally approved for temporary leave, you are still part of the vessel's crew and expected to be available.

Whether you're performing nightly or soaking up the sun ashore, the key is to stay flexible. Charter cruises can feel like a curveball, but sometimes, they're a gift.

cabin inspections may feel restrictive at first, but they exist to ensure safety and professionalism in a shared space.

Rules and expectations are communicated in several ways. During the onboarding process in the weeks prior to joining the vessel, you'll often be asked to review and electronically sign documents outlining the onboard rules, appearance standards, and behavioral expectations. Once onboard, you'll receive in-person training from senior officers and your managers as part of your embarkation. This is your opportunity to ask questions—if anything is unclear, speak up. It can

Table 5.1 Sample Entertainment Department Privilege Grid

Benefit	CD	Managers	Vocalists	Technicians
Cabin cleaning	Y	Y	Y	Y
Laundry	Y	Y	Y	Y - Uniform
Retail shops	Y	Y	Y	Y
Spa services	Y	Y	Y	Y
Pool	N	N	N	N
Guest gym	Y	Y	Y	N
Running track	Y	Y	Y	Y
Room service	Y	N	N	N
Family cruising benefit	Y	Y	Y	Y
Buffet restaurant	Y	Y	Y	Y
Specialty restaurants	Y	Y	Y	Y
Guest café	Y	Y	Y	Y
Guest bars & lounges	Y	Y	Y	Y - for job
Gelateria & Creperie	Y	N	N	N
Cigar lounge	N	N	N	N
Casino	N	N	N	N
Master account	Y	N	N	N
Guest laundry	N	N	N	N
Guest elevators	Y	Y (w/ guest)	Y (w/ guest)	Y (w/ guest)

(Actual privileges vary by cruise line.)

take time to absorb all the nuances of shipboard life, and those who are new to working at sea are typically given a little extra grace as they learn.

One framework that helps clarify the shipboard structure is the privilege grid—an internal document generated by shoreside HR that determines which crew members have access to certain areas and perks onboard. The grid outlines, based on rank and department, what you're allowed to wear, where you can eat or exercise, whether you can have a drink in a guest bar, or even what route you can take to walk through guest areas. For singers, privileges might vary widely depending on contract type. Production cast members and cruise administrators often enjoy more access than entry-level crew, but every role has its own set of guidelines. Understanding your position on the grid helps you avoid unintentional missteps and gives you a clearer picture of how the ship's hierarchy operates in practice. You will be provided with the grid upon embarkation, and the grid is typically posted in a visible location in your manager's office.

Hierarchy and Protocols

Cruise ships operate under a strict and well-defined hierarchy, not unlike a naval institution. Understanding this structure is essential not just for knowing who your boss is, but also for navigating ship life with professionalism and ease. From rank-based privileges to the way you address officers, protocol matters at sea.

The Chain of Command

Every department on a cruise ship has its own structure, but all departments feed into a central chain of command. For singers, this often means reporting to a cruise director, an entertainment manager, or both, depending on the line and your role. The entertainment department is part of the hotel division, which also includes food and beverage, housekeeping, shore excursions, revenue, and guest services. Above all of these sits the hotel director, who reports to the captain.

When addressing officers or senior staff, err on the side of formality in guest areas or official settings. Even if you're not directly interacting with senior officers daily, it's important to understand who's who and how the chain of command works. If an issue arises, go to your immediate supervisor first. Skipping the chain or complaining publicly before using proper channels is frowned upon and can damage working relationships.

Cruise ships use a ranking structure that influences everything from privileges to dress codes. Officers typically hold ranks with stripes on their shoulders and cuffs. Here's a quick breakdown of common officer stripes:

- Captain: 4 or 4.5 stripes
- Staff captain, chief engineer, and hotel director: 3.5 or 4 stripes
- Senior officers (e.g., safety officer, food and beverage manager, or cruise director): 3 or 3.5 stripes
- Mid-level officers (e.g., shore excursions manager or security officer): 2 or 2.5 stripes
- Junior officers (often includes production cast vocalists): 1 stripe

Who's Who Onboard—A Quick Guide to Ship Leadership and the EXCOM

Every cruise line has an executive committee (EXCOM)—a small team of senior officers who oversee the major departments onboard and make high-level decisions affecting both guests and crew. While you may not interact daily with them, knowing who they are helps you understand how the ship operates behind the scenes.

Core members of the EXCOM typically include the following:

- **Captain (or Master)**

The highest-ranking officer onboard. Responsible for the overall safety, legal authority, and operation of the vessel.

- **Staff Captain**

Second in command to the captain. Oversees the deck department, and manages all safety-related matters, including environmental and public health.

- **Chief Engineer**

Leads the entire engine department, overseeing all propulsion, technical systems, and energy production.

- **Hotel Director**

Heads the hotel department, which includes entertainment, food and beverage, housekeeping, shore excursions, guest services, and more.

- **HR Manager**

Responsible for crew welfare, discipline, compliance, and support. Oversees onboarding and documentation, and helps maintain a positive shipboard culture.

Figure 5.3 Member of the EXCOM greeting guests on deck.
Courtesy LWA/iStock.

Respecting Other Departments

It's easy to view your role as an entertainer as separate from the rest of ship operations, but success onboard often depends on respectful cross-department collaboration. Be courteous to housekeeping (they clean your cabin), security (they monitor safety and access), and food and beverage (who manage the messes). A good relationship with these teams can make your contract smoother, and a poor one can make it a lot harder.

If you're performing during a special event, you may be working with bar teams, cruise sales, or shore excursions, among other groups. Always approach these opportunities with a service mindset and a willingness to adapt to operational needs. Everyone onboard is juggling multiple responsibilities—you're not the only one working hard.

When in Doubt, Ask

Every ship, cruise line, and contract is different. When you're not sure what's appropriate—whether it's where to walk, what to wear, or who to report to—ask. Learning protocol takes time, especially if you're new to ships. What matters most is demonstrating professionalism, humility, and a willingness to learn.

Working with a Multinational Crew

One of the most unique and rewarding aspects of ship life is working alongside people from all over the world. It's not uncommon for a ship's crew to represent 30, 40, or even more than 60 nationalities, all living and working in close quarters. For singers used to working in relatively homogeneous professional circles, this diversity can be both eye-opening and enriching if approached with curiosity, humility, and respect.

Cultural Sensitivity Is Key

Cultural differences extend beyond language and food. They also show up in humor, social cues, body language, conflict-resolution styles, timekeeping, and concepts of personal space. What's considered assertive in one culture may be seen as aggressive in another. What feels like small talk to you might feel intrusive to someone else.

You're not expected to know every custom, but you are expected to approach differences with respect. Learn to listen more than you speak. If someone corrects you, accept the correction with grace. And if you're unsure about something—how to greet someone, whether it's okay to join a table in the mess, how to refer to someone formally—just ask. Curiosity is welcome; arrogance is not.

Language Barriers

English is the working language on most ships, and crew are expected to have a functional grasp of it. That said, many of your colleagues may speak English as a second, third, or fourth language. Be mindful of how you speak—avoid slang, idioms, or sarcasm that could easily be misunderstood. If you're not understood the first time, try rephrasing simply rather than raising your voice. It's also deeply appreciated when you try to learn a few words in your colleagues' languages—"hello," "thank you," or "good job" go a long way.

Respecting Cultural and Religious Practices

You'll likely work alongside crew who observe religious holidays, dietary laws, prayer rituals, or cultural norms that are unfamiliar to you. Respect is essential. Don't comment on what someone eats (or doesn't eat), wears, or believes. Ships do their best to accommodate various religious and cultural needs, including dedicated prayer spaces, special meals, and adjusted schedules during fasting periods like Ramadan.

Take time to learn about your coworkers' traditions—there's a good chance someone will invite you to a Diwali celebration, a Filipino karaoke night, or a holiday dinner featuring their home cuisine. These cross-cultural moments can be among the most rewarding parts of ship life.

Crew Cultural Events You Might Get Invited To

One of the most joyful aspects of life at sea is the chance to celebrate global cultures with your colleagues. Cultural events are usually organized by the onboard HR department as part of crew welfare programming and often include food, music, dance, and traditional dress.

Here are just a few that you might experience:

- **Filipino Independence Day (June 12)**
Expect karaoke, tons of food, and a whole lot of joy.

- **Diwali**
India's festival of lights often includes sweets, music, and dazzling decorations.

- **Indonesian Independence Day (August 17)**
Expect traditional games like sack races and cracker-eating contests, plus savory dishes like *nasi goreng*.

- **Brazilian Carnival**
Expect samba beats, costumes, and spirited dancing.

- **Eid al-Fitr**
The end of Ramadan is marked with feasting, sweets, and camaraderie.

- **Christmas around the World**
Ships with diverse crews often highlight how Christmas is celebrated in different countries, complete with regional treats and traditions.
Pro tip: If you've got a chance to attend, go! Even if you're not sure what to expect, attending these events shows respect for and interest in your colleagues' cultures and often includes delicious food and incredible music.

Figure 5.4 Crew bar set up for live music performance. Photograph by the author.

Working Styles and Expectations

Different cultures have different attitudes toward hierarchy, teamwork, and initiative. Some crew may defer to authority in ways you're not used to, while others may be very direct. Tensions sometimes arise—not out of malice but from mismatched expectations. The key is to remain open-minded and adaptable. Remember: There's more than one "right" way to communicate or solve a problem.

If conflict does arise, try to resolve it quietly and respectfully first. If that's not possible, escalate it through the appropriate channels—usually your department head or HR. Avoid gossip or passive-aggressive behavior. On a ship, word travels fast and reputations form quickly.

Diversity Is a Strength

While it can take time to adjust, working with a multinational crew offers incredible opportunities for growth. You'll learn about different ways of thinking, build empathy, and expand your worldview. Many performers say this aspect of ship life changed them more than the travel ever did. You may board the ship as a singer, but you'll have the opportunity to leave it as a global citizen.

Social Life, Mental Health, and Boundary Setting

Life on a cruise ship is a paradox: You're surrounded by people 24-7, yet it's possible to feel deeply isolated. The social dynamics onboard can be vibrant, intense, and emotionally charged, especially when your workplace, home, friend group, and romantic possibilities are all wrapped up in the same small steel bubble. For singers who often move between guest-facing glamour and below-deck crew reality, navigating this environment with self-awareness and boundaries is crucial.

Making Friends at Sea

You'll meet people quickly onboard—during training, mealtimes, and department duties. Shared experiences and tight quarters tend to accelerate friendships, and many singers find deep, lasting bonds with fellow crew. That said, friendships at sea can also be transient. Contracts end, people transfer ships, and not every connection becomes lifelong.

Being friendly, respectful, and open to new cultures will help you build relationships. Attend a crew event, join people exploring ashore, or simply sit at a different table in the mess once in a while. But also listen to your gut: If you need time to yourself, take it. Energy management is key.

Navigating Ship Life with a Partner or Children at Home

Cruise ship life doesn't happen in a vacuum. Many singers who work at sea do so while maintaining relationships, marriages, and even parenting responsibilities on land. It's not always easy—and it's rarely simple—but it is possible.

A reality that often goes unspoken is that cruise ships are still deeply shaped by traditional gender roles. On most passenger vessels, the ratio of men to women among crew skews quite high toward men. Of the estimated 1.2 million seafarers across the world, female seafarers constitute only 2 percent of the crewing workforce, and only an estimated 1.28 percent of STCW-certified seafarers globally are women.[1] While this is slowly shifting, it still has real-world consequences. Female performers with families may find fewer role models onboard who reflect their own circumstances. Women who do work at sea while raising children often rely on robust support systems at home: parents, siblings, or extended family who help with caregiving during their time away. These crew members carry not only the emotional weight of separation but also the mental logistics of planning school pickups, doctor visits, and birthdays, frequently from the other side of the world.

Long-distance partnerships also require thoughtful communication and shared goals. Some couples manage by both working at sea and syncing contracts and sailing together. Others work alternating contracts and rely on scheduled leave and port meetups to stay connected. For many, the ability to have at least two months of vacation between contracts and give their undivided attention to their partner while on land justifies the time spent away. Like in any long-distance relationship, it's the intentionality that matters—the effort to include your partner in your life at sea and to stay involved in life back home. There is no perfect formula, but being honest about your priorities and needs will help you determine whether cruise work can fit into your life holistically—not just professionally, but also personally.

Romance, Flings, and "Ship Fam"

Shipboard romance is famously intense and often short-lived. Some couples meet and stay together long-term, but more often, ship relationships have a built-in end date: sign-off day. Before diving in, be honest with yourself about your intentions, and remember that anything involving guests is forbidden (unless it is your approved guest from home).

Ships also tend to be highly social and, yes, promiscuous. The culture often follows a "work hard, play hard" rhythm, and it's not unusual for romantic entanglements to unfold quickly. Some crew treat ship relationships as casual fun, while others seek something more serious—either way, use good judgment and prioritize safety. Condoms are often provided free of charge by the onboard medical department. Be safe, be respectful, and don't take unnecessary risks.

While many relationships at sea begin casually, it's important to understand that not all relationships are treated the same, especially when there's a difference in rank. If you're dating someone who is your supervisor (or vice versa), your cruise line may require the relationship to be formally disclosed to human resources. This helps avoid conflicts of interest, favoritism, or perceptions of coercion. Failing to report it can result in disciplinary action for both parties.

Cruise lines also maintain strict sexual harassment policies. What might feel like harmless flirting in the crew bar can cross a line if it's unwanted or persistent. Consent must be clear, mutual, and continuous, and supervisors in particular are held to a higher standard when it comes to appropriate behavior. When in doubt, err on the side of professionalism and respect.

It's also important to know that crew gossip is real—and widespread. The smaller the ship, the faster news travels. Who you're seen with, what cabin you're in, who you're dating or breaking up with—it's all part of the rumor mill. The best protection? Make choices you don't feel the need to hide, but also lead by example: Avoid gossiping, respect others' privacy, and maintain professional boundaries, especially in public areas.

Your "ship fam" is your chosen support circle onboard. These friendships can be deeply meaningful, especially during long contracts. Just be mindful to not become emotionally dependent on a single person or clique. Keep your circle kind, grounded, and flexible.

The Unwritten Rules of Ship Dating

Sure, ship romances can be fun, intense, and memorable, but they come with their own unique playbook. Here are some unspoken truths and tips that seasoned crew know well:

1. What Happens in the Crew Bar ... Is Known by Breakfast
Ships are gossip factories. If you hook up with someone at night, expect it to be common knowledge by morning.

2. Privacy Is a Luxury, Not a Right
Everyone sees everything—who you walk with, who you sit with, which cabin you leave at 6:00 a.m. Choose partners (and moments) with this in mind.

3. Avoid Drama Triangles
Don't date within your own team or department if it's going to cause tension. And if someone just ended something with your roommate? Maybe wait a contract or two.

4. Cabin Swaps Are Sacred
Want to spend the night together? Be respectful of shared cabins and always communicate with roommates—yours and theirs.

5. Keep it Professional in Guest Areas
PDA is a no-go. Always prioritize the job and the guests. If you're having a lovers' quarrel, address it in private.

6. Use Protection—Always
Condoms are usually free from the medical center. There's no excuse—respect your health and your partner's.

7. Be Kind if or When it Ends

You still have to live and work within 200 to 400 yards of each other. Ghosting doesn't work on a ship. Communicate, be honest, and take the high road.

8. Ship Love Is Real, but So Is Ship Logic

Some relationships last forever. Most don't, and that's okay. Enjoy the relationship for what it is without assigning more meaning than it can carry.

LGBTQIA+ Life at Sea

Cruise ships are, by nature, diverse microcosms, but that doesn't always mean they're fully inclusive. For LGBTQIA+ crew members, ship life can be both liberating and challenging, depending on the ship's culture, leadership, and fellow crew.

Many cruise lines are actively working toward inclusivity, with sexual orientation and gender identity increasingly protected under antidiscrimination policies. That said, crews are made up of people from around the world, and many come from countries where being anything other than heterosexual is heavily stigmatized or even criminalized.

Paradoxically, that's part of why ships often become safe havens for queer crew members. Away from the expectations of home, many feel free to express their sexual identities for the first time. It's not uncommon, for example, for a male crew member from a conservative country to have a wife and children at home and a boyfriend onboard. These "dual lives" may seem surprising at first, but they reflect complex cultural and personal realities, and they're more common than you might think.

There's a strong, if often discreet, queer community at sea, especially within entertainment, hotel, spa, and retail departments. Informal gatherings, crew bar karaoke nights, or even just knowing looks on I-95 (the main crew corridor running the length of the ship) can foster a sense of solidarity. You'll find that while some crew members are very open about their identities, others keep things more private—and that's okay too.

For trans and nonbinary crew members, the experience varies widely. Many ships still operate with rigid gender-based systems for cabins, name tags, and uniforms, and not all companies have caught up with inclusive policies. If this applies to you, it's a good idea to reach out to your company's HR rep or crew staffing agency in advance to learn about available accommodations and support.

Pro tip: Seek out allies early—crew who demonstrate kindness, openness, and discretion. And if you ever experience discrimination or harassment, report it to HR and your onboard manager. Every crew member deserves a safe and respectful workplace.

Setting Boundaries in a Small Space

The hardest part of ship life might be that there is very little personal space. People will know when you come and go, where you're working, and who you're spending time with. That's why learning to set boundaries kindly and clearly is a key survival skill.

Some examples:

- You don't have to attend every crew party.
- You can say no to mess-table conversations if you need quiet.
- You can set limits on social media or video calls to preserve downtime.
- You can tell a colleague, "I'm off duty right now—may we talk later?"
- You can ask for a cabin swap or mediation if a roommate situation is affecting your well-being.

Boundaries are not rude—they're respectful. They allow you to bring your best self to the stage and the ship.

Essential Soft Skills for Success

Even if you're vocally exceptional, it's your soft skills that will determine how well you thrive at sea. Ship life is high-pressure, highly collaborative, and constantly changing, and the performers who succeed long-term are the ones who know how to adapt, communicate, and coexist with grace.

Flexibility and Adaptability

Schedules change. Shows are rescheduled. Port calls become surprise sea days. You may be asked to sing at a last-minute sail-away, or to step in for another performer who's ill. Instead of resisting change, lean into it with curiosity. On ships, the phrase "that's not my job" rarely flies—be the person who says, "No problem, I've got it."

Professionalism in Close Quarters

You're not seen just onstage—you're seen also in the mess, at drills, in the hallways, and in port. Being consistently courteous, punctual, and well-groomed matters. Gossiping, whining, or showing favoritism can damage your reputation fast. Understand that every hallway interaction can be part of an informal performance review.

Emotional Intelligence

On a ship, you'll encounter people from dozens of cultures, age groups, and belief systems. Learn to read the room, listen actively, and manage your emotions. When things go wrong—and they will—respond instead of reacting. And if you make a mistake, own it, apologize, and move forward.

Conflict Resolution

Disagreements are inevitable in a confined environment. Whether it's a roommate, castmate, or crew member from another department who you're disagreeing with, learn to address issues directly but respectfully. Don't let problems fester or gossip spread. If needed, involve your manager or HR. Mature communication earns respect fast.

Positivity and Team Spirit

Ship life isn't always easy, but a positive attitude makes a huge difference. Be the kind of person others want to be around. Celebrate your colleagues' wins. Offer help before it's asked for. Show up on time and with a smile. People remember how you made them feel, not just how you performed.

Cultural Humility

You don't need to know every custom or tradition, but you do need to approach differences with respect and curiosity. Avoid stereotyping, make room for other perspectives, and remember that being "the star" means nothing if you can't collaborate across cultures. Of course, at the heart of all these responsibilities is the core of your work: the performances themselves. In the next chapter, we'll explore the different types of performance opportunities singers may encounter at sea, from solo lounge sets to full-scale production shows. We'll also break down rehearsal schedules, performance rotations, and how to stay show-ready over the course of a contract.

Note

1   Eve Church, "Women in Maritime: The Stats You Need to Know," *Martide*, accessed August 15, 2025, https://www.martide.com/en/blog/women-in-maritime-stats-to-know.

6 Show Types and Rehearsal Realities

After the safety drills, the social hosting, and the structured life of shipboard routine, it can be easy to lose sight of why many singers pursue this path in the first place: the performances. At the heart of the job—regardless of your manifest status, contract length, or department affiliation—is the opportunity to share your voice with a global audience in a unique and constantly shifting environment.

This chapter breaks down the full spectrum of cruise ship performance life—from polished mainstage spectacles to relaxed acoustic sets—and helps singers understand the logistical, artistic, and professional demands of each type of performance. You'll also learn how rehearsals are handled both ashore and onboard, how to collaborate effectively with technical teams, and what it really means to stay performance-ready across months at sea. How you prepare, rehearse, and deliver that singing in the ever-changing world of cruise ship life is what sets you apart as a successful performer.

Cast-Driven Production Shows versus Individual Performances

Cruise ship singers fall into two primary performance categories: those who perform as part of mainstage production shows, and those who deliver individual or self-contained performances. While both types of performances involve singing for a live audience, the experience, preparation, and expectations differ in important ways. Understanding these differences is essential for knowing where your skills fit best and for managing your energy and expectations onboard.

Cast-Driven Production Shows

Mainstage production shows are high-energy, highly produced performances presented in the ship's largest theater venue. These shows are often cast-driven and performed by resident singers, dancers, and sometimes specialty performers, supported by a creative team both onboard and shoreside.

A typical production show might be a Broadway-style revue, a tribute show, a through-composed pop narrative, or a classical crossover concert with multimedia elements. Shows are typically 45 minutes in length, but this varies by cruise line and creative concept. Some lines, such as Royal Caribbean, have full-length Broadway musicals as part of their entertainment offerings, clocking in at 90 to 120 minutes in duration. Costumes, wigs, choreography, lighting design, video, automation, and props all work together to create a visually impressive and tightly structured performance. These shows are scripted, repeatable, and rehearsed to exact precision; once you're in the cast, the expectation is that every performance remains consistent, regardless of what port you are docked in that day or how tired you are.

Performance schedules vary by ship and itinerary. On some ships, production cast members perform two or three shows per cruise. On others, you might perform a rotation of four to six shows each voyage, sometimes with back-to-back show nights or double performance days. Cast singers are also often called upon to participate in additional onboard events—such as welcome-aboard shows, variety nights, or holiday performances—that may be added to the schedule on short notice.

This style of performing requires more than vocal ability. You'll also need to have or develop strong skills in stage movement and choreography (keeping in mind that there are dancers hired to carry the heaviest movement load), be comfortable with costume changes and headset microphones, and be ready to collaborate closely with dancers, A/V crew, and stage management. You may be expected to sing while executing choreography, do quick costume changes, or perform under unusual conditions (e.g., rocking ship, broken hydraulic stage lift, etc.).

Rehearsals for production shows can be intense. Many cruise lines rehearse casts on land for several weeks before embarkation, typically four to eight weeks depending on the number of shows. These rehearsals are conducted by directors, choreographers, musical directors, and production supervisors employed either directly by the cruise line or by third-party creative companies. Once onboard, rehearsals shift to "install": blocking the shows on the actual stage, integrating tech cues, and doing full dress runs before performing for an audience.

Singers who thrive in production shows are reliable, technically consistent, and able to maintain energy and professionalism across weeks or months of repeated performances. If you're used to self-producing your own shows, it may be an adjustment to give up creative control.

Figure 6.1 Live band and entertainment team leading a deck party.
Courtesy of the author.

Individual Performances

In contrast to cast-driven productions, individual performances refer to self-contained sets by singers working as guest entertainers, party-band vocalists, lounge soloists, step-on performers, or even performing cruise administrators. These performances vary widely in style, content, and format, and are often built around the performer's existing repertoire, voice, and personality. And as previously mentioned, rehearsals for individual shows are generally far more limited than those for cast-based performances.

Guest entertainers perform one or two mainstage shows per cruise—typically 45 minutes in length—and are expected to deliver polished, self-contained acts with minimal rehearsal onboard. They prepare their shows independently in advance, complete with custom charts for the house band or prerecorded backing tracks, often with click.

Step-on entertainers also fall under this category. These performers embark temporarily—typically while the ship is docked—for a one-time show, often themed to a particular port or region.

Party-band singers and lounge entertainers perform more frequently—typically every day with perhaps one night off per cruise depending on operational needs—and in a variety of informal venues around the ship. Sets are typically 45 minutes in length (including any banter with the audience and room for applause) and may range from jazz to Motown to Top 40 to themed tributes like ABBA night or British Invasion. These performers have more flexibility in choosing material, usually with the input of the bandmaster, but must maintain vocal stamina, adapt to quickly changing crowd dynamics, and often take on emcee duties during their sets.

Cruise administrators—particularly cruise directors and assistant cruise directors—may also be responsible for performing. This often includes singing solo material in a headlining performance, welcome shows, variety shows, or enrichment concerts, and sometimes participating in collaborative performances alongside production cast members or lounge musicians.

Singers in these roles usually rehearse independently or with their bandmates. Rehearsals are self-driven and ongoing—updating setlists, learning new songs, or polishing harmonies during sound checks or between performances. Unlike cast singers, these performers may change their material nightly depending on the crowd, which requires a well prepared and constantly refreshed repertoire. It is not uncommon for a lounge entertainer, for instance, to receive a request from a guest for a song that they do not know, which they will learn and have ready to perform by that night.

Figure 6.2 The author headlining a solo show.
Photograph by Kanstantsin Karatysheuski.

In addition to being musically versatile, resident individual performers must be adept at reading the room, adjusting on the fly, and serving as their own emcees, tech liaisons, and crowd wranglers. They often build strong rapport with guests, especially with those who return night after night, and can become key contributors to the social fabric of the cruise.

Bands, Charts, Tracks, Multimedia Elements, Microphones, and Monitors

While singing may be the centerpiece of your job, the success of a cruise ship performance relies heavily on what surrounds the performance. Whether you're singing with a live band, performing to prerecorded tracks, or synching video and lighting cues, you'll need to be musically and technically adaptable. This section explores the three pillars that shape most cruise performances—live musical accompaniment, track-based shows, and multimedia elements—as well as the gear that literally amplifies your voice: your microphone.

Live Bands and Charts

One of the greatest luxuries of cruise ship performing is the opportunity to work with talented live instrumentalists. Many cruise lines maintain onboard party bands, jazz trios, or orchestras or show bands, depending on the ship size and entertainment structure. The orchestra and show-band musicians often play for production shows and guest entertainers, while the party band and trios play lounge sets.

Working with a live band requires strong communication and rehearsal efficiency. As we have discussed, most band-backed performances are rehearsed in a single sound check, so you'll be expected to arrive prepared, with clearly marked charts, tempo indications, and arrangements that make sense for a live ensemble.

Good band charts should be legible and clearly indicate the following:

- Tempo and expression
- Intro and outro structure
- Cutoffs and fermatas
- Key changes, if applicable
- Solo sections or vamp cues

In today's cruise industry, charts are most commonly distributed as PDF files and loaded onto company-provided iPads, which musicians read from using an app called forScore. You can organize your solo show charts into a playlist for each instrument (keys, bass, drums, etc.) and AirDrop it to the bandmaster, who then forwards it to the other musicians in the band. This system is fast and standardized, and eliminates the need to carry folders of paper charts to ships.

That said, some entertainers still prefer or even insist on using paper charts, especially if they've made significant investments in custom arrangements. A professionally arranged 7-piece chart for a single song can easily cost US$700–$1,000, and understandably, many entertainers are protective of their creative property. They may hesitate to distribute digital versions for fear the charts will be shared too freely. However, the reality is that if a musician wants a digital copy of your chart, it's very easy to scan or photograph it directly to their iPad. In fact, many players do exactly that even when handed physical copies, because they prefer reading from a screen, often utilizing forScore.

The best approach is to be prepared to work in either format. If you're handing out paper, make sure the charts are clean, legible, and marked by part. If you're working digitally, organize and label your files clearly, and communicate with the bandmaster in advance to confirm delivery.

In addition to organizing setlists and displaying charts, forScore offers powerful features that can make rehearsals smoother and more efficient. You can attach a reference track to a chart, which is particularly useful if you're using a backing track with a click (which we will expand upon in the next section). This allows musicians to rehearse independently with the exact track they'll perform to, complete with the click in one ear and the music in the other. For songs performed strictly live, forScore also allows you to embed a metronome directly into the score, so each musician can practice with the correct tempo even without a conducting bandmaster present. These tools not only support musical preparation but also reduce the need for repeated rehearsal time, which is a precious commodity onboard.

Backing Tracks

Not all performances involve a live band. Prerecorded tracks are common in mainstage productions on cruise ships. Tracks provide consistent timing and precise musical structure, which can be vital when working with choreography, multimedia, or limited rehearsal time.

In many productions, backing tracks and live musicians merge seamlessly using a click track, an in-ear metronome fed to the band (but not the audience) that keeps everyone locked in time with the track. This allows the orchestra or rhythm section to play live while staying perfectly synced with prerecorded elements like extra instruments, vocals, or multimedia cues. Production cast singers often perform to full produced click-track mixes that include vocal cues, backing vocals, and instrumental parts arranged to match the show's blocking and choreography. These tracks are often synced with lighting and video cues,

What Should Your Backing Tracks Include?

- Create high-quality audio files: WAV or AIFF are preferable; MP3 is acceptable if necessary.
- Include one version with click (if applicable) and one without.
- When labeling tracks, use clear, consistent file names like these:
  - 01_Opening_Music.wav
  - 01_Opening_Music_withClick.wav

What Should Your Click Tracks Include?

- Have click in one channel, music in the other.
- Clearly indicate which channel (L/R) the click lives in.
- Be ready to test the tracks through the ship's sound system during tech run.

How Should You Deliver Your Tracks?

- Use a cloud-based link (Dropbox, Google Drive, etc.).
- Have tracks AirDrop-ready from a laptop, tablet, or phone.
- Use USBs as a backup only—many ships don't allow external drives for fear of viruses.

Pro Tips

- Make sure all tracks are volume-balanced—a sudden spike or drop mid-show will cause problems.
- Double-check for clean fade-outs and no dead space.
- Include a cue sheet for the A/V team with your preferred timing, levels, and start and stop notes—less is more!

Your tracks are your band—treat them like pros, and they'll support you like one.

meaning that timing is nonnegotiable—there's little room for improvisation or variation. As a singer, you may not hear the click yourself, but you'll be expected to follow the tempo without hesitation. Trust the band and stay in the pocket—they're listening to something you're not.

Guest entertainers may bring their own performance tracks, either as stand-alone audio or with visual elements like video backgrounds or lyric projections. In these cases, you'll often work closely with the A/V manager and bandmaster to align your files with the ship's playback system. Always ensure your tracks are labeled clearly, formatted correctly, and backed up on a physical drive or in the cloud.

Performing to track requires a slightly different vocal mindset: You need to be precise, and consistent. There's no band to vamp if you forget a line: The track is a conductor that will not wait for you.

Multimedia Elements

Cruise ships are the most technologically advanced performance spaces afloat, and many solo acts take full advantage of that with video backgrounds, lyric visuals, or cinematic storytelling synced to their shows. These elements are commonly used by guest entertainers and cruise administrators who perform solo shows, especially in large mainstage venues.

Video Backgrounds

If you plan to use video, you'll need to come fully prepared. Video backgrounds are usually organized along with backing tracks and click tracks in a playback software like QLab, which is industry-standard on most ships. A typical multimedia file package includes the following:

- High-resolution video files (1920 x 1080 unless otherwise specified)
- A version of your set file in QLab (if you're tech-savvy enough to program it yourself)
- Backing tracks with and without click
- Clear cue sheets that explain what happens and when

Refrain from bringing files on USB drives. Many cruise lines—especially larger fleets—do not allow onboard employees to insert thumb drives into shipboard computers due to virus risk. For this reason, you should prepare your show files in the following ways:

- Upload files to a cloud-based file-sharing service (Dropbox, Google Drive, WeTransfer, etc.).
- Have files available to AirDrop directly from a MacBook, iPad, or iPhone.
- Organize files by cue order so the A/V team can navigate quickly.

You'll also want to alert the A/V team well in advance—ideally during your initial communication with the cruise line, if you have any, or at least on embarkation day—that your show includes multimedia. They'll need time to check compatibility, download and import your files, and run a tech rehearsal before showtime.

What does a successful video background look like?

- The video should complement the song without distracting from you. Think subtle motion, abstract imagery, or location-based visuals that support the mood (e.g., a Paris street scene for "La Vie En Rose" or ocean waves for "Beyond the Sea").
- Avoid overly literal or flashy visuals that pull focus—no karaoke-style bouncing balls, unless you're doing an actual sing-along.
- Keep transitions smooth: Fades in and out work better than hard cuts or sudden blackouts.
- If lyrics are included (which is not standard), make sure they are readable from the back row, free of typos, and well-timed.
- Test the videos with your audio beforehand—the wrong frame rate or aspect ratio or incongruity with the audio can throw the whole performance off.
- There's no need to stick to one video for an entire song: Consider editing together multiple complementary videos that align with what is occurring musically.
- Avoid using in your visuals copyrighted or branded content such as Broadway show posters, movie stills, or corporate logos. We'll explore copyright and licensing more thoroughly later on, but as a general rule of thumb, stick to content you've created or licensed yourself.

Supporting Visuals

In addition to background videos for each musical number, you should also prepare three essential supporting visuals:

1 **Intro Screen:** A static or gently animated image displayed as guests arrive and take their seats. This typically includes your name and show title and occasionally a tagline. The intro screen sets the tone and is a marker for the A/V team that everything is ready.

2 **Outro Screen:** A closing image or animation shown after your final bow, often displaying your name and social media or website info. Consider adding a QR code to link to your strongest content. Some artists simply reuse the intro screen. The outro screen reinforces your brand as guests exit the theater.

3 **Holder Screen:** A clean and simple background, frequently with your name or logo, shown between songs while you're speaking to the audience. The holder screen keeps the visual environment alive without distracting from your banter or transitions.

These supporting screens add a layer of polish to your show and signal to both the A/V team and the audience that your performance is thoughtfully produced from beginning to end.

Pre- and Post-Show Music

If you're presenting a solo show, take time to consider what music you'd like playing as guests enter and exit the venue. This walk-in and walk-out music sets the mood, frames the show experience, and helps the audience transition in and out of the performance space. Prepare these files in advance in MP3 or WAV format and provide them to the A/V team with clear instructions.

You might choose instrumental versions of your show material to build anticipation or opt for vocal music in a similar style to set the tone (like classic jazz for a vintage cabaret show, or cinematic orchestration for a dramatic crossover program). Some artists even play recordings of their own studio work to introduce their voices before stepping onstage, which can be a great branding tool if the tone is casual or contemporary. Just be mindful: If your show opens with a dramatic reveal or vocal surprise, using your own voice beforehand may

---

QLab 101: What Singers Need to Know

What Is QLab?
QLab is a powerful playback software used on most cruise ships to control audio, video, lighting, and cues for performances. Think of it as the show's command center—every track, visual, and effect is programmed to run in a specific sequence, at specific times.

Do I Need to Know How to Use It?
Not necessarily. The A/V team onboard will operate QLab during your show. But you are responsible for providing materials in a way that integrates smoothly into their QLab sessions.

What Should I Bring?

- **Audio Files:** Backing tracks, with and without click (if used)

- **Video Files:** For projection on LED screens (MP4 or MOV, Full HD, 1920 x 1080, H.264 codec preferred)
- **Cue Sheet:** A clear document that explains what happens and when
- **Optional:** A preprogrammed QLab show file (QLAB4 or QLAB5 format), if you've worked with QLab before

How Should I Deliver QLab files?

- Avoid USB drives if possible.
- Upload files to a cloud-based folder or have files AirDrop-ready on your device.
- Label your files clearly (e.g., "01_Intro_Video.mp4," "03_BeyondTheSea_BackTrack.wav").

Pro Tip

Even if you've prepped everything perfectly, give the A/V team time to test and load your files during installation or sound check. Surprises during shows rarely go well at sea.

Table 6.1 Solo Show Materials Checklist

Music & Show Content	Audio & Visual Assets (as applicable)
☐ Set list	☐ Backing tracks
☐ Cue sheet	☐ Click tracks
☐ Show script	☐ Video background files
☐ Band charts (hard copy / forScore)	☐ Intro & outro video/image files
☐ Tech rider with stage plot	☐ Holder screen video/image files
	☐ Pre-/post-show music files
Wardrobe & Props	☐ Q-Lab file
☐ Performance outfit	☐ In-ear monitors
☐ Performance accessories	
☐ Props (if applicable)	**Storage & Backup**
☐ Mic sleeve (if desired)	☐ Laptop or tablet with digital files
☐ Mic belt (if desired)	☐ Cloud storage of digital files
	☐ USB backup of digital files
Documentation & Promotional Copy	
☐ Show take-on (~50 words)	**Merchandise (as applicable)**
☐ Performer bio (~100 words)	☐ CDs / DVDs / USBs for sale
☐ Show blurb (~50 words)	☐ Permanent marker for autographs
☐ Promotional photo (landscape)	
☐ Licensing (if applicable)	

spoil the effect. When in doubt, choose music that enhances your show's energy without giving too much away. It's a small detail that goes a long way in creating a polished, professional atmosphere.

Microphones

Your mic is your lifeline. Cruise ships primarily use two types of mics: headset (hands-free) microphones and handheld microphones. Each has its own benefits, drawbacks, and technical demands.

Headset Microphones

- These mics are common in production shows, especially for singers who dance or move.
- They provide consistent placement near the mouth, freeing the hands.
- Headset mics are susceptible to breath noise and plosives if not positioned properly.
- Mics are often routed through belt packs, which must be worn discreetly and securely.
- You'll typically be fitted for a personal headset at the start of your contract.
- Headset mics must be handled gently and stored carefully—your A/V team will brief you on proper care.

Handheld Microphones

- These mics are common for lounge, step-on, guest entertainer, and outdoor performances.
- They offer more control—they can be used to adjust dynamics, tone, and proximity.
- Handheld mics are more forgiving for vocalists who like to play with phrasing or mic distance.
- Handheld mics require good technique: Don't grip the grille (which distorts sound), and avoid pointing them at monitors to prevent feedback.
- Consider purchasing an inexpensive mic sleeve to match your performance attire.

Handheld Mic Technique Basics

- Keep the mic about 1–2 inches from your mouth for consistent volume.
- Pull slightly away on sustained high notes to avoid distortion.
- Use side angles to reduce "p" and "s" sounds (plosives and sibilance).

- Avoid tapping or handling the mic unnecessarily—it creates distracting noise.
- Trust your sound tech—they'll adjust your EQ and gain, so you don't have to push.

Note for Classically Trained Singers

Even if you have a strong operatic voice and were trained to sing acoustically, you will need to use a microphone on a cruise ship. Cruise ship theaters are not built for unamplified singing—even small venues are constructed with low ceilings and sound-absorbing walls, specifically to prevent noise from bleeding into adjacent spaces, which often include passenger cabins above, below, and nearby. No matter how powerful your voice, the room will swallow the sound, and balancing with backing tracks or live bands becomes impossible.

More importantly, cruise audiences expect sonically consistent shows. Singing one number acoustically and the next one with a mic breaks the experience. Use the microphone as an extension of your artistry and learn to work with it (and be grateful for how much you can rely on it when you're not at your vocal best)—it will elevate your impact and preserve your voice across many performances.

Pro tip: Most ships keep a handheld mic prepped and ready in the wings as a backup. If a headset or primary handheld fails during the show, an A/V tech will likely hand you the emergency mic from the side stage—or you may grab it yourself if there is no A/V tech stationed backstage. Stay calm, take it confidently, and keep going—the show must go on.

Monitors

On cruise ships, stage monitors—the speakers that allow you to hear yourself and your accompaniment—are your key to staying in tune, on the beat, and vocally safe. Depending on the venue, you may encounter the following:

- **Floor Wedges:** These are angled speakers at your feet that project sound back toward you. These are standard in lounges, band settings, and smaller mainstage setups. You'll usually get a basic mix of lead vocal, backing track, and band. Be mindful of your position—if you move too far off-axis or point your handheld mic toward the wedge, you risk feedback.
- **Side Fills and Ceiling Rings:** Side fills are larger speakers placed at the edge of the stage to help distribute sound more broadly—especially useful for cast shows or wide performance areas. The sound can feel different from what a wedge produces—more ambient—but it still plays a vital role in helping you stay oriented. On some smaller ships, especially in lounge-style venues with a dance floor in front of the stage, you may

also find ceiling-mounted monitors arranged in a ring above the dance floor. These are designed to project sound back toward the performer from overhead, compensating for the absence of floor monitors directly in front of the stage.

- **In-Ear Monitors (IEMs):** Most common in production shows or with tech-savvy guest entertainers, IEMs offer personalized audio delivered directly to your ears via wireless earpieces and a belt pack. They reduce ambient noise, prevent vocal strain, and allow for detailed, consistent mixes. That said, they take some getting used to—many singers find them isolating at first and may ask for a "room mic" feed to keep the mix feeling alive. Some singers prefer to wear one in-ear and keep one ear open to the room. This hybrid approach gives you clarity and pitch accuracy in one ear while preserving a natural sense of space in the other. The choice of ear often depends on your general stage position—for instance, if the drum kit is behind you and to the left, you might keep the left IEM in to dampen that sound slightly and avoid fatigue from cymbal wash. It's a personal decision, and you'll find what works best for your ears over time.

Whether you're performing with a live band, singing to carefully programmed tracks, or adding video and lighting elements to enhance your show, cruise ship performances are powered by a range of technical tools, and your success depends on how well you adapt to them. In the next section, we'll look at how these tools come together during rehearsals, tech runs, and live performances, and what it takes to stay prepared and consistent from install day to final bow.

Rehearsals, Performances, and Technical Preparation

The Install Period

The install is the onboard setup phase that takes place when a new cast or entertainment team joins the ship. It may last a few days or up to two weeks, depending on the scale of the shows and the availability of technical resources. This period is especially important for production show casts but can occasionally apply to party bands or new lounge acts.

What many first-time cruise-ship performers don't realize is that install happens while the ship is already sailing with guests onboard. That means the theater and other performance venues are still being used for regular entertainment—guest entertainer shows, enrichment lectures, game shows, and variety acts hosted by the entertainment team. As a result, stage time is extremely limited, and every minute counts.

Rehearsals during install usually take place during these times:

- In the morning and afternoon, after guests have gone ashore and before the evening's rehearsals and live programming begin
- On port days rather than sea days, since sea days are packed with guest-facing events
- In tight blocks, with meals sometimes delivered right to the theater so the cast and install team can eat quickly and stay on schedule

For production singers, install includes the following:

- Learning how to move on the actual shipboard stage, which may differ significantly from the land-based rehearsal venue
- Integrating choreography with real-world constraints (columns, railings, trapdoors, or moving lights)
- Costuming, quick-change rehearsals, and wardrobe fittings
- Working through cue-to-cue tech runs where lights, sound, video, and movement are timed and locked
- Doing emergency drills and safety training, which includes understanding muster duties and ship-specific procedures
- Completing training sessions for any additional hosting responsibilities, such as games and activities

Tech Runs versus Sound Checks

Understanding the differences between a tech run and a sound check is crucial, and knowing how to approach each one respectfully and efficiently will endear you to the A/V team and set you up for a strong performance.

Tech Run

A tech run is a full rehearsal onstage with lights, sound, and A/V cues, and may include costumes. It's especially critical for these types of performances:

- **Production Shows:** Syncing movement with lighting, click tracks, and video
- **Guest and Step-On Entertainers:** Practicing cues with the A/V team and house band
- **Variety Shows:** Where multiple acts must transition smoothly

In a tech run, you're not just checking the music—you're also walking through entrances and exits, transitions, and blackout cues. Your job is to hit your marks, follow direction, and give the team exactly what they need to ensure a smooth show.

Sound Check

A sound check is a shorter, more focused rehearsal, usually to set mic levels, balance instruments, and review one or two songs. For lounge entertainers, this often doubles as rehearsal time due to limited availability to practice in venues occupied by guests.

Tips for an effective sound check:

- Arrive early, warmed up, and ready to go.
- Know what songs you want to run—don't guess on the spot.
- Communicate clearly with the A/V team about what you need to hear in the monitors. That might include your own vocal level, or the levels of other voices, instruments, or tracks. Be specific and respectful: Saying "Can I get a bit more lead vocal in the center wedge?" or "Can we reduce the piano slightly in my in-ear?" is much more helpful than saying "I can't hear anything." A strong sound check sets you up for a successful performance.
- If you have specific blocking for a number, it's usually not necessary to act it all out—the A/V team is primarily concerned with how you sound, not where you'll be standing or moving. Focus on your vocal delivery and mic technique unless otherwise requested.
- Be efficient and polite—there may be another act waiting to sound-check after you.

Rehearsing for Different Performance Types
Production Casts

- Rehearsals during install are structured, are led by a director or bandmaster, and involve multiple departments (wardrobe, wigs, A/V, etc.).
- Expect regular brushup rehearsals once the show is up and running. A rehearsal usually happens on the same day as the performance (usually in the late afternoon or early evening depending on venue availability) and can vary in intensity depending on where you are in the contract: Early in the contract, brushups may involve full run-throughs, especially if spacing, vocal blend, or tech elements still need polishing. Marking is often encouraged to preserve show stamina.
- Later in the contract, as the show tightens, brushups are typically reduced to a cue-to-cue (jumping between specific transitions or sections), or in some cases, just a sound check and quick warm-up onstage.
- Rehearsal calls are mandatory and nonnegotiable.

Lounge Entertainers

- Rehearsals are self-managed and often informal, held during the day or built into sound check.
- You may rehearse in the actual lounge or venue where you perform, which presents its own set of challenges. Most lounges are open to guests nearly 24-7, so rehearsal time is typically limited to port days, when many guests are ashore.
- Even if there are only a few guests remaining onboard, it's important to rehearse mindfully. You may need to keep volume low or switch to an acoustic run-through. Rehearsals should always be cleared in advance with the bandmaster.
- Read the room: If the ship is docked but weather is poor and many guests are lingering indoors, you may need to find an alternate location (such as a crew bar or empty public lounge during off-hours) or postpone until a more suitable time.
- New songs are often added weekly, with each performer expected to learn their part independently, sometimes running harmonies during sound check or between sets.

Structure of a Typical Mainstage Performance

No matter the show, most cruise mainstage performances follow a similar flow:

1 **Call Time**
   - Call time is typically 30 minutes to 2 hours before showtime, depending on the production.
   - This allows time for mic fitting, warm-ups, wardrobe, and final notes.

2 **Preset**
   - Cast and crew place props, water, quick changes, and emergency items backstage.

3 **Mic Check**
   - The mic check is typically conducted from backstage.
   - A/V will call backstage and feed mic audio to the A/V booth.

4 **Take-On**
   - The cruise director welcomes the audience and introduces the act.

5 **Showtime**
   - This is the performance itself: most often one 45-minute set, sometimes two with intermission.

6 **Takeoff**
   - The cruise director returns to thank the audience and close the show.

- The takeoff is important for cuing applause and signaling a clean exit; on smaller ships, the cruise director usually leads the bows as well.

7 De-Greet

- On smaller ships, the performer may exit through the audience and greet guests at the door to thank them, take photos, or sign autographs.
- This step may be skipped on larger ships or if there is only a short break before a second performance of the show.

8 Strike and Reset

- All props and gear are cleared immediately to reset the space for the next performance, act, or event.
- Singers are typically responsible for reset of props and wardrobe, while the A/V team takes care of scenic elements.

Figure 6.3 Main theater on a premium cruise ship before a sound check. Photograph by the author.

It depends on your role.

Guest entertainers and cruise administrators usually have laundry privileges as part of their contracts. Their performance attire is cleaned by the ship's laundry team. They can also request pressing if needed.

Production cast members typically wear company-issued costumes. On smaller ships, one cast member is often designated as the wardrobe captain and is responsible for bringing all cast costumes to and from the onboard laundry. This role rotates or is shared depending on the contract.

Step-on entertainers aren't onboard long enough to need costume laundering.

Lounge entertainers may have varying privileges. Some contracts allow for laundry services, but more often, performers must wash their own performance attire using the crew laundry facilities.

Working with the Ship's A/V Team

Your relationship with the A/V team is one of your most important relationships on the ship. A/V professionals control your sound, your lighting, your backing track playback, your monitors, and frequently your entrances. Treat them like gold.

Tips for working with A/V techs:

- Learn their names, and say thank you often.
- Respect their space and schedules—don't ask for changes at the last second.
- Label your tracks, charts, and cues clearly.
- If something goes wrong mid-show, keep performing—they'll do their best to fix it on the fly.
- Don't overuse the talkback mic or make technical demands in front of an audience.
- A little kindness goes a long way—most A/V techs will move mountains for performers who treat them well.

No two performances at sea are exactly the same, but the principles of preparation, adaptability, and teamwork apply across the board. Whether you're rehearsing under show lights with a full cast or running harmonies into your phone between safety drills, your ability to honor the process—rehearsal, tech, and show—will define your consistency and reputation onboard (and on land—it's a tiny world).

Cruise audiences may not always appreciate the effort that goes into making a performance look seamless, but your tech team, your fellow entertainers, and your cruise director definitely will.

But before any of that happens, a bigger question has to be answered: What are you going to sing? Creating a cruise-ready show or setlist means understanding your audience, your environment, and the unique emotional rhythms of life at sea. In the next chapter, we'll look at how cruise ship shows are built—from repertoire selection and pacing to guest engagement and the key differences between land and sea audiences. Because on a ship, a great voice is only part of the equation. A great show is what people will remember.

7 Show Creation, Repertoire, and Engagement

Creating a compelling performance for a cruise ship is an art form all its own. While many of the same principles apply as performing on land—great singing, thoughtful repertoire, and strong stage presence—performing at sea involves unique considerations that go beyond what most singers encounter ashore. Audiences aboard cruise ships are diverse in nationality, age, and musical taste, and shows must cater to broad demographics while still maintaining artistic integrity. Additionally, logistical realities of life at sea—like limited rehearsal time, changing performance spaces, and varied acoustics—shape the way cruise shows are built, rehearsed, and delivered. This chapter will explore what makes cruise audiences distinct; how shows are constructed to meet their expectations; and how singers can navigate copyright, choose repertoire wisely, and create memorable experiences that keep guests coming back night after night.

Differences between Land and Sea Audiences

One of the most important mindset shifts for singers transitioning from land-based work to cruise ships is recognizing just how different the audience is. On land, audience members typically choose to see you—they've paid for a concert, booked tickets for a musical, or purchased entry to a jazz lounge. In contrast, cruise audiences are built in. They didn't come for you specifically—they came for a vacation. You are part of their package, and that changes how you approach the crafting of the performance.

A Global, Built-In Audience

Cruise audiences are some of the most diverse you'll encounter. On any given night, you may be singing to a mix of Americans, Canadians, Brits, Australians,

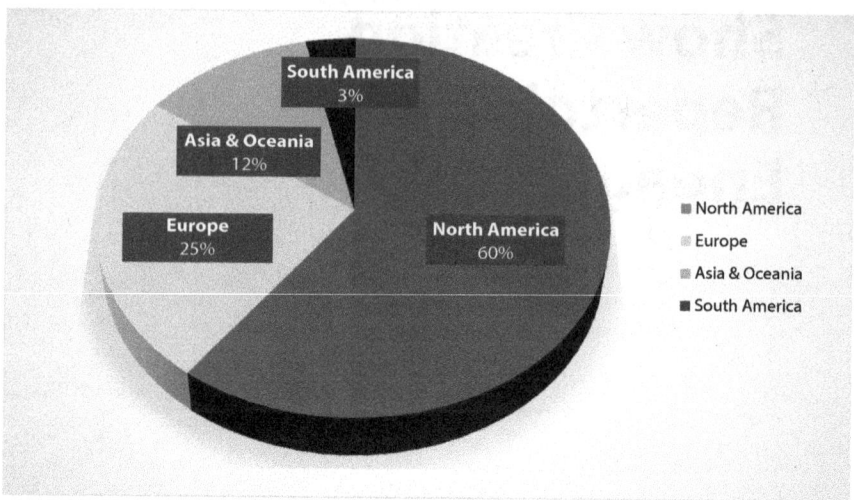

Figure 7.1 Passenger volume by source region for 2024.
Source: Cruise Lines International Association (2025).

Germans, Brazilians, and beyond. Their backgrounds, languages, and cultural expectations vary widely. One audience may be raucous and vocal; another may be polite and reserved. The same joke or song that lands spectacularly one night may earn only scattered applause the next.

This internationalism is also shaped by where and when the ship is sailing and how much the cruise costs. A boutique luxury vessel with higher fares cruising in Asia in the winter may attract wealthy, retired Australians during their summer who are looking for culture and sophistication that requires a relatively short flight from home. In contrast, a budget-friendly, mass-market cruise in the Caribbean during spring break is likely to attract families, college students, or first-time cruisers who may be more interested in dancing and daiquiris than Puccini. Understanding who your audience is—and where your ship is—allows you to tailor your tone, energy, and even repertoire (when you have the flexibility to do so).

Context Is Everything

Unlike in traditional venues, cruise audiences experience your show in the context of their vacation. They may have just come back from a full-day excursion: hiking a volcano, snorkeling a reef, or taking a wine-soaked walking tour through a medieval town. They may be sunburned, tired, or a few drinks deep. They've likely just indulged in a multicourse dinner (and perhaps two desserts). By the time they take their seats in the theater or lounge, they may be happy but not necessarily alert.

This is not to say that cruise ship entertainment needs to be "dumbed down." Far from it. But successful cruise entertainment does tend to lean toward the more commercial and easily digestible, not because guests lack taste, but because of the context in which guests are watching. Subtext-heavy theater songs or obscure historical works may be harder to process after a day in the sun and a bottle of wine. Clear storytelling, recognizable tunes, and charismatic delivery go a long way.

Guest Feedback and Proximity

Cruise performers don't exit through a stage door and disappear. You live among your audience. You'll see them at breakfast, pass them in hallways, even run into them in port. This proximity creates a unique feedback loop: Guests will often approach you directly to share what they loved (or what they didn't). Sometimes it's a simple "You were wonderful last night!" or a slightly more confusing "Why aren't you on Broadway?" Other times it's a well intentioned "You know what you should sing?" or "You really should smile more."

This dynamic demands a deepened sense of responsiveness and professionalism in performers. You learn to accept compliments graciously, handle criticism with poise, and navigate constant visibility. If you're someone who likes to vanish after a performance, ship life may feel invasive at first. But it also offers something rare: immediate insight into how your work is landing. For singers willing to listen— and filter wisely—this can be a fast track to artistic and professional growth.

In many ways, this level of public interaction is not unlike being a celebrity navigating fame, albeit on a smaller, floating scale. The audience recognizes you, watches your behavior, and often assumes familiarity. You become part of their vacation memories. How you conduct yourself in the buffet line or the guest fitness center may impact how your show is remembered. Performers who thrive in this environment tend to carry themselves with intention both on and off the stage.

Many guests will also choose to follow you on social media, tagging you in photos and videos and sending messages of appreciation, or keeping up with your career long after they've disembarked. Some may return on future cruises and seek you out specifically. Cruise ships may be temporary stages, but the relationships formed, and the impressions left, can be remarkably, even unexpectedly, enduring.

Know What You Can and Can't Control

It's important to recognize how much control you have over your repertoire. Production cast singers, for example, typically perform in predesigned shows with locked-in material, costumes, and direction. There is little room for personal taste or interpretation—these are branded products, created shoreside by creative teams long before cast members arrive for rehearsal.

In contrast, guest and step-on entertainers, cruise administrators who perform, and lounge entertainers often have more autonomy. If you're performing your own cabaret or set, you'll likely build your own show from scratch, choose your own songs, and shape the arc. That freedom comes with responsibility: You need to know your audience, consider the ship's brand and demographic, and create a show that works in this highly specific context.

Some solo entertainers thrive on this challenge, creating "plug-and-play" sets they can adapt to different regions, guest types, and atmospheres. Others struggle with the sheer variety of taste and the unpredictability of cruise audiences. The key is to strike a balance between your artistic identity and the needs of the people in front of you.

How Cruise Ship Shows Are Built

Before a single sequin is sewn or a note is sung, every cruise ship show begins with a question: What kind of entertainment experience best reflects our brand and delights our guests? Cruise ship shows are not simply chosen from a catalog or devised in isolation. They are strategically conceptualized to serve both aesthetic and commercial goals, shaped by the brand identity of the cruise line, the physical limitations of the ship, the tastes of expected guests, and the realities of budget and staffing.

Brand First: Entertainment as Identity

Each cruise line cultivates a distinct personality, and entertainment is key to how that identity is expressed. A luxury line with a European clientele may lean into classical crossover, high-end jazz, or stylishly reimagined musical theater, while a line targeting families or a younger demographic may opt for pop revues, jukebox musicals, or high-energy dance shows.

Creative teams—including directors, choreographers, music arrangers, costumers, lighting designers, and video editors—are often hired by in-house entertainment divisions or third-party production companies that specialize in cruise shows. Their mandate? Build a show that fits the ship, the space, the audience, and the brand. The process starts with research and brainstorming, not unlike designing a product launch.

Some of the core questions might include the following:

- What kind of music and storytelling will appeal to our typical guest?

- How can we differentiate ourselves from competitors while maintaining mass appeal?
- Can this show be adapted across multiple ships or fleets, or must it be unique?

Audience Demographics and Regional Itineraries

One of the most significant factors influencing show design is guest demographic, which fluctuates depending on the ship's price point, itinerary, and seasonal timing. A ship sailing out of Miami on short Caribbean loops may attract an entirely different crowd from one offering monthlong expeditions through Southeast Asia or the Mediterranean.

Creative teams build audience profiles based on this information. For example, a ship targeting active American retirees may favor nostalgic American hits from the 1950s to the 1970s with a storytelling thread, while a younger or more international audience might get a multilingual pop-rock spectacle with heavy visual effects. Some cruise lines even tailor shows to specific regional themes—like Latin nights in South America or operatic tributes in Italy—though this is less common as companies look to maximize reuse.

Designing for the Space: Theatrical Architecture at Sea

Cruise ship stages are notoriously unconventional. Some are proscenium theaters; others are thrust stages, theaters-in-the-round, or multipurpose spaces with movable seating. Shows must be tailored to the technical specs of each venue: stage size, fly space (if any), LED walls or scenic automation, and available lighting and audio infrastructure. Additionally, the cast size is often capped due to crew limits, safety requirements, and berth.

For instance, a flashy revue that might require a dozen singers and dancers on land may be reimagined for a smaller cast of multiskilled performers—singers who dance and dancers who can hold harmonies. Efficiency and adaptability are not just ideal—they're mandatory.

Budget, Reuse, and ROI

Creating a new production show is a major investment for a cruise line. It can cost anywhere from hundreds of thousands to over one million dollars when factoring in design, development, costumes, staging, licensing, tech programming, and installation. As such, the expectation is that a show will last several years, possibly transferring across multiple ships or being performed by several rotating casts.

Because of this, the return on investment (ROI) is a constant consideration. Can this show help retain guests or drive rebooking? Will it generate positive reviews or social media buzz? Will guests come back onboard and say, "I hope they're still doing that show"? These questions are baked into the early planning stages.

Some cruise lines mitigate risk by developing modular shows—productions that can be modified depending on the ship size or region. Others cocreate shows with known entities (e.g., Broadway composers, cirque-style troupes, celebrity performers, or even ballet companies) to leverage brand recognition and draw.

Aesthetic and Emotional Experience

Finally, cruise ship shows are designed not just to showcase talent, but also to evoke an emotional response. A successful production doesn't just fill a slot in the evening's programming—it also becomes a highlight of the cruise. As such, creative teams focus on emotional arc, pacing, musical impact, and even how the show will be remembered.

From Concept to Curtain: The Creative Workflow

Once a general show direction or theme is agreed upon—whether it's a Motown revue, a cinematic journey through film or music, or a stylish reinterpretation of the Great American Songbook—the actual creative build begins. This typically unfolds in phases and involves several departments working in tandem:

1. Creative Direction and Concept Development: A creative director or producer, often working for the cruise line or a third-party entertainment vendor, leads the charge. They may pitch multiple show ideas based on guest trends, branding goals, or successful past formats. These ideas are vetted by the cruise line's entertainment executives, and once a concept is approved, a full team is assembled to bring it to life.

2. Musical Direction and Arrangements: A music director and arranger steps in next, tasked with building the show's musical foundation. This involves selecting specific songs, transposing keys to suit cast vocal ranges, arranging medleys or transitions, and coordinating click tracks when needed. If a live band is used, the director also prepares full band charts. For track-based shows, audio is mixed and mastered to align with cuing systems for lights and video.

3. Choreography and Staging: A choreographer and a stage director collaborate with the music team to translate the show into visual storytelling. Numbers are blocked and choreographed with the ship's stage specs in mind (e.g., entrances, exits, trapdoors, and wing space).

Table 7.1 Top 50 Most Commonly Performed Songs on Cruise Ships

Song Title	Artist / Show	Typical Setting
"Dancing Queen"	ABBA	Dance Floor / Deck Party
"Celebration"	Kool & The Gang	Dance Floor / Deck Party
"I Gotta Feeling"	Black Eyed Peas	Dance Floor / Deck Party
"I Will Survive"	Gloria Gaynor	Dance Floor / Deck Party
"I'm So Excited"	Pointer Sisters	Dance Floor / Deck Party
"It's Raining Men"	The Weather Girls	Dance Floor / Deck Party
"Livin' on a Prayer"	Bon Jovi	Dance Floor / Deck Party
"Mustang Sally"	Wilson Pickett	Dance Floor / Deck Party
"September"	Earth, Wind & Fire	Dance Floor / Deck Party
"Superstition"	Stevie Wonder	Dance Floor / Deck Party
"Twist and Shout"	The Beatles	Dance Floor / Deck Party
"Uptown Funk"	Bruno Mars	Dance Floor / Deck Party
"Valerie"	Amy Winehouse	Dance Floor / Deck Party
"We Are Family"	Sister Sledge	Dance Floor / Deck Party
"Y.M.C.A."	Village People	Dance Floor / Deck Party
"American Pie"	Don McLean	Piano Bar / Sing-along
"Bohemian Rhapsody"	Queen	Piano Bar / Sing-along
"Brown Eyed Girl"	Van Morrison	Piano Bar / Sing-along
"Can't Help Falling in Love"	Elvis Presley	Piano Bar / Sing-along
"Friends in Low Places"	Garth Brooks	Piano Bar / Sing-along
"Hey Jude"	The Beatles	Piano Bar / Sing-along
"Let It Be"	The Beatles	Piano Bar / Sing-along
"New York, New York"	Frank Sinatra	Piano Bar / Sing-along
"Piano Man"	Billy Joel	Piano Bar / Sing-along
"Sweet Caroline"	Neil Diamond	Piano Bar / Sing-along
"Don't Stop Believin'"	Journey	Production Show
"Footloose"	Kenny Loggins	Production Show
"Hallelujah"	Leonard Cohen	Production Show
"My Way"	Frank Sinatra	Production Show
"One Night Only"	Dreamgirls	Production Show
"Proud Mary"	Tina Turner	Production Show
"Rolling in the Deep"	Adele	Production Show
"Shallow"	Lady Gaga & B. Cooper	Production Show
"Simply the Best"	Tina Turner	Production Show
"The Time of My Life"	Dirty Dancing	Production Show
"Don't Worry, Be Happy"	Bobby McFerrin	Pool Deck / Sailaway
"Happy"	Pharrell Williams	Pool Deck / Sailaway
"I'm Yours"	Jason Mraz	Pool Deck / Sailaway
"Is This Love"	Bob Marley	Pool Deck / Sailaway
"Kokomo"	The Beach Boys	Pool Deck / Sailaway
"Red Red Wine"	UB40	Pool Deck / Sailaway

"Three Little Birds"	Bob Marley	Pool Deck / Sailaway
"Walking on Sunshine"	Katrina & The Waves	Pool Deck / Sailaway
"Bailando"	Enrique Iglesias	Latin Night / Deck Party
"Despacito"	Luis Fonsi	Latin Night / Deck Party
"La Bamba"	Ritchie Valens	Latin Night / Deck Party
"Livin' La Vida Loca"	Ricky Martin	Latin Night / Deck Party
"Macarena"	Los Del Río	Latin Night / Deck Party
"Volare"	Gipsy Kings	Latin Night / Deck Party

4. Costume, Lighting, and Multimedia Design: Simultaneously, costume designers create looks that are glamorous but repeatable, while lighting and video designers build cue sequences to accompany the show. Multimedia is a major part of many cruise productions—large LED walls or projection systems are used to create flexible "virtual scenery" that can change with every number.

5. Casting and Rehearsal Materials: Casting is often done months in advance, either by the cruise line's internal casting team or by a third-party agency. Vocal scores, practice tracks, choreography demos, and staging maps are prepared ahead of rehearsals. Casting must be done with multiple factors in mind—vocal range, dance ability, endurance, stage presence, and versatility—since most performers will appear in multiple shows over the course of their contract.

6. Cast Rehearsals and Staging Labs: Once the show is fully conceptualized and cast, performers enter an intensive shore-based rehearsal period, usually lasting three to six weeks. These rehearsals take place at a studio or production facility affiliated with the cruise line, where the cast learns vocal arrangements, choreography, blocking, and transitions for multiple shows in repertory. Staging is often done on taped floors that mimic the ship's layout, and early tech elements are introduced to prepare the cast for life at sea. At the end of this period, performers are expected to arrive onboard performance-ready.

7. Tech Integration and Install: During the installation period onboard, the show is re-blocked and fine-tuned for the ship's theater. Tech cues are locked in, costumes are fitted, and any necessary adjustments are made for safety and flow. Quick changes and transitions are rehearsed fully in costume. This is also when final dress runs occur.

8. Ongoing Oversight and Updates: Even postlaunch, the show remains a living organism. Corporate teams may audit performances, update tracks or visuals, or send new cast materials. Brand-wide changes in tone, focus, or itinerary may lead to a show being refreshed or replaced entirely.

Copyright and Licensing Considerations

One of the most misunderstood—and often overlooked—aspects of performing at sea is the legal framework surrounding copyrighted music and media. On land, singers are often reminded to secure proper performance licenses, pay ASCAP or BMI fees, or avoid using unlicensed backing tracks or arrangements. But at sea, the rules can feel murky. Are you in international waters? Does the ship's flag state matter? Who is responsible for paying royalties? These are fair questions, and the answers depend on your role, your material, and the cruise line's structure.

Cruise Lines and Blanket Licenses

Most major cruise lines carry blanket performance licenses with the major performance rights organizations (PROs), such as ASCAP, BMI, and SESAC in the United States or PRS and SOCAN in the UK and Canada. These licenses cover the public performances of a wide catalog of music onboard, allowing production casts, bands, and lounge entertainers to legally perform most published songs in live settings.

This means that if you're singing a pop song, jazz standard, or Broadway hit from a licensed catalog, you're usually covered as long as it's a live performance. That said, these licenses only cover live performances. They do not automatically cover these:

- Prerecorded tracks or karaoke files
- Video projections or multimedia content
- Custom arrangements distributed or reused outside the performance

If your performance involves any of the above—especially if you're performing as a guest entertainer or lounge performer—you may be responsible for securing your own licenses.

Guest Entertainers and Self-Contained Shows

If you're a guest entertainer performing a self-contained show, the responsibility for copyright compliance may shift to you. While the ship's general performance license may cover your song choices, you are often expected to ensure that your tracks, multimedia content, and arrangements are properly licensed, especially if any of the following apply:

- You are using commercial karaoke or backing tracks purchased online
- Your show includes medleys or customized arrangements
- You use projected media, like film clips, photos, or artwork
- You intend to record and share your live performance

In these cases, you may need any of these types of licenses:

- A **mechanical license** for the right to reproduce and distribute a musical composition (e.g., on a track or video in physical or digital format)
- A **synchronization license** to pair music with visual media (e.g., a video clip in your show)
- A **master use license** to use a specific commercial recording (e.g., using a studio recording of Aretha Franklin)

You can obtain these through licensing platforms like the following:

- Easy Song (for mechanical, sync, and master rights)
- Songfile (for mechanical licenses)

Estimated costs:

- Mechanical licenses: US$15 to US$30 per song
- Sync licenses: US$25 to more than US$200 per song, depending on use and platform
- Master use licenses: US$100 to more than US$500 per song, depending on the artist and the rights holder

When you license music through one of these platforms, the royalties owed to the rights holders are included in your fee. You're paying not just for permission to use the material, but also to ensure that the original creators are compensated. However, some karaoke and backing-track providers do not include these rights in the purchase price. Always read the fine print or ask the vendor directly. Best practice: If you're ever unsure whether something is licensed, either replace it or license it yourself.

Production Shows: Licensing Handled by the Cruise Line

If you're performing in a production show designed by the cruise line or a third-party entertainment company, you won't be involved in licensing at all. The creative team that built the show will have already done the following:

- Selected music from cleared catalogs
- Paid for synchronization rights for video or projection elements
- Created arrangements within legal usage

Your job as a singer is to perform the material as staged. You don't need to worry about copyright while doing the show onboard because the cruise line has already cleared the necessary rights for that specific performance context.

However, if you plan to use any footage, audio recordings, or visuals from those shows later—for example, in a demo reel, on YouTube, on your website, or on social media—you may be stepping outside the scope of the cruise line's licensing agreement.

The original license covers the live performance on the ship, not additional use or distribution. Beyond the live performance, you may need to license the music, get permission from the cruise line to use footage, and be sure you're not violating performer or company privacy policies.

Cover Songs and Arrangements

Cruise lines' blanket licenses do cover live performance of covers. You're free to sing Adele, Sinatra, or Sondheim onboard—live. But if you record yourself singing those songs and plan to post the video online, you may need additional rights, like a mechanical license for the audio and a sync license for pairing it with video.

This also applies to custom arrangements of copyrighted songs. It's one thing to create a fresh take on a standard for live performance on the ship—that's generally covered under the cruise line's license. But if that arrangement is distributed or reused outside of its original intended performance context, you may be infringing on the original copyright.

In cruise terms, let's say you create a jazz reharmonization of "Yesterday" by The Beatles for your lounge set or guest entertainer show. That's perfectly legal to perform live onboard under the cruise line's blanket license.

But if you

- send that arrangement to another performer,
- publish the arrangement or upload the sheet music online,
- use the arrangement in a monetized YouTube video, or
- adapt the arrangement into another setting entirely (e.g., a wedding performance)

then you are distributing or reusing a derivative work, which requires explicit permission from the copyright holder. This usually means obtaining a derivative work license, or arrangement rights, directly from the publisher.

When in doubt, always assume that arranging is a creative act that requires permission, unless you're staying entirely within live performance under an active blanket license.

What about International Waters?

There's a popular myth that copyright doesn't apply in international waters. This is false. Cruise ships are subject to the laws of their flag states, and cruise companies follow international copyright treaties to avoid serious legal consequences. Whether your ship is docked in Europe, is crossing the Atlantic, or is anchored off a private island, the safest approach is to assume this: If you couldn't legally use it on land, you can't use it at sea without a license.

What Is Fair Use, and Does it Apply to Me?

You may have heard of something called "fair use"—a legal doctrine in US copyright law that allows for limited use of copyrighted material without permission under certain conditions. But here's the key: Fair use applies rarely to public performances and almost never to cruise ship entertainment.

Fair use typically protects things like these:

- Education use (e.g., quoting a passage in a classroom)
- Commentary and criticism (e.g., reviewing a song and playing a clip)
- News reporting
- Parody or satire (e.g., a musical parody with clearly transformative purpose)

Cruise ships are commercial, public, and designed to entertain, so they don't qualify as fair use. Even using just ten seconds of a copyrighted song in a paid performance still requires a license.

Crafting Setlists for Sea Audiences

Choosing what to sing at sea isn't just a question of personal taste—it's also a strategic decision. Whether you're building a 45-minute guest entertainer show, curating a themed set for the lounge, or prepping for an audience participation night, you must choose songs that resonate with an unpredictable, multicultural, often exhausted audience on vacation. The right setlist can turn a casual listener into a lifelong fan. The wrong one might clear a lounge.

It's always important to remember that cruise audiences didn't come for your show—they came for the ship. That means you often need to win them over quickly and build trust that your performance is one worth staying for.

Recognizable, but Not Predictable

Guests are moved most by songs they recognize, but that doesn't mean you should stick to the obvious. The sweet spot lies in blending familiarity with surprise: delivering crowd-pleasers, yes, but in fresh and compelling ways.

Successful setlists often include the following:

- Songs that evoke strong emotion (e.g., "Hallelujah," "My Way," or "Time To Say Goodbye")
- Clever medleys or mash-ups that show artistry and musicality
- Regional nods (e.g., Piaf in France, ABBA in Scandinavia, or Bob Marley in the Caribbean)
- One or two deep cuts placed strategically after the audience is engaged

Consider Vocal Demands and Scheduling

Setlists should also consider the physical realities of shipboard performance.

You might be singing under any of the following conditions:

- In dry, recycled air
- After a long day ashore
- Over a lively cocktail crowd
- Multiple nights in a row, in various venues

Build in variety to protect your voice—alternate between power ballads, midrange storytelling pieces, and spoken pattern. Think about acoustic energy too: Some songs play better in a theater, others in an intimate lounge or noisy bar.

Variety Is the Spice of Life

Especially for lounge entertainers, rotation is essential. Many guests sail for a week or more and will come to see you multiple times. Repeating the same setlist is one of the fastest ways to lose your audience.

- Lounge singers should aim to carry 300–400 songs, depending on their contracts and expected weekly appearances.
- Pianist-vocalists, who perform solo across various parts of the day, often carry 400–500 songs, including pop, jazz, Broadway, and international standards.
- Some cruise lines require singers to have a minimum number of sets or songs when applying, so tracking and organizing your repertoire by artist and genre is vital.

Unlike theatrical or guest entertainer work, there's no expectation that lounge entertainers perform from memory. While singing without a music stand or screen can enhance audience engagement, it's industry standard (and completely acceptable) to use an iPad or tablet to manage lyrics, chords, and setlists. Guests are generally understanding, as long as you maintain eye contact, connect between songs, and don't bury your face in the screen.

Figure 7.2 Main show lounge on an ultra-luxury cruise ship set for a Halloween event. Photograph by Kanstantsin Karatysheuski.

Themed Nights and Special Events

Cruise lines love theme programming, and singers who can jump in with appropriate material become indispensable:

- Seventies nights
- French or Italian evenings
- Broadway cabarets
- Jazz after dark
- And much more! (My husband performed in a set for an anniversary of the moon landing.)

Have a handful of themed mini-sets ready to go. Bonus points if you can pull them off with tracks and little prep, or in collaboration with the ship's musicians.

Crafting a 45-Minute Solo Show

If you're a guest entertainer, step-on performer, or cruise administrator preparing a stand-alone solo show, you will formulate your show depending on your venue and audience size. A well-balanced 45-minute set typically includes around 10 songs with applause, transitions, audience interaction, and light banter between numbers.

But context is key:

- On smaller ships, the audience is physically closer and emotionally more invested. These guests tend to crave connection. They want to know who you are, where you've performed, what a certain song means to you, and why you chose it for them. In these intimate venues, banter is an important part of the show. Don't be afraid to share a story, dedicate a song, or respond in real time to audience reactions.
- On larger ships, the experience is less personal. You're likely performing in a multilevel theater to an audience seated far away. You won't see facial expressions, and you may not feel a connection. These crowds want polish, power, and pacing—not a life story. The best approach here is to let the music do the talking. Use minimal, well-rehearsed banter—just enough to transition, reset the mood, or land a punch line. Keep the pacing brisk, the vocals tight, and the energy high.

Think of it this way: On small ships, your stories are part of the experience. On big ships, they're an intermission.

How to Structure a Show Arc

Whether you're crafting a lounge set or a headline show, the shape of your set matters.

1. **Start with Impact:** Grab attention with something upbeat, familiar, and vocally confident.

2. **Build Variety:** Alternate tempos and moods to hold interest.

3. **Drop into Depth:** Include a ballad or emotionally rich number mid-set.

4. **Reignite Energy:** Follow slow moments with something rhythmic or humorous.

5 **Finish Strong:** End with your showstopper or sing-along crowd-pleaser.

Always think like a host: How do you want people to feel as they leave?

Table 7.2 Design Your Own 45-Minute Show

1. Opener – High energy & recognizable *"I want to grab their attention with…"*	**6. Unexpected deep-cut** – Lesser-known gem *"They'll be glad they heard…"*
2. Follow-up – Keep momentum going *"Once I've got them, I'll keep it up with…"*	**7. Medley or mashup** – Suprise arrangement *"Time to show off some creativity with…"*
3. Style shift – New tempo or genre *"I'll show them a different side of me with…"*	**8. Rebuild energy** – Fun, rhythmic, or funny *"Let's lift the vibe back up with…"*
4. Regional nod – Connect with your port *"I want to reference our location with…"*	**9. Climatic vocal feature** – big notes & flair *"I give them the big moment with…"*
5. Emotional anchor – A ballad with depth *"I invite them to feel something deep with…"*	**10. Finale** – Sing-along or standing ovation *"I want to sing or get on their feet with…"*

Engaging Cruise Audiences

Even the best setlist falls flat without strong audience engagement. On cruise ships, the ability to read the room, adjust your energy, and connect authentically can turn a good performance into a night guests remember for the rest of their vacation—or even their lives.

Reading the Room

Flexibility is everything. What worked last night may not land tonight. Singers with considerable artistic autonomy, such as lounge entertainers, should consider the following:

- Is the crowd lively or sleepy?
- Are they chatty or silent?
- Do they laugh easily or seem more reserved?
- Are they singing along? Are they glued to your every word or scrolling Instagram?

Be ready to swap out a ballad for an up-tempo number, cut a story short, or add an audience participation moment. Cruise ship entertainers succeed when they prioritize the guest experience over their own artistic agendas.

Connection over Perfection

Cruise guests value connection more than polish. While strong vocal technique and musicality are expected, they don't matter much if you're emotionally disconnected. Warmth, spontaneity, and genuine joy go a long way.

Some of the most impactful engagement strategies include these:

- Making eye contact—even in a large theater, this can be felt
- Greeting returning guests by name when appropriate (especially effective for lounge entertainers or cruise administrators)
- Adjusting your pacing based on audience response
- Offering a personal anecdote that sets up a song
- Dedicating a number to someone in the crowd

Even just saying "Welcome back, nice to see some familiar faces" helps people feel seen.

Engagement by Role

Engagement strategies will look different depending on your role onboard:

Production Cast Singer

You are part of a tightly staged show, and your primary engagement tool is performance quality. Your eye contact, physical energy, vocal delivery, and ability to project personality within choreography all count. Meet and greets, embarkation welcomes, or cast-led events are where personal engagement can happen more freely, but onstage, your job is to connect within the bounds of direction.

Lounge Entertainer

You have the most direct, repeated access to guests, and the most room to shape the energy of the room. This is what your role includes:

- Reading the crowd in real time
- Taking and managing song requests
- Acknowledging regulars by name or with a wave

- Changing your vibe to match the room: a chill jazz set for predinner drinks, sing-alongs post-dessert

For lounge entertainers, your charm is as important as your chops.

Cruise Administrator

You're already a familiar face on the ship—from the daily schedule to trivia or game shows—so your performance engagement can lean heavily on that rapport. Mentioning earlier events, inside jokes, specific guest interactions, or shared experiences about the port or even the weather makes your performance feel integrated into the voyage. You also represent the company directly, so your tone should strike a balance between warmth and professionalism.

Guest Entertainer

You're new. The guests don't know you yet. That means your job is to build trust fast. Here is the best way to do this:

- Start with a well-known, high-energy number.
- Let your banter reveal who you are (a bit about your background, where you're from, or a funny travel or ship anecdote).
- Warmly acknowledge that you're just joining the voyage, and thank them for making you feel welcome.

Your show is a first impression. Make it count.

If you have more than one show during the voyage, your second appearance allows for a deeper level of engagement. You might reference a moment from your first show, offer a different side of yourself musically or personally, or even respond to guest feedback. Just don't assume that everyone in the audience saw your first show. It's common to ask: "Who was at the last show?" A quick show of applause helps you adjust your tone and content accordingly. Think of your second show not as a sequel, but as another opportunity to leave a lasting impression.

Step-On Entertainer

Depending on where the ship is sailing, your act may be in another language, and your English may not be fluent. That's okay—music is universal, and the cruise director often sets the tone by framing your appearance. Audiences will lean in if you do the following:

- Project warmth and an eagerness to share your culture and story
- Use physicality and expression to tell the story

- Use one or two simple phrases in English (e.g., "Thank you very much!" or "Enjoy!")

Even the most seasoned cruisers often say these performances can be the most authentic and moving of their trips.

Meaningful Participation

Incorporating audience participation—when done well—creates magic:

- Call-and-response (asking, "Is anybody here from New York?")
- Simple sing-alongs ("Sweet Caroline" or "Can't Help Falling In Love")
- Asking questions (saying "Have you ever felt this way?" before a ballad)
- Recognizing special occasions (anniversaries, birthdays, solo travelers, or repeat cruisers)

Pro tip: Always keep participation optional. Never pressure or embarrass guests. The goal is to make them feel included—not exposed.

After the Show

One of the most unique things about cruise ship performing is that you live with your audience. Many guests will approach you after a performance to say thank you, request songs, ask questions about your background, or tell you that a certain song you performed is significant to them.

Postshow mingling is usually optional, but it's one of the best ways to do the following:

- Build genuine connection
- Receive live feedback
- Be remembered (and recommended) long after a cruise ends

Just make sure to set boundaries when needed and always keep things professional.

Choosing repertoire, understanding your audience, and delivering engaging performances are at the core of singing at sea. Whether you're building theme nights, crafting emotional arcs, or mastering the art of mid-show banter, you have the job of bringing joy, connection, and quality entertainment to an ever-changing audience. The more strategically you plan your sets—and the more authentically you engage—the more memorable your performances will be.

Creating and delivering an engaging show is only part of what it means to be a singer at sea. Unlike land-based gigs, cruise contracts often come with a host of nonperformance responsibilities tied to your status as a member of the ship's crew. Whether they're participating in safety drills, attending guest sail-away events, or hosting onboard activities, singers must expect to contribute to the overall cruise experience. In the next chapter, we'll explore what it means to be on the crew manifest and how these additional duties factor into your daily life and professional identity onboard.

8 Singer Duties on the Crew Manifest

Life at sea as a singer offers exciting performance opportunities, but your role onboard extends far beyond what happens onstage. Unlike land-based entertainment jobs, cruise ship performers must understand and adapt to the unique environment of shipboard life, one governed by maritime law, ship policies, and company expectations.

As we have discussed, an essential starting point is understanding how you will be classified while onboard. A singer can be onboard under one of three distinct statuses: crew, guest, or visitor. Each designation comes with its own set of privileges, restrictions, and expectations.

This chapter will examine the additional duties singers may be asked to perform as part of a ship's broader community. You'll also learn how to balance these duties with your primary responsibility: delivering outstanding performances.

Understanding the Differences between Crew, Guest, and Visitor Statuses

When you accept a singing contract at sea, perhaps the first and most important distinction you'll encounter is whether you are considered crew, guest, or visitor. This status shapes nearly every aspect of your shipboard life: where you live, what you are allowed to do, when and where you dine, how you interact with guests and crew, and even which doors you can pass through.

Crew Status

As previously mentioned, most singers hired as part of a ship's production cast, lounge entertainment team, resident party band, or cruise administration are classified as crew members.

As a crew member, you are an essential part of the operational and cultural fabric of the ship. You will have an official seaman's contract (and yes, the term "seaman" is still widely used for all genders, unfortunately), be listed on the crew manifest, and be expected to follow a strict set of rules governing everything from conduct to appearance.

Being crew comes with both responsibilities and privileges:

- **Cabin Assignment:** Crew accommodations vary by cruise line and role. Singers and cruise administrators are typically placed in single or double crew cabins located in designated crew areas below the guest decks.

- **Crew Facilities:** You will have access to the crew gym, crew mess (dining hall), crew bar, recreation rooms, smoking areas, and outdoor space. Some cruise lines also offer wellness and enrichment programs specifically for crew, such as group fitness classes and tours ashore.

- **Movement Restrictions:** Crew must use crew stairwells, elevators, and corridors, and are often prohibited from "roaming" guest areas when off duty unless specific rules allow it.

- **Guest-Area Access:** Depending on your role and the cruise line's policy, certain crew—especially singers and cruise administrators—may have select guest-area access. This can include permission to dine in guest restaurants, visit guest bars, or work out in the guest gym, when those areas are not busy with paying guests. These permissions are considered privileges and can be revoked at any time. They are usually communicated in a privilege or benefits grid prepared by the HR department shoreside. A copy of the grid is given to the crew member upon sign-on, and the grid is posted in a visible location in the entertainment office.

- **Code of Conduct:** Most cruise lines have strict behavioral expectations. This includes guidelines for interacting with guests, restrictions on fraternization, and adherence to appearance and uniform standards. These expectations are typically taught through a mandatory online course to be completed prior to the first day of employment or onboard within the first week or two after sign-on.

- **Alcohol and Substance Policies:** Crew members must adhere to very strict alcohol consumption rules. The legal blood alcohol content (BAC) limit for crew onboard is typically 0.04 percent at all times, both on duty and off duty. Many cruise lines enforce random drug and alcohol testing. A violation can result in immediate dismissal and repatriation at the crew member's expense.

There is also a legal element: Under international maritime law, the ship's captain and staff captain are responsible for the health, safety, and behavior of every crew member onboard. Your crew status places you within this chain of command.

Guest Status

Singers who are contracted for short-term engagements or special performances may sail under guest status. This designation applies primarily to guest entertainers but can also include artists or vocalists hired for special events or promotional voyages.

Performers with guest status are not listed on the crew manifest and are not considered crew members. However, they must still comply with ship policies, including safety requirements and codes of conduct.

Guest status comes with significant privileges that are more aligned with those of regular passengers:

- **Accommodation in Guest Staterooms:** Singers with guest status typically stay in rooms located on higher decks with more space and amenities than crew cabins.
- **Full Guest Access:** This includes use of passenger dining rooms, bars, lounges, pools, and public spaces.
- **No Additional Duties beyond Contracted Performances:** However, some cruise lines may request or suggest social appearances, dining-table hosting, or meet and greets.
- **Onboard Perks:** These can include complimentary laundry service, free Wi-Fi, beverage packages, and discounts in the onboard shops and on shore excursions. The exact perks vary widely by cruise line and contract terms.
- **Greater Independence:** These singers have more autonomy over their schedules, with fewer mandatory meetings or check-ins compared to crew.

There are also important restrictions:

- Guest entertainers do not have access to crew areas or crew-only facilities such as the crew mess, bar, or recreation areas.
- Many cruise lines prohibit entertainers on the guest manifest from gambling or participating in any revenue-generating activities onboard such as casino play, bingo, or lottery games. This restriction is designed to avoid any potential conflicts of interest or issues of perceived fairness among guests.

Because of their short-term contracts and elevated status, guest entertainers are often held to exceptionally high standards for punctuality, preparation, and overall conduct. Their reputations may determine whether they are rehired for future engagements.

Day-Visitor Status

A unique third category exists for individuals who are invited onboard temporarily while the ship is docked. This group includes step-on entertainers, as well as travel agents, inspectors, and friends and family visiting crew. Singers in this group are classified as day visitors, and unlike crew or guest entertainers, they do not appear on the ship's manifest because they do not sail with the vessel overnight.

Key aspects of the day-visitor status include the following:

- **No Overnight Accommodation:** These singers leave the ship before it departs the port.
- **No Official Inclusion on the Ship's Manifest:** These singers' visits are temporary and tied to the ship's time in port.
- **Access to Guest Dining Venues:** This applies to meals during their time onboard, enjoying the same food service as paying guests.
- **No Access to Crew Facilities:** Day-visitor singers are also often restricted to designated guest and performance areas.
- **No Entitlement to Onboard Perks:** Day-visitor singers do not receive perks commonly extended to guest entertainers, such as complimentary laundry, beverage packages, Wi-Fi, or shop discounts.
- **Shortened Onboarding Process:** This is because day-visitor singers are not considered part of the sailing operation team.

To be approved for a day visit, most visitors must submit a visitor-pass request in advance, usually initiated online via a secure link sent by a cruise administrator onboard. The request form requires personal information, including government-issued identification details (with a passport strongly encouraged), which must also be brought to the ship on the day of the visit. This paperwork typically must be completed as early as possible, but at a minimum three days prior to the visit to allow the ship's security team to provide the visitor's information to the local port agent. The port agent ensures that the visitor is granted clearance to enter the port and access the vessel.

Upon arrival at the port, day visitors must pass through standard security screening that is similar to screening for embarking guests. Once at the gangway, visitors are photographed by ship security personnel and issued visitor badges, which must be worn at all times while onboard (apart from during rehearsals or performances).

While this category provides flexibility for performers to gain experience and exposure without committing to a full cruise contract, it does require the ability to adapt quickly to a ship's protocols and schedule.

Mandatory Safety Training and Responsibilities

Cruise lines take safety very seriously. As a singer sailing under crew status, you will be required to complete a comprehensive set of safety trainings and responsibilities under SOLAS (Safety of Life at Sea) regulations. Even those sailing under guest status must participate in certain mandatory drills and briefings. Understanding these requirements—and treating them seriously—is an essential part of being a professional performer at sea. While these requirements may seem far outside the scope of a singer's job description, cruise lines expect every crew member to be fully capable of responding to emergencies with calm, clarity, and precision.

Emergency Duties and Muster-Station Assignments

As a crew member, you'll be assigned a muster station—a designated gathering point for passengers during emergencies—and a specific emergency role. These assignments vary by ship and position but may include the following:

- Acting as a muster assistant, helping to direct and account for passengers
- Serving as a stairway guide to ensure safe and orderly evacuation
- Assisting with the preparation of lifeboats or life rafts (less common for singers but possible)
- Reporting to a specific team such as the fire squad or first-aid team (usually reserved for trained personnel)

You'll participate in mandatory safety drills, often weekly or biweekly. These drills are usually announced beforehand and treated with the same level of seriousness as an actual emergency. Not knowing your role or failing to participate can result in disciplinary action, up to dismissal.

Cruise administrators carry specific emergency responsibilities, primarily focused on guest communication and coordination. In an emergency, the cruise director most often serves as the voice of the bridge, delivering public announcements. Their role is highly visible and focuses on maintaining order, offering reassurance, and relaying instructions from the captain and staff captain. The assistant cruise director assumes these duties if the cruise director is unavailable or incapacitated, but under normal circumstances, the assistant cruise director is also assigned a secondary safety role.

This may include the following:

- Taking calls on the bridge from various emergency-response teams (e.g., firefighting, medical, or evacuation units) and relaying updates directly to the staff captain

Figure 8.1 Crew member overseeing guests at a muster drill.
Courtesy Eyesonmilan/Shutterstock.

- Overseeing muster-station control, acting as a communication liaison between muster stations and the evacuation control center

These roles require excellent communication skills, situational awareness, and a clear understanding of the ship's emergency protocols. While these responsibilities may not be performance related, they demonstrate how cruise entertainment staff are deeply integrated into the overall safety structure of the vessel.

Safety Requirements for Guest Entertainers and Day Visitors

Singers sailing under guest status are not typically assigned emergency duties, but they are still required to attend passenger safety drills and must familiarize themselves with evacuation procedures. In rare emergency situations, guest entertainers may be asked to assist under the direction of senior staff.

Day visitors, including step-on entertainers, are generally exempt from drills due to their short onboard durations. However, they must follow any instructions given by ship safety personnel during their visits, especially in the event of an emergency.

Ongoing Safety Training during Your Contract

It's important to understand that safety training doesn't end after embarkation. Additional training sessions may be conducted throughout your contract, depending on the itinerary and the operational demands of the ship's sailing region.

Here are some examples:

- If your ship is transiting through a piracy risk zone, such as the Gulf of Aden, you may be required to attend a piracy response training to understand what actions to take in the event of a pirate attack.
- If your ship is traveling to Antarctica or other polar regions, you may undergo training on cold-water survival and extreme-weather preparedness, which are essential in the case of emergencies in those environments.

These trainings are mandatory, may be introduced on short notice, and are part of your ongoing responsibility as a crew member.

The Performer's Role in Safety Culture

Though singers may not view themselves as part of the traditional ship-operations team, they play a crucial role in the ship's safety culture. Performing artists are often highly visible and can help set the tone for guests and fellow crew alike. Participating in drills with professionalism, asking questions when needed, and staying informed about your emergency role reinforces your value onboard—not just as an entertainer, but also as a reliable and responsible part of the larger team.

Requirements for Hosting Activities, Socializing, and Interacting with Guests

Performers on cruise ships are not just entertainers—they're also brand ambassadors. Especially for singers listed on the crew manifest, the role extends well beyond the performance venue. Cruise lines expect crew-status performers to contribute to the overall guest experience by being visible, approachable, and engaged in ship life. This is a major shift from most land-based gigs, where the performer's job ends when the show is over.

Guest-facing responsibilities vary greatly depending on the cruise line and entertainment structure—be sure to check with your hiring body to clarify what will be required of you. The following are some common expectations you may encounter.

Hosting Shipboard Activities

Singers may be asked to host or cohost daily events that fall outside of traditional performances. These can include the following:

- Trivia contests
- Karaoke nights
- Line dancing or ballroom dance lessons
- Arts and crafts
- Bingo and game shows
- Ship tours
- Sports and recreation
- Language classes
- Choir conducting
- Theme-night events (e.g., Seventies discos, country hoedowns, Gatsby parties, or ABBA nights)
- Sail-away parties, deck games, or dance parties

These activities are designed to energize the ship, help guests engage, and build personal connection between passengers and the onboard entertainment team. Performers who are charismatic, outgoing, and comfortable with a mic in informal settings tend to excel in these moments.

While participation is expected, the specific activities you're assigned to host often consider your unique strengths and personality. Whoever is in charge of activity scheduling—whether it's the activity manager, assistant cruise director, cruise director, or entertainment manager—will usually collaborate with you to find hosting opportunities that align with your comfort zone and skill set. For example, a singer with a background in dance might lead a themed dance class, while someone with improv experience might shine while hosting game shows or bingo. This kind of thoughtful scheduling not only enhances guest enjoyment but also helps you feel confident and authentic in your role.

Socializing with Guests

Social interaction is often an unwritten perk of the job, especially for singers in lounge settings, party bands, and production casts. While there is a delicate balance between being friendly and being too familiar, singers are generally expected to do the following:

- Engage in casual conversation after performances
- Be warm, professional, and positive in guest areas
- Attend special events like captains' welcome receptions, loyalty guest events, or officers' BBQs

- Host dining tables
- Represent the brand with grace and approachability

These moments help guests feel seen and valued, and that emotional connection often leads to better show attendance, higher satisfaction scores, and repeat cruise bookings. Your social presence contributes directly to the success of the cruise and the bottom line of the company. That said, be sure that any additional responsibilities that fall outside the scope of performing are clearly communicated to you prior to you beginning your contract. It is vital that you know exactly what your role onboard will entail.

Guest Interaction for Cruise Administrators

For cruise directors, assistant cruise directors, entertainment managers, and other cruise administrators, guest interaction is not just encouraged—it's also a core responsibility. These roles are highly visible and serve as the face of the cruise line onboard.

Daily duties often include the following:

- Hosting main events such as welcome-aboard shows, sail-aways, and game shows
- Making daily public announcements heard throughout guest areas
- Working the room at parties, receptions, and specialty dinners
- Greeting guests during initial embarkation to offer a warm first impression and throughout the cruise, frequently upon the return of large tours in port
- Being constantly accessible and approachable in guest areas throughout the day

Cruise administrators build rapport with guests to create a sense of comfort and community from day one. Their presence is central to the emotional tone of the cruise. Because of their leadership roles, administrators are expected to maintain consistently high standards of conduct. They must also walk a fine line between being warm and accessible and still projecting authority and professionalism, particularly during moments of disruption or unexpected changes to the itinerary.

Knowing the Boundaries

While sociability is encouraged, there are clear boundaries in place to protect both guests and crew. All performers and cruise staff must be aware of the line between being approachable and professional versus being overly familiar or informal.

Most cruise lines have policies that do the following:

- Prohibit fraternization or personal relationships with guests
- Restrict consumption of alcohol in guest areas (or allow it only in moderation under specific conditions)
- Expect crew to always act as representatives of the company, even when off duty

A good rule to follow is this: If you're in a guest area, you're on the clock in terms of conduct. Your tone, demeanor, and appearance matter—even if you're just getting a coffee at the café or walking through a lounge.

Socializing for Guest Entertainers

Singers sailing under guest status may not be contractually obligated to socialize, but many still choose to do so strategically. Appearing at postshow meet and greets, mingling at receptions, or sitting with guests during hosted dinners can generate more audience members at their shows and elevate the impact of a performance.

Socializing for Step-On Entertainers

For step-on entertainers, guest-socialization requirements are typically minimal to nonexistent. Since these performers are brought onboard temporarily—usually only while the ship is docked in port—once the performance concludes, step-on entertainers are generally expected to pack up and disembark quickly, often with limited time for postshow guest interaction. Because these performers are day visitors and are not on the ship's manifest, the ship cannot officially sail until step-on entertainers have left the vessel. This also means the gangway cannot be lifted or secured until all visitors have disembarked, making timely departure a top priority.

Standard protocol requires all day visitors to disembark at least one hour prior to the ship's scheduled departure, though in some cases, exceptions may be made for step-on entertainers if disembarkation is tightly coordinated with the bridge and port agent.

As a result, while a brief thank-you, farewell, or photo may be possible, step-on entertainers are rarely required—or even able to—participate in extended guest socialization, and their contracts typically do not include this expectation.

Balancing Additional Duties with Performance Demands

As a singer, you have the primary responsibility of delivering exceptional performances, but the additional duties you take on—whether hosting, training, safety drills, or social events—can significantly fill up your days. Balancing these expectations without burning out is one of the most important skills to master as a cruise ship performer.

The Reality of a Full Schedule

Many first-time singers are surprised to learn just how full a day at sea can be, even when they're not performing that evening.

A typical week might include the following:

- Participating in multiple safety drills or training sessions
- Hosting trivia, karaoke, and themed parties
- Participating in photo ops and meet-and-greets
- Attending loyalty receptions, specialty dinners, or officer-hosted events
- Rehearsing new material or doing tech runs or music brushups
- Having personal warm-up and practice time
- Fitting fitness, laundry, rest, and basic self-care around the above

It's not unusual for singers to find that their "off" days aren't exactly off—their days are just free of stage time. This is particularly true in the early stages of a contract when you're still adjusting to the rhythm of ship life and building your presence with guests and crew.

Time Management Is Key

To thrive in this environment, singers must develop strong time-management habits. Here are some best practices:

- Keep a planner or digital calendar and set alarms on your phone to stay on top of your call times, hosting slots, and drill schedules.
- Schedule rest as intentionally as work. Even a thirty-minute nap can be a game changer during back-to-back days at sea.
- Communicate proactively with your company manager if your schedule is becoming unsustainable or if a duty is interfering with necessary vocal rest.
- Batch tasks when possible, like doing laundry while studying lyrics or warming up discreetly while walking to your venue.

Table 8.1 Example of a Sea Day Schedule for Resident Entertainment Roles

Time	Production Cast Vocalist	Lounge Entertainer	Cruise Director
7:00	Get ready	Sleep in	Workout
8:00	Breakfast	Breakfast	Get ready & breakfast
9:00	Get ready	Get ready	Office work & meetings
10:00	Host dance class	Practice	Film daily TV show
11:00	Host sports/arts & crafts		Serve at guest brunch
12:00	Lunch	Lunch & Soundcheck	Announcements & host trivia
13:00	Break	Pool deck set	Lunch
14:00	Assist with bingo	Workout	Office work
15:00	Break	Nap	Nap
16:00	Host trivia	Get ready for evening	Get ready for evening
17:00	Warm-up	Soundcheck	Office work
18:00	Tech rehearsal	Pre-dinner lounge set	Cocktail parties/host table
19:00	Costumes & makeup	Dinner	
20:00	Production show performances	Evening lounge sets	Host production shows
21:00			
22:00	De-greet guests; prop & costume clean-up		Visit lounges
23:00	Room service dinner	Free time	Office work
24:00	Free time		Crew bar

- Guard your vocal health—avoid unnecessary talking, warm up and cool down consistently, and know when to say no to loud social events if they affect your voice.

Performers who pace themselves wisely tend to perform more consistently and avoid the mid-contract burnout that can plague even the most talented singers.

Asking for Support

One of the best ways to stay afloat (pun intended) is to remember that you're part of a team. If you're feeling overextended, do the following:

- Speak to your manager respectfully but directly.
- Ask for adjustments that protect your vocal or mental health.
- Offer alternative solutions (e.g., "Could I host trivia on a nonperformance day instead?").
- Be honest—but not dramatic—about your needs.

Most entertainment teams genuinely want their performers to succeed and will do their best to accommodate reasonable requests. The key is to communicate early and stay collaborative.

Cruise Administrators and the Double Workload

For cruise directors, assistant cruise directors, and entertainment managers, this balancing act is even more intense. These roles require long hours, constant visibility, and high-stakes multitasking.

Cruise administrators are often managing the following responsibilities:

- Running activities from morning until late at night
- Managing daily scheduling and team communication
- Making ship-wide announcements and managing complaints
- Handling sudden changes due to weather, logistics, or medical emergencies
- Participating in leadership meetings and safety drills
- Attending every mainstage show, often while still hosting events in between

It's a demanding rhythm, and success requires both personal discipline and a strong support team. Cruise administrators set the tone for the entire department, and their ability to manage the workload with grace and humor makes a major impact on morale.

The Bigger Picture

Life at sea as a singer means being more than just a performer—you are also a crew member, a host, a safety-trained team player, and a visible ambassador of the brand. Whether classified as crew, guest, or day visitor, each role comes with a distinct set of responsibilities and expectations that extend far beyond the stage.

While understanding your additional responsibilities as a singer on the crew manifest is essential, it's just one part of the equation. In the next chapter, we'll shift focus to the business of singing at sea: the contracts that govern your work, how you get paid, additional ways to earn income onboard, tips for saving money while living on a ship, managing your online presence responsibly, and planning a long-term, sustainable career in this unique environment.

9 The Business of Singing at Sea

By now, you've learned what kinds of singing jobs exist at sea, how to land them, and how to prepare for life and work onboard. But behind every successful cruise ship singer is a solid understanding of the business side of the industry. This chapter pulls back the curtain on what many first-time performers don't realize until they're already mid-contract: Cruise ship singing is as much a business decision as it is an artistic one.

Compensation structures, onboard expenses, and long-term career strategies will vary between cruise lines, agencies, and roles; and unfortunately, you won't find a union rep onboard or a booking agent to guide you through the fine print. Today's performers must navigate everything from managing personal finances during contracts to maintaining a digital presence on social media.

This chapter won't just help you make informed decisions: It will also help you build a sustainable and strategic career. Whether your goal is to cruise for a few years or to parlay shipboard experience into bigger opportunities on land or to build a life on ships, understanding the business of singing at sea is key to your success.

Pay Structures and Financial Realities at Sea

Before you pack your bags and set sail, it's important to understand how you'll actually get paid for your work at sea and how that income fits into your broader financial life. Cruise ship contracts offer steady, sometimes tax-free, income, but the details vary widely depending on your role, your country of residence, and the cruise line's policies. In this section, we'll break down the essentials: how and when you'll be paid, how taxes typically work for cruise ship singers, and what financial realities you should prepare for so your time at sea strengthens your financial foundation.

How You'll Actually Get Paid

The days of ship crew getting paid in wads of US cash and hiding it under their mattresses are, for better or for worse, long gone. Today's cruise ship performers are paid through a range of digital systems and international banking platforms. The method of payment depends on your role, your hiring agency, and the cruise line's internal structure, with variations in timing, fees, and level of accessibility.

Production Cast Vocalists and Cruise Administrators

- **What You're Paid Through:** You're paid through onboard crew payroll systems (such as Brightwell, Salary@Sea, OceanPay, or MXM).
- **How it Works:** You receive a physical debit card onboard linked to your payroll account. Funds are deposited biweekly or monthly.
- **How to Access Funds:**
  - Use crew-designated ATMs onboard to withdraw cash without fees.
  - Transfers to home bank accounts are available via the payroll system's web portal or app. (Fees and conversion rates apply.)

Lounge Entertainers

- **What You're Paid Through (Depending on Cruise Line and Agency):**
  - You may be paid via direct bank transfer from an entertainment agency (most common for duos, party bands, and piano bar entertainers).
  - Or you may be paid through an onboard crew payroll system (more common if the entertainer is considered a full crew member or part of a long-term onboard music team).
- **How it Works:**
  - Agency-based payments are wired biweekly or monthly, often in US dollars or local currency depending on the agency's location.
  - Ship-based payments follow the same structure as that for production cast vocalists and cruise administrators: payroll card, onboard ATM, and optional transfers.

Guest Entertainers

- **What You're Paid Through:** You're paid either via a booking agent (most common) or directly from the cruise line.
- **How it Works:**
  - Larger cruise lines typically pay the agent, who then pays the performer (often via wire transfer and minus a 15 percent commission).

- Some lines, particularly smaller luxury brands, may pay the artist directly via bank transfer (shifting the requirement to the artist to pay their agent the 15 percent commission).
- **Timing:** Payments often net 30 or 60 days after the performance. Payments may be delayed if paperwork (e.g., travel receipts) is not submitted properly.

Step-On Entertainers

- **What You're Paid Through:** You are paid one of two ways, depending on how the act was booked:
  1 **Through a Local Port Agent or Tour Operator:** Performers are often paid directly via cash or check onboard by the cruise director or assistant cruise director, usually after the performance.
  2 **Through a Talent Agency:** The cruise line's shoreside office pays the agency, and the agency pays the performer, typically via wire transfer and minus a 15 percent commission. Payment is subject to the agency's invoicing schedule and may take several weeks.

Taxes at Sea: What Performers Need to Know

One of the biggest surprises for cruise performers is realizing that tax withholding is inconsistent and often nonexistent, especially if your contract is administered outside your home country.

US Citizens and Residents

- If you're hired by a US-based company like Royal Caribbean Group (headquartered in Miami) and you're listed as an employee, your wages may be subject to withholding.
  - In that case, you'll likely receive a W-2 at tax time, with federal (and sometimes state) income tax already deducted.
- If you're hired as an independent contractor, you won't have any taxes withheld. You may receive a 1099-NEC, or no forms at all, and are responsible for reporting your full income and paying self-employment tax.

Canadian Citizens and Residents

- Canadian cruise performers generally do not receive a T4 unless they are hired by a Canadian company.
- All cruise income must be reported on your Canadian tax return as foreign-earned income.

- You are responsible for tracking your earnings and paying tax on that income in Canada, even if it's in a foreign currency.

Contracts Administered Abroad

- Cruise lines like Azamara, which is headquartered in the United States but administers contracts through offices in Mumbai, do not withhold taxes for any nationality.
- You are paid in full and must declare all earnings in your country of residence.
- You will not receive a tax form (e.g., W-2 or 1099-NEC), and the cruise line is not required to report your earnings to your home country.

What This Means for You

- Track your income meticulously. If no taxes are withheld, you are still responsible for reporting that income to your country's tax authority and paying applicable income and self-employment taxes.
- Consider hiring a tax professional familiar with foreign-earned income, especially if you work multiple contracts in a year or if you work across different cruise lines.
- US citizens may qualify for the foreign earned income exclusion (FEIE) under IRS rules (Form 2555), but this depends on how much time you spent abroad and on other criteria.
- No matter where you're paid from, you are not exempt from income taxes just because you're working at sea.

Saving and Supplementing Your Income

One of the biggest financial advantages of working on a cruise ship is how much you are able to save. With housing, meals, and transportation provided, many performers put aside far more money at sea than they ever could on land. But financial success onboard requires intention, awareness, and a bit of discipline.

This section will walk you through practical ways to save money during your contract, including how to avoid hidden costs, manage onboard spending systems, and take advantage of perks like free shore excursions and onboard medical care. We'll also explore additional ways singers can supplement their income onboard, whether by taking on extra responsibilities like vocal or dance captain, participating in revenue-generating events, or performing in bonus headlining shows outside their primary contracts. Used wisely, a cruise contract can be far more lucrative than the initial salary figure would suggest.

Smart Ways to Save Money Onboard

Avoid Paying for What's Free

Meals in the mess (and in select guest venues, depending on your contract) are included. Buying meals at specialty restaurants onboard, ordering daily premium coffee, or getting food ashore quickly chips away at your earnings. Stick to included meals for your daily routine and save guest dining for the occasional treat.

Be Strategic about Wi-Fi and Phone Use

Cruise Wi-Fi is expensive and often slow. Crew get discounted rates (and some cruise lines do provide Wi-Fi for free), but rates can still add up fast over a long contract. Use free Wi-Fi in port (typically available in cruise ship terminals) or buy local SIM cards or eSIMs where possible. Download content ashore to avoid large streaming fees. Additionally, many cruise lines allow crew members to use WhatsApp for free while connected to the crew Wi-Fi network. Prioritize using Wi-Fi for staying in touch with friends and family.

Watch Out for Roaming Charges

Roaming charges can sneak up quickly if your phone connects to a local network. Choose a phone plan that includes global roaming—such as T-Mobile (United States) or Vodafone (Europe)—to avoid surprise charges. Some travelers use Google Fi Wireless or Holafly eSIMs as flexible global options.

Crew-Bar Spending Adds Up

The crew bar offers cheap drinks, but small charges accumulate fast when they're billed to your crew account and no cash or bank cards pass hands. Consider setting a weekly or monthly spending limit for social nights.

Bring Your Own Essentials

Pack toiletries, over-the-counter meds, and detergent. Buying these items on the ship or during short port stops is often more expensive and selection may be limited, depending on where the ship is in the world.

Know What the Slop Chest Offers

Most ships have a slop chest—a small, crew-only store that sells necessities like these:

- Laundry detergent
- Soap, shampoo, and razors

- Over-the-counter medications
- Snacks and instant noodles
- Sodas and nonalcoholic beverages

Prices are typically lower than in guest shops, but higher than what you'd pay on land. Inventory is also limited, and it's not always restocked regularly, so don't rely on the slop chest as your only supply source. Treat the slop chest as a backup, not your primary resource. You'll save more by bringing what you need with you, especially personal care items that may be difficult to find in port.

Don't Shop for Sport

Guest boutiques can be tempting, but impulse buys (snacks, clothing, or gadgets) add up. Stick to a monthly budget for nonessentials and track your spending.

Use Crew-Specific ATMs

Withdraw cash from designated crew ATMs onboard to avoid transactional fees. If you're paid via a payroll system, minimize conversion and transfer fees by sending home money in larger, less frequent batches.

Escort Shore Excursions for Free Tours

Many cruise lines encourage crew (and occasionally guest entertainers) to escort guest shore excursions. You act as a representative of the cruise line, help guests navigate the tour, and complete a short survey or report about the tour. In the rare case of an incident, you would be required to document it. While you don't get paid for escorting excursions, you get to go on tours for free—a great way to experience high-value excursions without spending a cent.

How You're Charged for Things Onboard: Crew versus Guests

Whether you're buying a snack, signing up for a wine tasting, or getting a massage at the spa, you will pay for nearly all onboard purchases through your onboard account, not pay in cash or with a debit or credit card. But the way the charges are handled varies depending on your role and sometimes your cruise line.

Crew Members

If you are a crew member, you are issued a crew ID card, which doubles as your spending card. This allows you to make purchases at the crew bar, in onboard shops, and in guest areas (where permitted), and even pay for specialty services like dining or spa procedures.

Here's how those charges may be settled:

- On some cruise lines, charges are automatically deducted from your paycheck.
- Other cruise lines allow you to link a credit card, and your balance is charged to it on payroll day.
- Some cruise lines require you to visit the crew purser's office and settle your balance manually, either in cash or by using your payroll debit card (e.g., via Brightwell, Salary@Sea, OceanPay, or ShipMoney).

Most cruise lines cap crew spending around US$200. If you hit your limit and don't settle the balance, your spending privileges may be frozen until payment is made. If you want to make a larger purchase, you can preload your account with additional funds to increase your spending limit—which is helpful if you want to buy things like fine jewelry, electronics, or designer merchandise from the guest shops while onboard.

Guest Entertainers

If you're a guest entertainer, you are issued a guest key card, just like passengers.

- All purchases—Wi-Fi, drinks, dining, laundry, or medical services—are added to your guest folio.
- You must settle your folio in full before disembarking, using a credit card, a debit card, or cash.
- You typically do not have access to the crew bar or slop chest, unless you are granted special privileges by the cruise director or entertainment manager.

Pro tip: Always review your folio before the last day. If your card was not set up properly at embarkation, charges may accumulate without your knowledge, and you'll be held responsible at disembarkation. Most cruise lines give you the ability to check your folio balance via your stateroom television.

Additional Ways to Make Money

Serve as a Vocal, Dance, or Wardrobe Captain

On smaller ships or in leaner entertainment departments, performers are often asked to take on additional responsibilities beyond singing. These extra duties can offer small financial bonuses and demonstrate your reliability and leadership potential.

- **Vocal Captains:** These leaders help maintain vocal health and musical integrity throughout the contract. They may run warm-ups, facilitate brushup rehearsals, and relay notes from the bandmaster or music supervisor shoreside.
- **Dance Captains:** These captains are responsible for keeping choreography clean, leading rehearsals when needed, and ensuring cast consistency.
- **Wardrobe Captains:** Wardrobe captains support costume changes and laundering, steaming, and organizing accessories, especially during production shows with fast quick changes and limited crew backstage.

These roles may come with weekly stipends, end-of-contract bonuses, or one-time payments depending on the cruise line and how the role is defined in your contract. Be sure to clarify expectations up front and advocate for compensation if the task falls outside your original job description.

Help with Revenue-Generating Activities

- Cruise lines occasionally ask singers to assist with events like the following:
  - Bingo
  - Art auctions
  - Wine tastings or mixology classes
- These may offer small per-event bonuses or commissions if your involvement helps drive guest participation or sales.

Perform Extra Shows

- On some ships, lounge entertainers or production cast vocalists may be invited to headline solo shows in the main theater.
- If a headline performance is outside your original contract, it may come with a performance fee or bonus, depending on the cruise line. (Note that most contracts stipulate that the performer must perform additional shows "per the discretion of the cruise director" without additional compensation.)
- These opportunities are often determined by programming needs or guest demographics—be ready with a polished set and promo materials if asked.

Sell Merchandise (Guest Entertainers Only)

- Guest entertainers often sell CDs, USB drives, download cards, or small branded items to supplement their performance fees.

- Sales usually happen in either of these venues:
  - Just outside the theater after the show
  - In the onboard gift shop, which may host a designated signing session
- Step-on entertainers are usually not allowed to sell merchandise, as onboard shops are allowed to operate only while ships are at sea in international waters. Selling in port would require portside customs clearance and fee payment, which is typically prohibited.

What Not to Do

- Don't perform unsanctioned gigs for private parties, weddings, or other paid events without cruise-director approval.
- Don't sell your own merchandise unless you're a contracted guest entertainer and have obtained explicit approval.
- Don't run informal side businesses (e.g., giving music lessons, doing haircuts, or selling snacks). These are violations of most shipboard conduct policies and can result in termination.

Saving at sea is less about strict sacrifice and more about conscious decision making. Most performers can save a significant portion of their income by simply taking advantage of what's included and avoiding unnecessary extras. And while cruise ships won't make you rich overnight, every bonus opportunity and bit saved can tip the scales toward a financially successful contract.

Navigating Social Media

Social media can be a powerful asset for cruise ship singers. It allows you to document your travels, promote your work, stay connected with your community, and, if well done, build a personal brand that supports future opportunities. But it also comes with responsibilities and risks. Because you are a contracted performer, your online presence reflects not only on you but also on the cruise line, your entertainment agency, and sometimes even your fellow castmates.

This section will help you use social media in a way that feels authentic and artistically fulfilling while respecting onboard policies, protecting your reputation, and staying aligned with the brand you're temporarily representing.

Know the Rules: Cruise Line Policies on Social Media

Most cruise lines have clear policies—often buried in your contract or onboarding documents—about what crew may or may not post online. These rules exist to protect guest privacy, brand image, and operational security.

Common restrictions include the following:

- No photos or videos of guests without consent.
- No behind-the-scenes content from restricted areas unless explicitly approved.
- No real-time reporting of ship location, delays, emergencies, or onboard incidents.
- No complaints about your job, itinerary, or living conditions.
- No use of the cruise line's name or hashtags in a way that implies official endorsement.

Some cruise lines also prohibit filming content for monetized platforms (e.g., TikTok UGC, YouTube vlogs, sponsored Instagram Reels) unless preapproved by corporate.

Pro tip: If you're unsure, ask your cruise director or entertainment manager what's appropriate. When in doubt, err on the side of discretion—your job could depend on it.

Branding Yourself while Representing the Cruise Line

Even though you're working for a brand, you're also building your own brand. Cruise contracts offer unique content opportunities—sunsets on Santorini, backstage moments in full makeup, or rehearsals at sea. But it's essential to strike a balance between showcasing your experience and respecting the environment you're in.

- **Tone Matters:** Celebrate your journey without sounding like you're advertising or, worse, complaining.
- **Highlight the Work:** Posting clips from rehearsals, show-ready selfies, or spotlight moments helps future employers see you in action.
- **Be Gracious:** Tag your musicians, thank your production team, and acknowledge the broader team effort behind every performance. Evaluate a post as if you expect everyone on the ship to see it.

The best performers on social media are those who appear professional, collaborative, and proud—not self-important.

What to Share, What to Skip

Good ideas for posts include the following:

- Snippets from your performances (when allowed)
- Port-day adventures and travel content
- Show posters or performance schedules (if already shared publicly)

- Candid but respectful backstage moments
- Reels or carousels about ship life (with care and context)

Avoid sharing the following:

- Unflattering or unauthorized footage of other performers
- Anything that reveals passenger faces without consent
- Behind-the-scenes images in restricted areas
- Complaints about your contract, the cruise line, guests, or other crew
- Confidential information, including security protocols or internal memos

Growing Your Following while at Sea

The cruise world offers a built-in content calendar: new ports every few days, performances several nights per week, and beautiful venues to document your journey. Here's how to use that to your advantage:

- Be consistent—post regularly, even if it's just stories.
- Use location tags and ship-relevant hashtags.
- Collaborate with fellow entertainers.
- Engage with followers: Answer questions, share behind-the-scenes stories, and keep the tone warm and approachable.
- Post with intention—share your artistic identity, not just your itinerary.

Influence without Overstepping

Some performers lean into the "travel influencer" aesthetic, which is fine, as long as it doesn't compromise your job. However, if you're posting public-facing content from your cruise contract, follow these guidelines:

- Avoid appearing as a spokesperson for the cruise line unless you've been officially approved to do so.
- Disclose gifts or sponsorships (e.g., "Thanks to [Brand] for this luggage I'm using on tour!") if posting as an influencer.
- Don't film monetized or branded content using ship spaces without permission.

Even a well-meaning post can cause problems if it violates policies or raises concerns about professionalism. Use your platform with care and know that cruise lines do monitor online content.

Used wisely, social media can elevate your cruise experience beyond the ship. It can reconnect you with old fans, attract new opportunities, and help you reflect in real time on what you're building. Just remember: You're not just representing yourself—you're also part of a floating brand. Navigate both with grace, and your digital presence will become one of your strongest assets at sea and beyond.

The business side of singing at sea can be complex, but when navigated well, it can offer extraordinary rewards. Understanding the financial structures behind different types of contracts, knowing how and when you're paid, budgeting for life onboard, and leveraging small but meaningful opportunities can help set you up for long-term security and artistic freedom.

We've also seen how your digital presence—how you represent yourself and the cruise line online—can influence future bookings, industry perception, and your ability to be rehired. But no matter how sharp your branding, how solid your contract, or how fast your career acceleration, none of it matters without your voice. Which brings us to a topic at the very heart of a singer's success at sea: vocal health and longevity.

In the next chapter, we'll dive into the unique vocal demands of cruise work, explore how to care for your instrument in constantly changing environments, and discuss strategies for staying healthy, consistent, and resilient across long contracts, multiple venues, and sometimes grueling performance schedules. Because in the end, your most valuable business asset isn't your social media feed, your resume, or even your talent—it's your voice.

10 Vocal Health and Longevity

No matter how charming your stage manner is or how thrilling your high notes may be, your career at sea hinges on one thing above all: your ability to stay vocally healthy. Unlike in land-based gigs, where you may be able to cancel a show or call in a sub, cruise ship performers don't have understudies. The show must go on, and that means your vocal health isn't just a priority—it's a necessity.

The unique demands of ship life, with its dry, recycled air, unpredictable schedules, late nights, noisy environments, and limited access to vocal-health specialists, can take a toll. Even seasoned professionals can be surprised by how quickly vocal fatigue sets in without consistent maintenance and care.

This chapter will explore how to keep your voice and body in peak condition for the long haul. From hydration and warm-ups to managing illness and preventing burnout, we'll cover real-life strategies for sustaining a career at sea without blowing out. Because singing at sea isn't just about surviving a contract—it's also about building a sustainable, joyful career that you can carry across oceans and years.

Why Vocal Health Is Different at Sea

Singing on a cruise ship may come with glamorous destinations and enthusiastic audiences, but the environment itself presents a host of vocal-health challenges that performers don't always anticipate, especially if they're used to working on land.

Dry, Recycled Air

Most ships operate with industrial HVAC systems that recirculate dry, air-conditioned air 24-7. This environment can dehydrate your vocal folds even if you're drinking plenty of water. For singers, it means the body must work harder to stay lubricated, and a single skipped steam or warm-up can result in noticeable vocal fatigue. Add in changing climates from port to port, and your respiratory system is constantly adjusting.

Constant Background Noise

Ships are noisy places. Engine hum, hallway chatter, deck parties, and even the sea itself create a level of ambient noise that requires you to speak louder than you normally would. Over time, this low-grade strain on the voice—especially for singers who are also expected to engage with guests—can lead to chronic fatigue or injury.

Inconsistent Schedules

Late-night sets, early-morning trainings, port days, time-zone changes, and last-minute calls can wreak havoc on your sleep schedule and recovery time. Cruise schedules often fluctuate with itinerary changes, weather, or operational needs. Consistent rest is important for both physical and mental health, and without it, even well-trained voices can become strained or vulnerable to illness.

Lack of Vocal Health Resources

While cruise ships typically have onboard medical teams, they are not specialists in vocal health. There are no ENTs, laryngologists, or voice therapists onboard, and if you need to be scoped or receive vocal therapy, you will need to wait until you reach a port with the right facilities.

Social Demands and Guest Interaction

As we previously touched upon, cruise contracts often involve socializing with guests and participating in events where you're expected to be "on." Whether it's welcome parties, hosting duties, or simply being recognized in public spaces, the cumulative vocal and energetic load can add up quickly. Learning how to protect your voice while still being personable is a critical skill.

Everyday Maintenance and Preventative Care

When you're performing regularly in an unpredictable environment like a cruise ship, you need to make vocal maintenance a consistent and intentional part of your day. While every singer develops their own unique routine based on their voice, schedule, and preferences, there are some universal strategies that can help keep your voice resilient, your energy up, and your body primed to support your singing, even in the middle of the ocean.

Warm Up, Cool Down—Every Time

Warming up your voice isn't optional when you sing at sea. A consistent warm-up helps prepare your instrument for the wildly different acoustic environments you will confront. Include gentle onset exercises, like soft "ng" humming or light "gee" or "goo" on a descending five-note scale, to engage the vocal folds without force. Follow these with semi-occluded vocal-tract exercises like lip trills or straw

Steroids, Silence, and a Showstopper

Here's a glamorous behind-the-scenes truth: Sometimes your vocal folds stop phonating mid-note and you just hope the audience thinks it's a tech issue!

While cruise directing for Azamara, I caught a vicious respiratory virus that had already steamrollered half the crew. It tanked my singing voice just in time for my solo show, of course. Since the show was near the end of the cruise, I couldn't swap nights with another act. I had to go on.

I took myself to medical, where the nurse gave me a shot of steroids right in the butt. I had never taken steroids before to reduce vocal-fold swelling (I always worried it would mask symptoms and lead to more damage), but desperate times, and so on.

Cut to me absolutely *slaying* rehearsal. Glorious. Effortless. Vocally bulletproof.

But at exactly the six-hour mark—midway through my final song—I started dropping sound like a bad Wi-Fi connection. I'd begin a big, dramatic note, and halfway through … silence. Then suddenly: voice again! It was like watching a car try to start in the dead of winter. I silently prayed the audience thought it was a mic cutting out, not my folds staging a coup.

I somehow pulled off the final high note, bowed like a queen, then disappeared to my cabin, ordered room service, and entered a vow of total vocal silence for the next eight hours.

The takeaway: At sea, you don't get understudies. Sometimes, it's technique, tenacity, and a shot in the butt that get you through.

phonation, light sirens, or voiced fricatives like "vvv" or "zzz" to promote efficient airflow and reduce tension. Finish up with some resonance balancing to fine-tune where the sound vibrates in your face and skull, like buzzing on an "ng" and then transitioning into an "ee" or "ay" to feel the shift in resonance.

If your role onboard includes a lot of speaking—such as if you're a cruise director or entertainment manager—it can be tempting to skip your warm-up entirely. After all, your voice may feel like it's in a constant state of use. But even then, just a few gentle exercises like the ones listed above are still essential. They help bring balance and coordination back to the voice and prevent fatigue from creeping in unnoticed.

Equally important is a vocal cooldown after your show or sets. A few minutes of gentle humming, sighs, or straw phonation can help reduce post-performance swelling and signal to your voice that the workday is over.

Hydration, Hydration, Hydration

Cruise ships are *dry*. The HVAC systems pull moisture from your body and your vocal folds, and you'll often be in air conditioning both day and night. Hydrate from the inside (aim to drink 2–3 liters of water per day) and consider external hydration as well: a personal steam inhaler, hot showers, and a travel humidifier for your cabin.

A vocal-friendly upgrade many singers swear by is a nebulizer—a handheld device that delivers isotonic saline mist directly into the lungs and upper airway. Unlike steaming, which hydrates surface tissue through heat and moisture, nebulizing offers internal hydration that can help soothe irritated tissue and reduce inflammation. Just be sure to use saline made for inhalation, not tap water or essential oils.

Keep in mind that alcohol and caffeine are both dehydrating. That doesn't mean you can't enjoy them, but balance them with extra water and be especially mindful the day before a show.

Fuel and Rest

What you eat affects how you sing. Heavy, greasy meals before a show may lead to reflux, while acidic or spicy foods can irritate the throat. Learn your body's triggers and adjust accordingly.

Sleep is another major factor. The ship's schedule can throw your rhythm off—late sets, early excursions, crew drills—so you may need to get strategic about rest. Even short naps or consistent wind-down rituals can make a difference. When you're tired, your vocal folds are too.

Movement Is Maintenance

Keeping your body in motion isn't just good for your health—it also supports your vocal technique. Whether it's a gym session, yoga on deck, dance classes, exploring a port, or just a walk around the promenade deck, movement helps you stay limber, breathe better, and manage stress. Even if you're not dancing in your shows, singing itself is a physical act, and if your body is stiff, sluggish, or out of alignment, your singing will reflect it.

The Motion of the Ocean

The ship is always in motion, even when it's docked. Whether you're feeling the gentle sway caused by waves lapping at the pier, or full-blown swells in open sea, your body is constantly making micro-adjustments to stay balanced. Over time, this subtle effort can wear you out more than you realize.

Learning to stabilize your core without holding unnecessary tension is key. Adjust your stance in real time, conserve energy on rough sea days, and remember that grace under pressure includes knowing when to simplify your movement and let the ship do its thing.

Know When to Say No

Sometimes the best thing you can do for your voice is not use it. That might mean skipping karaoke night with guests or ducking out of a crew party when your voice is feeling fragile. Vocal health is a long game and learning to set boundaries, especially in a culture of constant social interaction, is one of the most powerful tools in your kit.

Remember that you don't need to be sick to rest. Build in recovery days during which you minimize speaking, prioritize nutrition and hydration, stretch or walk instead of doing a full workout, and let your nervous system relax. You are your instrument—treat yourself accordingly.

Mental Health Matters

It's easy to underestimate how much your mental and emotional health affects your voice. Loneliness, burnout, over-socialization, and lack of personal space are common on ships and can manifest vocally as tension, fatigue, or inconsistency. Build small rituals that help you reset such as journaling, meditation, breath work, or even watching your favorite show on your morning off. Talk to someone if you're struggling: Many cruise lines offer onboard mental-health resources, and peer support goes a long way.

Performing in Rough Seas

Performing in rough seas is a rite of passage. Whether you're trying to belt a ballad while gripping a mic stand like a lifeline or attempting choreography with the grace of a tipsy flamingo, you will have your technique and your sense of humor tested.

Here are tips for staying grounded in rocky conditions:

- Widen your stance and keep your knees slightly bent—think "ready position" in sports.
- Anchor your weight over both feet rather than shifting or crossing legs.
- Simplify your blocking and avoid unnecessary movement, especially on platforms or stairs.
- Use props or set pieces to help stabilize yourself (mic stands are VIPs in this situation).
- Adjust your breathing. Stay low and grounded; high, shallow breaths make balancing harder.
- Keep smiling—audiences are usually extra impressed by your poise and professionalism under pressure.

Most production-show teams follow a progressive scale of adjustments depending on conditions:

- **Step 1:** Swap heels for flats, especially for female cast members.
- **Step 2:** Remove lifts, jumps, or any unstable choreography.
- **Step 3:** Scrap the dancing entirely and have the cast sing it straight.
- **Step 4:** Cancel the show altogether—a rare but sometimes necessary call. If conditions are so extreme that the show can't be performed safely, it's likely the audience wouldn't be able to get to the theater safely either—or wouldn't want to sit through a show in the first place.

There's no shame in standing still and delivering a killer vocal—or in not performing at all if safety is at stake. If you do stumble, recover with flair and move on. The show must go on, and it usually does, wobbles and all.

When You're Sick or Injured

It's every singer's nightmare: waking up with swollen vocal folds, a raspy voice, or, worse, no sound at all. Unfortunately, your options are limited, the schedule is tight, and there's no backup cast waiting in the wings.

When I was offered my first ship contract, one of the very first things my producer brought up wasn't the repertoire or the costume fittings—it was how to perform when the ship is rocky.

He told us, "The worst thing you can do is fight it. If you lock your knees and try to hold yourself rigid, you're more likely to fall. The key is to move *with* the ship." Then he added a tip I've never forgotten: "Just pretend you're drunk."

Naturally, I took a full method-acting approach to that one. (Kidding! Though I may have done some independent research in the crew bar.) But he was right—when you sway with the ship instead of bracing against it, you stay balanced.

Report Early, Don't Push Through

The biggest mistake singers make is trying to "push through" illness. On a ship, that choice can have real consequences, not only for your vocal health but also for the health of everyone around you. If you feel yourself getting sick, report it to the onboard medical team immediately. Not only is this a professional responsibility, but also most cruise lines require it under public health protocols.

Even if the medical team can't offer a vocal diagnosis, they can treat infections, help with inflammation, and in some cases provide medication to ease symptoms or prevent escalation. And importantly, it creates a medical record, which could be useful if you need to cancel a performance or receive medical disembarkation.

Be Honest with the Entertainment Team

Cruise directors and entertainment managers appreciate honesty and notice when performers try to "fake it." If your voice is compromised, loop your leadership in early. You may be able to swap your performance night, shorten your set, drop the hardest numbers, or get creative with programming. The more notice you give, the more options the team has to help you succeed. If you do have to go on, be smart: Use your best technique, simplify your vocal choices, avoid risky effects (like growling), and don't push for volume. Microphones exist for a reason.

Limited Resources, Creative Solutions

There are no laryngologists or speech therapists onboard. If you need vocal rehab, a strobe exam, or anything more specialized, you'll have to wait until the ship reaches a major port with the appropriate facilities, assuming time and scheduling allow. That's why prevention and knowing your voice are so crucial.

Until then, you'll have to get creative: Saline nebulizers, steam, vocal rest, hydration, naps, and vocal pacing can all buy time until proper treatment is available.

When It's More Than a Cold

Injury also happens, whether it be slipping onstage, throwing out your back, or developing repetitive strain from constant tech rehearsals or show runs. In these cases, the medical center will assess you and possibly sign you off duty temporarily. Depending on the injury and the length of your contract, you may recover onboard or be medically disembarked. In very rare cases, singers have been evacuated for serious illness or injury, but the bar is high. Most of the time, you'll be expected to recover onboard while still contributing where possible. If you are still able to carry out your assigned safety duty, you are deemed still fit to be onboard. It's a humbling reminder that cruise work is not just glamorous—it's also physically and mentally demanding, and not without risk.

Understand How Onboard Medical Works

Getting sick or injured at sea is stressful enough—don't let confusion over costs make it worse. Medical access onboard varies significantly depending on your employment status.

If you're on the crew manifest:

Medical care onboard is included at no cost to you. This covers the following:

- Consultations with the ship's doctor or a nurse
- Treatment for routine illnesses or minor injuries
- Medications dispensed onboard
- Follow-up care as needed
- Referrals to medical facilities ashore, when necessary, including transportation and coverage of the visit, as long as it's approved by the ship's doctor and deemed medically necessary

If you're on the guest manifest:

You are treated as a guest, which means the following:

- All medical care onboard must be paid out of pocket.

- This includes even minor consultations and over-the-counter meds.

- Charges will be added to your onboard folio, and it's up to you to seek reimbursement from your agent, insurance provider, or home health-care plan.

Cruise line reality check: On many cruise lines, the medical department is considered a revenue-generating department. Yes, really—medical staff often have targets to meet per cruise and will bill you even for small services if you're not listed as crew.

Pro tip: Always carry international health insurance that covers cruise work and clarify medical-expense policies in your contract.

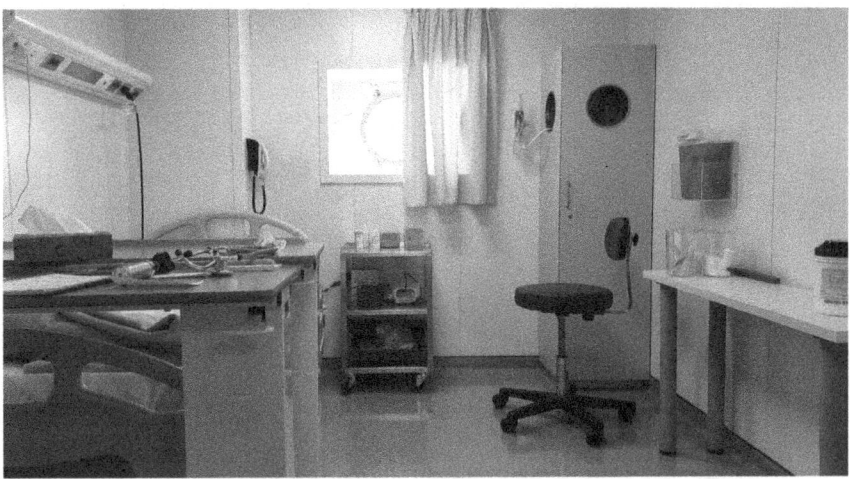

Figure 10.1 Examination room in a cruise ship medical center.
Courtesy Ihor Koptilin/Shutterstock.

Cruise ship singing is equal parts passion and endurance. You will be asked to sing in less-than-ideal conditions: while adjusting to jet lag, in dry air, during rocky seas, or with a cold that hit half the cast. There will be nights when adrenaline gets you through and mornings when only technique and discipline keep you from vocal trouble.

What separates the good from the great at sea isn't just talent. It's also consistency. It's preparation. It's knowing how to care for the body that houses your instrument, and how to advocate for yourself when something feels off. Your voice is not just how you entertain—it's also how you work, how you connect, and how you thrive.

On a ship, the voice can't be separated from the vessel. You're living and working in a unique, 24-7 environment that affects not only your health, but also your mental well-being, your relationships, your identity, and your day-to-day experience. Once you've learned to thrive onboard, the next question becomes this: How do you build on that momentum? In the next chapter, we'll explore how to make the most of your time at sea, whether your goal is to extend your cruise career, use your time aboard as a launchpad, or take everything you've learned and sail confidently into your next chapter on land.

11 Making the Most of the Experience

By the time you've settled into ship life—learned the rules, found your rhythm, and figured out how to sing when the stage is swaying—you may start asking a deeper question: "Now that I'm here, how do I make this mean something?" Whether you're doing one contract or building a long-term career, you will make choices that can shape your artistry, your mindset, your network, and your future. In this chapter, we'll explore how to use the cruise experience intentionally: as a tool for creativity, connection, and transformation while you're onboard and long after you disembark.

Travel as a Tool for Artistic and Personal Growth

One of the most extraordinary aspects of singing at sea is the travel—not as a tourist, but as a working artist embedded in the world. You won't just visit places: You'll also wake up in them, walk their streets, perform for people who call them home, and begin to feel the subtle rhythms of different cultures beneath your feet. Over time, travel isn't just a perk of the job: It also becomes a wellspring of artistic inspiration and personal transformation.

Artistic Inspiration Everywhere

Exposure to different cultures, landscapes, and musical traditions naturally fuels your creativity. A morning visit to a cathedral in Italy might inform how you sing sacred music. A Kabuki performance in Japan might shift how you think about extended vocal techniques. A conversation with a guest from another country could lead to a song choice you never would have considered. Your art becomes broader, more textured, and more human when you let travel seep into it. Keep a notebook or voice-memo log. Sketch song ideas. Record ambient sounds. Journal. Sing in a new space just to hear what it does to your voice. The world becomes your conservatory if you let it.

Learning to See Differently

Living in different ports, even briefly, reshapes your perspective. You'll become more aware of how other people live, think, celebrate, and struggle. Things you once took for granted may become stranger; things that once seemed foreign may start to feel familiar. This softening and stretching of worldview is one of the great gifts of ship life and it seeps into your performance whether you notice it or not. It can also teach empathy. When you experience beauty and hardship side by side in new places, you become a more emotionally honest and nuanced performer. Travel won't just give you stories—it will also help you understand the weight of the stories you tell through song.

Travel as a Mirror

There's also a solitary beauty to the kind of travel singers do at sea. Yes, you're surrounded by crew, but you'll spend time alone in ports, cafés, temples, and markets with nothing but your thoughts. You'll learn what comforts you, challenges you, and moves you. Travel becomes a mirror: It reflects who you are when all your usual reference points are gone.

Many singers return home from ships not only with stronger resumes, but also with a clearer sense of self. If you treat travel as more than a photo op—if you show up with curiosity and humility—it can change your life in ways no classroom ever could.

Figure 11.1 Spending free time ashore in Kotor, Montenegro. Courtesy frantic00/Shutterstock.

Creative Ways to Document Your Travels

You'll see so much during your time at sea that it's easy for it all to blur together. Whether you're in it for one contract or ten, keeping a creative record of your journey can help you stay present, inspired, and grounded. Here are some simple, low-pressure ways to document your travels while you're onboard (that don't involve social media):

- **One-Line-a-Day Journal:** If keeping a traditional journal feels too daunting or time consuming, try writing one sentence per port— what you saw, felt, ate, or sang. You'll be surprised how much a single detail can spark a memory later.

- **Postcards to Yourself:** Buy a postcard in each port and write a note about your day. Mail it to your home or save it in your luggage as a time capsule.

- **Voice-Memo Travel Logs:** Talk to yourself on a walk through town. Describe where you are, what you're hearing, or how a place makes you feel.

- **Sketchbook or Scrapbook:** Even if you don't think of yourself as visually creative, collect ticket stubs, pressed flowers, or little sketches of your surroundings. Imperfection is part of the charm.

- **Port-Day Playlist:** Keep a running playlist of songs that remind you of specific places or moods. One day, hearing the songs again will bring you right back.

- **Small Souvenirs:** While magnets are popular with crew members to adorn magnetic cabin walls, their weight can add up come the end of a port-intensive contract. Consider collecting small and light mementos such as pins and patches or purchasing a coin purse for local currency.

Pro tip: Don't aim for perfect. Aim for real. Whether you look back a year from now or a decade later, these little records will mean more than you can imagine.

Using Time at Sea Strategically

When you first start singing at sea, you may feel like your whole life has become adjusting to ship life, finding your footing, and delivering performances. But once the initial learning curve levels out, you may find something unexpected and precious: time. With no commute, limited distractions, and fewer daily obligations than most land-based artists, you may find ship life offers a rare chance to work on your future while living in the present.

Build Your Resume Onboard

Every show you perform, every themed set you build, every collaboration you join is a legitimate performance credit. Document these credits. Keep copies of your show orders, contracts, and any media coverage or ship programs that mention you. Take photos and videos of your performances and collect material that can later be used in audition reels, grant applications, social media content, or teaching portfolios.

Beyond singing, note any additional responsibilities you take on: hosting, arranging music, leading rehearsals, helping with special events, or doing cross-department collaborations. These experiences demonstrate versatility and professionalism that will help build a well-rounded resume.

Pursue Creative Side Projects

Do you have a passion project that always got sidelined on land? Maybe a solo cabaret, a role, a language, or a certification? Sea time can be the perfect environment to finally begin or finish it. Bring digital copies of vocal scores you want to learn, download writing software, or start a simple creative routine you can stick to.

Some singers use their free time during contracts to write books, plan solo shows, create new arrangements, or even work on a degree remotely. Others explore photography, start teaching online, or develop wellness routines that transform their bodies. Whatever your focus is, use the quiet moments to inch it forward.

Develop Habits You Can Take Home

Discipline is baked into ship life—drills, call times, duties, routines. That structure can help you develop habits that stick with you long after you disembark. Whether they're daily warm-ups, journaling, hydration, or fitness routines, these habits are easier to build in the contained world of a ship.

Bringing Friends and Family Onboard

One of the most rewarding—though occasionally complicated—perks of working at sea is the ability to share the experience with your loved ones. Whether it's inviting a parent to see you perform, hosting a partner in your cabin, or showing a friend around the ship during a day in port, having friends and family onboard can be a grounding, joyful part of your contract. But as with all things at sea, there are rules that vary by cruise line, ship, rank, and department. Here's what you need to know:

Visitor Passes for Port Days

Like the requirements for step-on entertainers to join a ship, a crew member must request a visitor pass for a guest to come onboard for a few hours while the ship is docked. Visitor passes are limited, must be approved in advance, and are subject to ship and port security clearance.

The guest will need to show a valid government-issued ID at the gangway, and the crew member usually must escort the guest at all times while the guest is onboard. Visitor passes typically allow access to public areas only, and the visitor must disembark most often an hour before the ship sets sail. No overnight stays are allowed.

Having a Guest Stay in Your Cabin

Crew members with single cabins may be allowed to have a friend, partner, or family member stay with them for a few nights or even for a few cruises. This approval process usually involves the following:

- Filling out a guest authorization form or a cruise request form
- Submitting the visitor's passport details
- Getting sign-off from your division head, your department head, the HR manager, and sometimes the captain

Not all roles or cabin types qualify for this, so check with your crew administrator early. If you are a singer on the guest manifest, you will likely have the ability to have someone sail with you for free or for a small fee for the duration of your engagement. Check with your agent for cruise-line specifics.

Discounted Sailings for Friends and Family

Another popular option is to book your loved ones on a greatly discounted guest cruise fare, especially on itineraries you're already working. These fares allow your guests to stay in guest staterooms, enjoy full guest privileges, and attend your performances. It's one of the most generous perks of ship life, but it's not available to everyone and not necessarily available right away.

Friends-and-family sailing benefits typically kick in only after you've completed a probationary period, the length of which varies by cruise line. In most cases, this means a minimum of ninety days, but some cruise lines require up to six months or more. The policy may also differ depending on your department, position, or contract.

That said, it's also important to understand that priority is always given to "revenue guests," those paying full fare. Even if your discounted-cruise request is submitted and approved well in advance, your guest will be denied boarding at the last minute if the ship becomes overbooked or full-paying guests claim remaining cabins. I've seen it happen multiple times, including to my own husband. Approval may also be delayed until just one or two weeks before sailing, giving the cruise line more time to sell cabins at full price. For this reason, friends and family planning to sail on a crew rate should always have a backup plan, including refundable airfare and flexible accommodations in the embarkation port, in case they're turned away.

Onboard Etiquette

When inviting someone onboard, remember that you're still at work. Your guests represent *you*, and any inappropriate behavior on their end could reflect poorly on you. Remind your guests of dress codes, restricted areas, and social norms onboard. Avoid guest-and-crew PDA, and don't try to sneak someone where they shouldn't be (e.g., the crew bar). They *will* get caught. Done right, though, having someone onboard can be incredibly special. Having them watch you perform, sharing your day-to-day world, and sailing together can help bridge the emotional gap between ship life and home life.

Planning a Long-Term Career at Sea

Some singers treat cruise contracts as one-time adventures. Others discover that life at sea offers not only artistic fulfillment but also long-term professional stability. If you find yourself drawn to ship life, your next step is learning how to build a career out of it.

This section explores how to plan for longevity in cruise entertainment, whether you're aiming to climb the onboard ranks, diversify the kinds of contracts you accept, or eventually transition into leadership roles ashore or at sea.

Think in Contracts, Not Years

Cruise ship careers rarely follow traditional year-by-year timelines. Instead, they unfold in contracts that last three to nine months for onboard crew, one week for guest entertainers, and one day for step-on entertainers. Long-term planning means learning to think in contract cycles rather than in terms of seasonal or annual goals.

For production cast vocalists and lounge entertainers, this means doing the following:

- Planning at least one contract ahead, especially if you want to return to the same cruise line or ship
- Keeping your materials current—headshot, resume, reel, medical paperwork, and STCW certificates—so you're always ready for rehire
- Using time between contracts to rest, reset, and grow your skills or repertoire

For cruise administrators, planning looks a bit different:

- You are typically assigned a permanent ship and rotation upon hire.
- Your schedule is consistent, which allows for structured long-term planning but can reduce flexibility for freelance work or short-notice projects on land.
- Use your time off strategically—to rest, upskill, network, build shows, or represent the brand in training or recruiting efforts.
- Stay informed about changes across the fleet, especially if you plan to transfer ships or move into a senior leadership role.

For guest and step-on entertainers, the schedule can be more sporadic and often less predictable. Staying in close communication with your agent and keeping travel documents and performance materials ready to go allows you to say yes to last-minute bookings.

Know the Growth Paths Available

There are many ways to evolve professionally at sea. Here are a few common career progressions:

Within Your Role

- A lounge entertainer builds a following and is rebooked on prime itineraries or luxury ships.
- A cast singer is promoted to lead vocalist, vocal captain, or company manager.

- A guest entertainer increases their weekly fee and expands to new cruise lines.

Between Roles

- A cast member becomes a guest entertainer by developing their own shows.
- A lounge entertainer transitions into bandmaster.
- A singer of any type becomes a cruise administrator.
- A cruise administrator moves into a corporate role shoreside or becomes a guest entertainer.

Cruise lines are often loyal and favor internal promotion. They appreciate the safety of hiring someone who understands the brand and has proven they can thrive at sea.

Pay Attention to Your Reviews

On ships, your reputation isn't just built onstage—it's also recorded, reported, and remembered.

A production cast singer, lounge entertainer, or cruise administrator typically receives a formal end-of-contract performance evaluation from their onboard supervisor, often the cruise director or entertainment manager (or the hotel director if you *are* the cruise director or entertainment manager). These reviews assess professionalism, punctuality, vocal consistency, adaptability, and guest interaction. They become part of your internal record and play a major role in future casting and promotions within the fleet.

If you're a guest entertainer or step-on entertainer, while formal evaluations may not be standard, your name and performance will appear in the cruise director's end-of-voyage (EOV) report. These reports are often distributed onboard to the EXCOM, and shoreside to the cruise line's corporate office and the agencies and production companies responsible for casting. Positive mentions can fast-track a rebooking; negative ones may cost you future work. If you would like to know what feedback has been given about your performance, speak with your agent.

Guests also weigh in. End-of-cruise surveys often include comment sections asking about standout entertainment, and many cruise lines closely monitor which performers are mentioned by name. One glowing review—or one complaint—can influence hiring decisions across the fleet.

Here's how to keep your reviews strong:

- Maintain professionalism on and off stage.
- Be gracious with guests, even when you're tired.
- Show adaptability when technical or scheduling issues arise.
- Support your fellow performers and the entertainment team.

After you've been hired once, your next contract won't be decided in an audition room—it will be decided in someone's inbox.

Plan for the Gaps

Even if you're aiming for a long career at sea, you will have gaps between contracts, sometimes longer than you expect. To bridge these gaps, do the following:

- Keep multiple income streams (e.g., teaching, gigging, and studio work).
- Set financial goals—save during contracts so you're not financially strained between them.
- Stay connected—maintain relationships with agents, casting directors, recruiters, and your fellow crew.

Contracts may be delayed, canceled, or changed, so flexibility is essential.

Keep Learning (Even on Breaks)

The performers who thrive long-term are the ones who invest in their growth:

- Learn new vocal styles or instruments.
- Study languages relevant to common cruise itineraries or guest demographics.
- Take courses in leadership, sound design, or even hospitality.

Adding new tools to your kit makes you more valuable on future contracts and keeps the work exciting.

Set Boundaries, Not Just Goals

It's easy to fall into the rhythm of contract after contract without thinking about how the work aligns with your personal goals. Ask yourself the following questions:

- How many contracts per year do I want to do?
- What do I need emotionally, physically, and financially between contracts?

Figure 11.2 Enjoying the open deck and the breeze on a day at sea.
Courtesy BraunS/iStock.

- Do I want to pursue land-based performance opportunities in parallel?
- What kinds of contracts are sustainable for my voice, my relationships, and my physical and mental health?

Some singers thrive doing back-to-back contracts; others prefer a seasonal rhythm. There's no single path: The key is making sure you are the one choosing yours.

Transitioning to Land Life after Singing at Sea

No matter how long you perform at sea, be it one contract or twenty, there will come a time when you ask, "What's next?" Transitioning back to land life can be both exciting and disorienting. After months or years of structure, purpose, applause, and port calls, reentry to "normal" life can feel like culture shock. But with intention and reflection, you can use your time at sea as a powerful springboard into your next chapter, whatever that looks like.

Your Cruise Experience Is Real Experience

Don't underestimate the value of your cruise contracts. You've performed professionally, traveled internationally, collaborated across cultures, adapted to constant change, and maintained vocal health under unpredictable conditions. That's not just valid—it's also impressive. Whether you're pursuing auditions, teaching, arts administration, or a total career pivot, learn how to frame your ship experience in ways that resonate with land-based employers:

- Emphasize consistency and discipline ("Performed six nights per week for diverse global audiences").
- Highlight teamwork and adaptability ("Collaborated with international cast and crew in high-pressure environments").
- Mention the bonus skills you gained: event hosting, show building, social media management, leadership, and so on.

Prepare for the Emotional Letdown

Cruise contracts can feel like dopamine roller coasters—applause nearly nightly, new cities every day, built-in community. Coming home to stillness, routine, and fewer performances can lead to a post-contract crash. That's normal. Give yourself space to adjust and resist the urge to compare your land life to the highlight reel of ship life.

Stay in the Loop

Even if you step away from ships, you may want to return later. Fortunately, you'll be in a great position to do so. Once you've completed your first contract, you are a trained and certified seafarer, which makes you far more valuable to cruise lines than someone brand new to the industry. You've already cleared many of the onboarding hurdles: safety certifications, medicals, onboard procedures, and ship-life adjustment. That means you can often be rehired quickly, even after taking time away.

Keep your materials up to date—resume, headshot, demo reel, STCW certificates, medical paperwork—and check in with your agency or casting contacts periodically. Letting them know you're open to future opportunities can keep doors open for the next season or even the next sailing. If you maintain a good reputation and professional relationships, your return to ships can be as seamless as picking up where you left off.

What Comes Next Is Yours to Define

Some singers go on to Broadway or the West End, regional theater or touring, voice-over work, teaching, or graduate school. Others transition into music direction, casting, or cruise staff roles. Some never work on ships again, and some come back five years later with new skill sets and fresh perspectives.

The skills you've built at sea—resilience, adaptability, and global awareness—are assets in any setting. Take time to reflect on what you've gained, what you loved, what you never want to do again, and how this experience fits into your larger artistic life.

A career at sea offers more than a chance to sing—it also offers a chance to grow. The performers who thrive onboard are those who approach the experience with curiosity, adaptability, and a sense of purpose. Whether your time on ships lasts one contract or becomes a defining chapter in your artistic life, it's what you make of it that matters most. From port days to performance days, from conversations in the mess to standing ovations, every moment onboard can teach you something if you're paying attention.

In the final part of this book, we'll step back and look at the big picture: What have we learned? Is singing at sea right for *you*? And what should you do next if you feel ready to step onboard?

Conclusion: Is Singing at Sea Right for You?

As we reach the end of this book, it's time to reflect on the journey we've taken—through the unique world of cruise ship entertainment, the demands and rewards of life at sea, and the many pathways open to singers beyond the shoreline. Whether you began this book with curiosity, ambition, or uncertainty, you now have a comprehensive understanding of what it means to build a singing career aboard a cruise ship. In this final section, we'll revisit the key takeaways, consider whether this career path aligns with your personal and artistic goals, and outline practical next steps for getting started—or for confidently choosing a different course. The stage is set. The ship is waiting. Where you go from here is entirely up to you.

Is This Your Gig?

Cruise-ship performing is not a one-size-fits-all career. For some singers, it becomes a deeply fulfilling way to travel the world while building financial stability and expanding their artistry. For others, the structure, isolation, or unpredictability make the career an ill-fitting match. Both outcomes are valid. The goal is not to convince you to set sail—it's to help you decide, with clarity and confidence, whether this path aligns with your goals, values, and lifestyle.

Here are a few questions to ask yourself:

Do I enjoy performing for a wide range of audiences who often have different expectations and tastes from my own?

Cruise ship audiences are diverse in age, nationality, and musical taste. One night you may be singing jazz standards, the next pop hits or musical-theater favorites. The more musically flexible you are, the more employable—and successful—you'll be.

Am I okay with creating entertainment that prioritizes broad appeal, consistency, and repetition over innovation or interpretation?

Cruise ship singing also invites deeper reflection on your long-term artistic goals. If your primary aim is to build character-driven roles in theatrical productions, explore new music, or work with live orchestras in acoustic settings, cruise work may not align fully with your creative aspirations.

Am I comfortable living communally, sharing tight spaces, and operating within a strict chain of command?

Cruise ships are not democratic environments. You'll be expected to follow rules, attend mandatory trainings and drills, and be visibly professional at all times, while simultaneously having little to no personal space. If you value independence above structure, ship life could prove frustrating.

Do I enjoy travel, not just the *idea* of travel?
Being in a new port every day sounds glamorous, but many days are spent rehearsing, performing, or resting. You may not always have the time or energy to explore. It helps to enjoy the rhythm of movement as much as the destinations themselves.

Can I handle extended time away from home?
Cruise contracts mean time away from loved ones, pets, apartments, and communities. While technology helps bridge the gap, homesickness is real. Some singers find extended time away freeing, while others struggle with the separation and feel emotionally drained. The romanticism of travel wears off fast if your emotional needs go unmet.

Am I self-motivated, emotionally resilient, and able to handle isolation well?
Ship life can be wonderful, but it can also be isolating, intense, and unpredictable. While cruise ships are filled with people, they can feel incredibly lonely, especially in your first few weeks. Your success may depend more on your mindset and emotional stamina than on your vocal technique. The performers who thrive are those who self-regulate their emotional health, take initiative in social situations, and know how to recharge.

Can I accept that for all its beauty, ship life is a job—not a paid vacation?
If you go in with eyes wide open, the rewards can be incredible. But if you expect a tropical break with light singing duties, you'll be disappointed. The singers who return again and again do so because they accept that the work is part of the adventure, not a distraction from the fun.

If you find yourself answering yes to most of these questions, you may be an excellent candidate for cruise ship life. And if your answer is "maybe," that's okay too. Many singers take a single contract to explore the world and test their limits, then return to land life with new skills and insights.

Steps for Getting Started

If you've read this far and feel a sense of excitement, readiness, or even healthy nervousness, that's a good sign. There are practical actions you can take today to begin your journey. You don't need to have everything figured out, but taking small, incremental steps will move you closer to the stage, the ship, and the experience.

Choose Your Track

- Decide which type of role best suits you: production cast member, lounge entertainer, guest entertainer, step-on entertainer, or cruise administrator.
- Be honest with yourself about your current strengths, your lifestyle, and what type of gig will set you up for success, not stress.

Research Agencies and Cruise Lines

- Familiarize yourself with the major players in the industry—casting and crewing agencies, cruise lines, and production companies.
- Visit cruise-line entertainment websites, talent-booking pages, audition postings, and LinkedIn or social media profiles of cruise ship performers and casting associates.
- Consider attending showcases or conferences that include cruise ship casting representatives.

Get Connected

- Reach out to colleagues who have worked at sea—ask thoughtful questions and listen to their stories.
- Join social media groups or online forums for cruise performers.
- Subscribe to casting calls, agency newsletters, and audition boards that list cruise-related work.

Update Your Materials

- Prepare a clean, professional resume highlighting your vocal training, performance credits, and special skills (like dance or movement, instruments, or languages).

- Select clear high-quality headshots or promotional photos that reflect your personality, performance style, and brand.
- Create or refresh your vocal demo reel—include contrasting vocal selections and live performance footage.

Prepare Logistically

- Make sure your passport is valid for at least six months beyond your anticipated start date.
- Begin budgeting for required medical exams, visas, background checks, or certifications.
- Start organizing your digital files (e.g., scanned documents, demo reels, and references) so you can apply quickly when the opportunity arises.

Start Applying and Stay Open

- The path to your first contract may take time, or it may appear suddenly.
- It's common to audition more than once before being hired, so treat the process as a marathon, not a sprint.
- Remain flexible. You may get booked on a ship you've never heard of or to perform styles you didn't expect.
- What matters is that you're prepared, grounded, and ready to make the most of it.

A cruise-ship singing career is not just about travel or paychecks or resume additions. It's also about transformation. It asks you to become more than a vocalist—it asks you to become someone who can sing in a dozen styles, take feedback with grace, collaborate with people from everywhere, and stand steady while the floor beneath you literally moves.

This life is not always easy. You'll get tired. You'll feel isolated. You'll miss birthdays, weddings, anniversaries, and the ordinary comforts of home. But you'll also witness sunsets that feel like private miracles. You'll sing to strangers who become lifelong friends. You'll stretch your capacity for music, culture, endurance, and joy. And through it all, you'll gain things that can't be taught in a studio or written into a song: a deeper sense of yourself, a clarity of purpose, and a confidence that comes only from navigating the unknown and finding your balance.

Whether you decide to board the ship or take another path entirely, you now carry something valuable: perspective, preparation, and the power to choose with intention. That's what this book is meant to offer—not a sales pitch or a guarantee, but a map. One that honors the art, the work, the freedom, and the grit required to sing at sea.

Figure 12.1 The author celebrating a final sunset at sea.
Photograph by Margarita Navas.

Wherever your voice takes you next—whether to a luxury liner or a land-based stage, a teaching studio or a creative sabbatical—go forward with confidence. The sea isn't for everyone, but if it calls to you, you'll know. And if it does, I hope you'll answer with your whole heart.

Bon voyage!

Appendix A: Glossary of Ship Terminology

Formal and Operation Terms

aft—Toward the back (stern) of the ship.

anchorage—A designated area where ships can anchor offshore, used when the ship cannot dock directly at the port.

ballast—Water stored in tanks to help stabilize and balance the ship.

berth—The location where the ship docks; a bed on the ship.

bow—The front end of the ship.

bridge—The ship's navigation and command center.

bulkhead—A wall within the ship.

cabin—A private, enclosed room on a ship typically used for sleeping and relaxation.

captain (or master)—The highest-ranking officer who commands the vessel.

chart—A nautical map used for navigation.

charter—When a ship is hired for private use by an outside group or organization.

code words—Verbal signals used over the ship's PA system to alert crew to specific emergencies.

concessionaire—A third-party contract worker who is not directly employed by the cruise line.

crew drill—Mandatory safety training for the crew, usually held weekly.

crossing—Navigating from one geographical location to another over a substantial body of water.

current—The flow of ocean water.

deck—A floor level on the ship.

deck plan—A diagram showing the layout of spaces on each floor level.

DECT (digital enhanced cordless telecommunications) phone—Mobile telephone used by crew members that connects onboard only.

designated person ashore (DPA)—A shoreside official appointed by the cruise line who serves as the primary contact for safety and compliance between the ship and company management.

disembarkation—The process of leaving the ship.

dock—Where the ship is moored in port.

dry dock—A maintenance period when the ship is taken out of water for repairs and refurbishment.

embarkation—The process of boarding the ship.

engine room—The area that houses the ship's engines and mechanical systems.

EXCOM (executive committee)—A small team of senior officers who oversee the major departments onboard and make high-level decisions.

F&B (food and beverage)—The department onboard that oversees all aspects of providing food and drinks to guests and crew.

flag state—The country under which a ship is registered.

formal night—A designated evening when formal attire is worn by guests.

forward—Toward the front (bow) of the ship.

galley—The ship's kitchen.

gangway—The ramp or stairway used for boarding or exiting the ship.

gastrointestinal illness (GI)—An inflammation of the stomach and intestines causing nausea, vomiting, diarrhea, and stomach cramps.

general emergency signal (GES)—An alarm consisting of seven short blasts followed by one long blast on the ship's whistle and internal alarm system.

harbor master—A port official responsible for the safe and efficient movement of ships within a harbor.

hull—The part of the ship that sits in the water.

in-port manning (IPM)—The responsibility of a minimum number of crew to stay onboard while a ship is in port.

international waters—The areas of the sea that are not under the jurisdiction of any one country.

itinerary—A detailed plan outlining the specific destinations a ship will visit.

keel—The bottommost longitudinal structure of the ship.

knot—A unit of speed equal to one nautical mile per hour.

lido deck—Typically the pool deck and a central guest-recreation area.

lifestyle cruise—A euphemism for adult-only cruises.

lines—Ropes used to secure the ship when docked.

list—When the ship leans to one side or the other due to imbalance.

manifest—A detailed list of all passengers onboard, typically subdivided into guests and crew.

MARSEC (maritime security levels)—A three-tier system of security levels used in port and aboard ships.

mess—A designated dining area for crew members.

midship—The middle part of the ship.

mooring—The act of securing the ship to a dock using lines.

muster—To assemble for safety purposes.

muster drill—A mandatory safety exercise conducted before the ship sails at the beginning of a cruise.

muster station (or assembly station)—The designated location where passengers and crew gather during an emergency.

nautical mile—A unit measuring distances at sea, equal to 1.15 miles or 1.85 kilometers.

onboarding—The process of integrating a new crew member to a cruise line.

outbreak prevention plan (OPP)—A set of instructions to prevent outbreaks from occurring on a ship and how to stop any spread.

personal protective equipment (PPE)—Specialized clothing and gear to protect a crew member from harm while working.

pilot—A local navigator who comes aboard to guide the ship into or out of port.

pilot station—A designated area where harbor pilots board or leave the ship.

pitch—The up-and-down motion of the ship's bow and stern.

port—A harbor where a ship docks; the left side of the ship when facing forward.

port of call—A scheduled stop at a port during a cruise.

propeller—A device that propels the ship through water.

purser—An officer responsible for financial administration and accounting onboard.

quarters—An area of cabins and living spaces.

repositioning cruise—A one-way voyage in which a ship travels from one geographical region to another.

roll—The side-to-side motion of the ship.

rudder—A steering device at the stern used to control the ship's direction.

Safety of Life at Sea (SOLAS)—An international treaty created by the International Maritime Organization (IMO) to set minimum safety standards for ships.

sea day—A day when the ship is at sea and does not stop at any ports.

seafarer—A crew member working on a ship.

shoreside—Company personnel and operations located on land.

shorex (shore excursions)—The department that organizes tours in port for guests.

sign-on/sign-off—The process of beginning or ending a contract aboard a ship.

slop chest—A store onboard that sells a selection of general goods for crew.

stabilizers—Mechanical fins used to reduce the ship's roll.

starboard—The right side of the ship when facing forward.

stateroom—A guest cabin.

station bill—A document listing each crew member's emergency duties.

stern—The back of the ship.

steward—A crew member responsible for maintaining the cleanliness and comfort of a cabin.

tender—A small boat that ferries guests to and from shore when the ship is anchored instead of docked.

thruster—A small propeller near the bow or stern used for sideways movement.

turnaround day—The day when one cruise itinerary ends and another begins.

vessel—A general term for a watercraft larger than a boat.

wake—The wave effect created by a ship moving through water.

waterline—The line on the hull where the ship meets the surface of the water.

watertight door—A heavy, sealed door to prevent water from flooding between compartments.

Ship Entertainment Terms

charts—Written sheet music for singers and musicians.

click track—The metronome pulse delivered through in-ear monitors.

deep cut—A lesser-known song by a popular artist.

enrichment lecturer—A guest speaker offering educational talks on topics like history, science, or travel.

guest entertainer—An independent performer contracted for a short period to present a self-contained act.

install—The period of rehearsing a new show onboard.

load-in—The process of bringing onboard show equipment.

lounge entertainer—A singer or musician who performs in venues such as piano bars and lounges.

monitor—A speaker or in-ear headphone that allows performers to hear themselves, other singers and instruments, and tracks.

production cast—The resident cast of singers and dancers hired for multi-month contracts.

sail-away set—A musical performance scheduled at departure.

set—A scheduled block of live performance time, typically lasting forty-five minutes.

sick track—A prerecorded vocal audio used when a singer is unable to phonate.

signature show—A professionally produced show featuring a cast of entertainers.

sound check—A brief rehearsal focused on adjusting sound levels and quality.

step-on entertainer—A local performer brought onboard for a short duration while the ship is docked.

strike—The process of tearing down and dismantling show equipment.

take-on/take-off—The opening or closing lines used to bookend a show or event.

tech run—A full run-through of a show with lights, sound, and any multimedia elements.

theme night—A scheduled night of the cruise with a specific concept or era.

Crew Slang and Shipboard Lingo

babaloo—A fool or idiot.

banana—A scolding or discipline from your supervisor.

capo—Slang for "boss" (from the Italian word for "military captain").

crew bar—The crew's social hub where off-duty crew members hang out.

debark—Crew shorthand for disembarkation.

de-greet—A mash-up of "departure" and "greet" referring to saying goodbye to guests as they leave a venue.

going to church—Going to the crew bar.

I-95—The main crew corridor running the length of the ship on a lower deck.

jiggy-jiggy—Engaging in romantic or sexual activity.

mafia—A close-knit community of crew who come from the same country.

mamagayo—A crew member pretending to work.

paisano—A fellow crew member from the same country.

pax—Crew shorthand for passengers.

taka-taka—To gossip or talk senselessly.

tranquillo—A command to calm down or chill out.

Appendix B: Cruise Line Information

1AVista Reisen

- Parent Company: Privately owned
- Fleet: 12 ships (~120–180 pax each)
- Category: Premium river
- HQ: Cologne, Germany
- Language: German
- Website: https://www.1avista.de
- Hiring: 1AVista Reisen—https://www.1avista.de/ueber-uns/karriere

Adora Cruises

- Parent Company: China Cruises Limited
- Fleet: 2 ships (~2,600–5,246 pax each)
- Category: Mainstream
- HQ: Shanghai, China
- Language: Mandarin
- Website: https://www.adoracruises.com
- Hiring: Alpha Magsaysay—https://www.alphamagsaysaycareers.com
- Casting: Selection International Entertainment—https://www.selectionie.com

AIDA Cruises

- Parent Company: Carnival Corporation & plc
- Fleet: 12 ships (~1,200–6,600 pax each)
- Categories: Mainstream, premium
- HQ: Rostock, Germany
- Language: German
- Website: https://www.aida.de
- Hiring and Casting: AIDA Careers/Casting—https://www.aida.de/careers

AMADEUS River Cruises

- Parent Company: Lüftner Cruises
- Fleet: 16 ships (~140–180 pax each)
- Category: Luxury river
- HQ: Innsbruck, Austria
- Languages: English, German
- Website: https://www.amadeus-rivercruises.com
- Hiring: AMADEUS Careers—https://www.amadeus-careers.com

AmaWaterways

- Parent Company: Privately owned
- Fleet: 29 ships (~140–160 pax each)
- Category: Luxury river
- HQ: Calabasas, California
- Language: English
- Website: https://www.amawaterways.com
- Hiring: AmaWaterways—https://www.amawaterways.eu/careers

Ambassador Cruise Line

- Parent Company: Njord Partners
- Fleet: 2 ships (~1,200–1,400 pax each)
- Category: Premium
- HQ: Purfleet, England, UK
- Language: English
- Website: https://www.ambassadorcruiseline.com
- Hiring: BSM Cruise Services—https://careers.schultecruise.com
- Casting: Peel Entertainment—https://www.peeltalent.com

American Cruise Lines

- Parent Company: Privately owned
- Fleet: 27 ships (~90–180 pax each)
- Category: Premium river
- HQ: Guilford, CT
- Language: English
- Website: https://www.americancruiselines.com
- Hiring: ACL Careers—https://www.aclcareers.com

A-ROSA River Cruises

- Parent Company: Duke Street
- Fleet: 15 ships (~202–242 pax each)
- Category: Premium river
- HQ: Rostock, Germany
- Languages: German, English
- Website: https://www.arosa-cruises.com
- Hiring: A-ROSA River Cruises—https://jobs.arosa-cruises.com

AROYA Cruises

- Parent Company: Cruise Saudi
- Fleet: 1 ship (~3,362 pax)
- Category: Ultra-luxury
- HQ: Jeddah, Saudi Arabia
- Languages: Arabic, English
- Website: https://www.aroya.com
- Hiring: The Columbia Group—https://aroyaonboardcareers.com
- Casting: Live Business—https://www.livebusiness.co.uk

Atlas Ocean Voyages

- Parent Company: Mystic Invest Holding
- Fleet: 3 ships (~200 pax each)
- Category: Ultra-luxury expedition
- HQ: Fort Lauderdale, FL
- Language: English
- Website: https://www.atlasoceanvoyages.com
- Hiring: Atlas Ocean Voyages—https://www.linkedin.com/company/atlascruises/jobs

Avalon Waterways

- Parent Company: Globus family of brands
- Fleet: 26 ships (~128–166 pax each)
- Category: Premium river
- HQ: Littleton, CO
- Language: English
- Website: https://www.avalonwaterways.com
- Hiring: Avalon Europe—https://avaloneurope.eu/careers

Azamara Cruises

- Parent Company: Sycamore Partners
- Fleet: 4 ships (~694 pax each)
- Category: Luxury
- HQ: Miami, FL
- Language: English
- Website: https://www.azamara.com
- Hiring: V.Ships—https://azamara.vcrew.com
- Casting: RWS Global—https://www.rwsglobal.com

Carnival Cruise Line

- Parent Company: Carnival Corporation & plc
- Fleet: 29 ships (~2,190–6,631 pax each)
- Category: Mainstream
- HQ: Doral, FL
- Language: English
- Website: https://www.carnival.com
- Hiring: Carnival Jobs—https://jobs.carnival.com
- Casting: Carnival Entertainment—https://www.carnivalentertainment.com

Celebrity Cruises

- Parent Company: Royal Caribbean Group
- Fleet: 15 ships (~100–3,260 pax each)
- Category: Premium
- HQ: Miami, FL
- Language: English
- Website: https://www.celebritycruises.com
- Hiring: Royal Caribbean Careers—https://careers.royalcaribbeangroup.com
- Casting: Celebrity Cruises Entertainment—https://www.celebritycruisesentertainment.com

Celestyal Cruises

- Parent Company: Searchlight Capital
- Fleet: 2 ships (~1,266–1,512 pax each)

- Category: Mainstream
- HQ: Piraeus, Athens, Greece
- Languages: English, Greek
- Website: https://www.celestyal.com
- Hiring: Celestyal Cruises—https://www.linkedin.com/company/celestyal-cruises/jobs

Century Cruises

- Parent Company: Gaund Holding Group
- Fleet: 5 ships (~400–650 pax each)
- Category: Premium river
- HQ: Chongqing, China
- Languages: Mandarin, English
- Website: https://www.centurycruise.com
- Hiring: Century Cruises—https://www.linkedin.com/company/century-river-cruises

Club Med

- Parent Company: Fosun International
- Fleet: 1 ship (~386 pax)
- Category: Luxury
- HQ: Paris, France
- Languages: French, English
- Website: https://www.clubmed.us
- Hiring: Club Med Jobs—https://www.clubmedjobs.com

Color Line

- Parent Company: Color Group AS
- Fleet: 4 ships (~2,000–2,600 pax each)
- Category: Ferry
- HQ: Oslo, Norway
- Languages: Norwegian, English
- Website: https://www.colorline.com
- Hiring: Color Line—https://www.colorline.no/om-oss/jobb-i-color-line
- Casting: Belinda King Creative Productions—https://www.belindaking.com

Costa Cruises

- Parent Company: Carnival Corporation & plc
- Fleet: 12 ships (~2,260–6,554 pax each)
- Category: Mainstream
- HQ: Genoa, Italy
- Languages: Italian, English
- Website: https://www.costacruises.com
- Hiring: Costa Crociere Careers—https://career.costacrociere.it
- Casting: Peel Entertainment—https://www.peeltalent.com

CroisiEurope

- Parent Company: Privately owned
- Fleet: 50 ships (~16–200 pax each)
- Category: Luxury river
- HQ: Strasbourg, France
- Languages: French, English
- Website: https://www.croisieuroperivercruises.com
- Hiring: CroisiEurope—https://www.linkedin.com/company/croisieurope/jobs

Crystal Cruises

- Parent Company: Abercrombie & Kent
- Fleet: 2 ships (~606–740 pax each)
- Category: Ultra-luxury
- HQ: Hallandale Beach, FL
- Language: English
- Website: https://www.crystalcruises.com
- Hiring: V.Ships—https://crystal.vcrew.com

Cunard Line

- Parent Company: Carnival Corporation & plc
- Fleet: 4 ships (~2,061–2,996 pax each)
- Category: Luxury
- HQ: Southampton, England, UK
- Language: English
- Website: https://www.cunard.com

- Hiring and Casting: Cunard Careers—https://www.cunardcareers.co.uk/careers

Disney Cruise Line

- Parent Company: The Walt Disney Company
- Fleet: 6 ships (~2,700–4,000 pax each)
- Category: Premium
- HQ: Celebration, FL
- Language: English
- Website: https://disneycruise.disney.go.com
- Hiring and Casting: Disney Careers—https://www.disneycareers.com/en/disney-cruise-line

DouroAzul

- Parent Company: Mystic Invest Holding
- Fleet: 11 ships (~100–130 pax each)
- Category: Luxury river
- HQ: Porto, Portugal
- Languages: Portuguese, English
- Website: https://www.douroazul.com
- Hiring: DouroAzul Careers—https://www.douroazul.com/opportunities

Emerald Cruises

- Parent Company: Scenic
- Fleet: 11 ships (~128–180 pax each)
- Category: Premium
- HQ: Zug, Switzerland
- Language: English
- Website: https://www.emeraldcruises.com
- Hiring: Scenic Careers—https://www.scenic.com.au/careers
- Casting: Rising Stars Talents—https://risingstars-talents.com

Excellence Cruises

- Parent Company: Twerenbold Reisen Gruppe
- Fleet: 8 ships (~140–180 pax each)

- Category: Premium river
- HQ: Weinfelden, Switzerland
- Language: German
- Website: https://www.mittelthurgau.ch
- Hiring: Excellence Cruises—https://www.mittelthurgau.ch/ueber-uns/jobs

Explora Journeys

- Parent Company: MSC Group
- Fleet: 2 ships (~900–996 pax each)
- Category: Ultra-luxury
- HQ: Geneva, Switzerland
- Language: English
- Website: https://www.explorajourneys.com
- Hiring: MSC Careers—https://careers.msccruises.com/explorajourneys
- Casting: The Agency Excellent Entertainment—https://excellententertainment.biz

Four Seasons Yachts

- Parent Company: Four Seasons Hotels and Resorts and Marc-Henry Cruise Holdings LTD
- Fleet: 1 ship (~190 pax)
- Category: Ultra-luxury
- HQ: Miami, FL
- Language: English
- Website: https://www.fourseasonsyachts.com
- Hiring and Casting: Four Seasons Yachts Careers—https://careers.fourseasonsyachts.com

Fred. Olsen Cruise Lines

- Parent Company: Bonheur
- Fleet: 3 ships (~600–700 pax each)
- Category: Premium
- HQ: Ipswich, England, UK
- Language: English
- Website: https://www.fredolsencruises.com
- Hiring: Fred. Olsen Cruise Lines—https://www.fredolsencruises.com/careers
- Casting: Pop Up Global—https://popup-global.com

Hapag-Lloyd Cruises

- Parent Company: TUI Group
- Fleet: 5 ships (~230–500 pax each)
- Categories: Luxury, expedition
- HQ: Hamburg, Germany
- Languages: German, English
- Website: https://www.hl-cruises.com
- Hiring: sea chefs—https://www.seachefs.com

Holland America Line

- Parent Company: Carnival Corporation & plc
- Fleet: 11 ships (~1,400–2,600 pax each)
- Category: Premium
- HQ: Seattle, WA
- Language: English
- Website: https://www.hollandamerica.com
- Hiring: Holland America Line—https://www.hollandamerica.com/en/us/about/our-company/careers
- Casting: RWS Global—https://www.rwsglobal.com

Hurtigruten

- Parent Company: Hurtigruten Group
- Fleet: 16 ships (~250–600 pax each)
- Category: Expedition
- HQ: Tromsø, Norway
- Languages: English, Norwegian
- Website: https://www.hurtigruten.com
- Hiring: Hurtigruten Group Careers—https://www.hurtigruten.com/en/careers

Lindblad Cruises

- Parent Company: Lindblad Expeditions Holdings, Inc.
- Fleet: 17 ships (~50–150 pax each)
- Categories: Expedition, luxury
- HQ: New York, NY
- Language: English

- Website: https://www.expeditions.com
- Hiring: Lindblad Careers—https://www.expeditions.com/careers

Marella Cruises

- Parent Company: TUI Group
- Fleet: 5 ships (~1,800–2,000 pax each)
- Category: Premium
- HQ: Luton, England, UK
- Language: English
- Website: https://www.tui.co.uk/cruise
- Hiring: TUI Careers—https://careers.tuigroup.com/en/marella-cruise
- Casting: RWS Global—https://www.rwsglobal.com

Margaritaville at Sea

- Parent Company: Margaritaville Enterprises/Bahamas Paradise Cruise Line
- Fleet: 1 ship (~1,300 pax)
- Category: Mainstream
- HQ: Deerfield Beach, FL
- Language: English
- Website: https://www.margaritaville.com
- Hiring: Margaritaville at Sea Careers—https://www.margaritaville.com/careers
- Casting: Maybury Webb Creative, Inc.—https://kmwcreatives.com

Mein Schiff

- Parent Company: TUI Group and Royal Caribbean Group
- Fleet: 7 ships (~2,500–2,900 pax each)
- Category: Premium
- HQ: Hamburg, Germany
- Language: German
- Website: https://www.meinschiff.com
- Hiring and Casting: sea chefs—https://www.seachefs.com

Mitsui Ocean Cruises

- Parent Company: MOL Cruises, Ltd.
- Fleet: 1 ship (~524 pax)

- Category: Premium
- HQ: Tokyo, Japan
- Language: Japanese
- Website: https://www.mitsuioceancruises.com
- Hiring: V.Ships—https://mitsui.vcrew.com
- Casting: Belinda King Creative Productions—https://www.belindaking.com

MSC Cruises

- Parent Company: MSC Group
- Fleet: 22 ships (~2,500–6,700 pax each)
- Category: Mainstream
- HQ: Geneva, Switzerland
- Languages: English, Italian, Spanish, French, German
- Website: https://www.msccruises.com
- Hiring and Casting: MSC Careers/Entertainment—https://www.careers.msccruises.com

Mystic Cruises

- Parent Company: Mystic Invest Holding
- Fleet: 3 ships (~200 pax each)
- Category: Expedition
- HQ: Porto, Portugal
- Language: English
- Website: https://www.mysticcruises.com
- Hiring: Mystic Invest—https://www.mysticcruises.com/opportunities

Norwegian Cruise Line

- Parent Company: Norwegian Cruise Line Holdings Ltd. (NCLH)
- Fleet: 20 ships (~2,000–4,500 pax each)
- Category: Mainstream
- HQ: Miami, FL
- Language: English
- Website: https://www.ncl.com
- Hiring: NCL Careers—https://careers.ncl.com
- Casting: NCLH Creative Studios—http://nclhcreativestudios.com

Oceania Cruises

- Parent Company: Norwegian Cruise Line Holdings Ltd. (NCLH)
- Fleet: 8 ships (~684–1,250 pax each)
- Category: Premium
- HQ: Miami, Florida
- Language: English
- Website: https://www.oceaniacruises.com
- Hiring: NCL Careers—https://careers.ncl.com
- Casting: NCLH Creative Studios—http://nclhcreativestudios.com

Paul Gauguin Cruises

- Parent Company: Compagnie du Ponant
- Fleet: 1 ship (~330 pax)
- Category: Luxury
- HQ: Marseille, France
- Languages: English, French
- Website: https://www.pgcruises.com
- Hiring and Casting: Paul Gauguin Cruises—https://www.pgcruises.com/careers

Phoenix Reisen

- Parent Company: Phoenix Reisen GmbH
- Fleet: 44 ships (4 ocean, 40 river; ~100–1,200 pax each)
- Category: Premium
- HQ: Bonn, Germany
- Language: German
- Website: https://www.phoenixreisen.com
- Hiring: sea chefs—https://www.seachefs.com

P&O Cruises

- Parent Company: Carnival Corporation & plc
- Fleet: 7 ships (~1,800–5,200 pax each)
- Category: Mainstream
- HQ: Southampton, England, UK
- Language: English
- Website: https://www.pocruises.com

- Hiring: P&O Cruises—https://www.pocruisescareers.co.uk
- Casting: Headliners Theatre Company—https://www.instagram.com/headlinerstheatrecompany

PONANT

- Parent Company: Ponant Explorations Group
- Fleet: 13 ships (~32–264 pax each)
- Category: Expedition
- HQ: Marseille, France
- Languages: French, English
- Website: https://en.ponant.com
- Hiring: Ponant Explorations Group—https://en.ponant.com/careers

Princess Cruise Line

- Parent Company: Carnival Corporation & plc
- Fleet: 16 ships (~2,000–4,300 pax each)
- Category: Premium
- HQ: Santa Clarita, CA
- Language: English
- Website: https://www.princess.com
- Hiring: Princess Cruises—https://www.princess.com/careers
- Casting: Princess Cruises Entertainment—https://www.princesscruisesentertainment.com

Regent Seven Seas Cruises

- Parent Company: Norwegian Cruise Line Holdings Ltd. (NCLH)
- Fleet: 6 ships (~490–750 pax each)
- Category: Ultra-luxury
- HQ: Miami, Florida
- Language: English
- Website: https://www.rssc.com
- Hiring: NCL Careers—https://careers.ncl.com
- Casting: NCLH Creative Studios—http://nclhcreativestudios.com

The Ritz-Carlton Yacht Collection

- Parent Company: Marriott International, Inc.

- Fleet: 3 ships (~298–448 pax each)
- Category: Ultra-luxury
- HQ: Miami, FL
- Language: English
- Website: https://www.ritzcarltonyachtcollection.com
- Hiring: The Ritz-Carlton Yacht Collection—https://careers. ritzcarltonyachtcollection.com/en
- Casting: East West Entertainment Group—https://www.eastwestevents.ae

Royal Caribbean International

- Parent Company: Royal Caribbean Group
- Fleet: 28 ships (~2,000–7,600 pax each)
- Category: Mainstream
- HQ: Miami, FL
- Language: English
- Website: https://www.royalcaribbean.com
- Hiring: Royal Caribbean Careers—https://careers.royalcaribbeangroup. com
- Casting: Royal Caribbean Productions—https:// royalcaribbeanentertainment.com

Saga Cruises

- Parent Company: Saga Group Ltd.
- Fleet: 2 ships (~999 pax each)
- Category: Premium
- HQ: Folkestone, England, UK
- Language: English
- Website: https://travel.saga.co.uk
- Hiring: Saga Careers—https://www.saga.co.uk/careers
- Casting: Belinda King Creative Productions—https://www.belindaking. com

Scenic Luxury Cruises & Tours

- Parent Company: Scenic Group
- Fleet: 16 ships (15 river, 1 ocean; ~140–228 pax each)
- Category: Luxury
- HQ: Newcastle, New South Wales, Australia
- Language: English

- Website: https://www.scenic.com.au
- Hiring: Scenic Careers—https://www.scenic.com.au/careers

Seabourn Cruise Line

- Parent Company: Carnival Corporation & plc
- Fleet: 7 ships (5 ocean, 2 expedition; ~264–600 pax each)
- Categories: Ultra-luxury, expedition
- HQ: Seattle, WA
- Language: English
- Website: https://www.seabourn.com
- Hiring: Seabourn—https://www.seabourn.com/en/us/about/careers
- Casting: Belinda King Creative Productions—https://www.belindaking.com

SeaDream Yacht Club

- Parent Company: Privately owned
- Fleet: 2 ships (~112 pax each)
- Category: Ultra-luxury
- HQ: Oslo, Norway
- Language: English
- Website: https://seadream.com
- Hiring: SeaDream Yacht Club—https://seadream.com/about/careers

Silversea Cruises

- Parent Company: Royal Caribbean Group
- Fleet: 13 ships (6 ocean, 7 expedition; ~100–728 pax each)
- Categories: Ultra-luxury, expedition
- Headquarters: Fontvieille, Monaco
- Language: English
- Website: https://www.silversea.com
- Hiring: V.Ships—https://silversea.vcrew.com
- Casting: Jean Ann Ryan Productions—https://www.jeanannryanproductions.com

Star Clippers

- Parent Company: Star Clippers Ltd.
- Fleet: 3 ships (~170–227 pax each)

- Category: Luxury
- HQ: Monte Carlo, Monaco
- Language: English
- Website: https://www.starclippers.com
- Hiring: Star Clippers—https://www.starclippers-career.com

Swan Hellenic

- Parent Company: Swan Hellenic Ltd.
- Fleet: 3 ships (~150–190 pax each)
- Category: Expedition
- HQ: Nicosia, Cyprus
- Language: English
- Website: https://www.swanhellenic.com
- Hiring: V.Ships—https://swanhellenic.vcrew.com

Uniworld River Cruises

- Parent Company: The Travel Corporation (TTC)
- Fleet: 19 ships (~120–160 pax each)
- Category: Luxury
- HQ: Los Angeles, CA
- Language: English
- Website: https://www.uniworld.com
- Hiring: Uniworld Careers—https://www.uniworld.com/careers

Victoria Mekong Cruises

- Parent Company: Thien Minh Group (TMG)
- Fleet: 1 ship (~70 pax)
- Category: Expedition river
- HQ: Ho Chi Minh City, Vietnam
- Languages: English, Vietnamese
- Website: https://www.victoriamekong.com
- Hiring: Thien Minh Group—https://tmgroup.vn/jobs

Victory Cruise Lines

- Parent Company: Privately owned
- Fleet: 2 ships (~190 pax each)

- Category: Expedition
- HQ: New Albany, IN
- Language: English
- Website: https://victorycruiselines.com
- Hiring: Victory Cruise Lines—https://victorycruiselines.com/careers

Viking Cruises

- Parent Company: Viking Holdings Ltd.
- Fleet: 92 ships (10 ocean, 80 river, 2 expedition; ~190–930 pax each)
- Categories: Luxury, expedition
- HQ: Basel, Switzerland
- Language: English
- Website: https://www.viking.com
- Hiring: Viking Careers—https://www.vikingcareers.com
- Casting: Blackburn International—https://www.blackburninternational.com

Virgin Voyages

- Parent Company: Virgin Group & Bain Capital
- Fleet: 4 ships (~2,770 pax each)
- Category: Premium
- HQ: Plantation, FL
- Language: English
- Website: https://www.virginvoyages.com
- Hiring: Virgin Voyages—https://www.virginvoyages.com/careers
- Casting: Virgin Voyages Entertainment Casting—https://www.leaveyourlegasea.com

VIVA Cruises

- Parent Company: Scylla AG
- Fleet: 10 ships (~140–190 pax each)
- Category: Premium river
- HQ: Düsseldorf, Germany
- Languages: English, German
- Website: https://www.viva-cruises.com
- Hiring: Scylla Hotel Operations—https://www.scylla.com/career

Vodohod

- Parent Company: UCL Holding
- Fleet: 25 ships (~200–300 pax each)
- Category: Premium river
- HQ: Moscow, Russia
- Language: Russian
- Website: https://www.vodohod.com
- Hiring: Vodohod—https://www.vodohod-cruises.com/about/careers

Windstar Cruises

- Parent Company: Xanterra Travel Collection
- Fleet: 6 ships (~148–342 pax each)
- Category: Luxury
- HQ: Seattle, WA
- Language: English
- Website: https://www.windstarcruises.com
- Hiring: Viking Crew—https://www.vikingcrew.com

Appendix C: Cruise Ship Entertainment Agencies

The Agency Excellent Entertainment

- Website: https://www.excellententertainment.biz
- Location: London, England, UK
- Represents: All entertainers

Artists Provider Talent Agency

- Website: https://artistsprovider.com
- Location: Santiago de Compostela, Spain
- Represents: Singers, musicians

Blackburn International

- Website: https://www.blackburninternational.com
- Location: Camberley, England, UK
- Represents: All entertainers

Cindy Thompson Entertainment

- Website: https://cindythompsonentertainment.com
- Location: East Preston, England, UK
- Represents: All entertainers

Cruise Talent

- Website: https://www.cruisetalent.com
- Location: Bristol, England, UK
- Represents: All entertainers

Don Casino Entertainment Agency

- Website: https://www.dcptalent.com
- Location: Miami, FL
- Represents: All entertainers

The Entertainment Consultancy

- Website: https://www.theentertainmentconsultancy.com
- Location: North Yorkshire, England, UK
- Represents: All entertainers

Gary Parkes Music

- Website: https://www.garyparkes.com
- Location: London, England, UK
- Represents: All entertainers

G.L. Berg Entertainment

- Website: https://www.glberg.com
- Location: Minneapolis, MN
- Represents: All entertainers

International Event Bookings (IEB)

- Website: https://internationaleventbookings.com
- Location: Miami, FL
- Represents: Step-on entertainers

iStage Group

- Website: https://www.istagegroup.com
- Location: Sunderland, England, UK
- Represents: Singers, musicians, dancers

Landau Music

- Website: https://www.landaumusic.com
- Location: Solana Beach, CA
- Represents: Singers, musicians

Lime Entertainment

- Website: https://lime.inc
- Location: Ardsley, NY
- Represents: All entertainers

MMEC Entertainment Solutions

- Website: https://www.mmec.com
- Location: Las Vegas, NV
- Represents: All entertainers

Peel Entertainment

- Website: https://www.peeltalent.com
- Location: North Yorkshire, England, UK
- Represents: All entertainers

Premier Entertainment International

- Website: https://premierentertainmentint.com
- Location: Cork, Ireland
- Represents: Singers, musicians

Proship Entertainment

- Website: http://www.proship.com
- Location: Montreal, Quebec, Canada
- Represents: All entertainers

Rising Stars International

- Website: https://www.risingstars.com.ua
- Location: Kharkiv, Ukraine
- Represents: All entertainers

RWS Global

- Website: https://www.rwsglobal.com
- Location: New York, NY
- Represents: All entertainers

Scarlett Entertainment

- Website: https://scarlettentertainment.com
- Location: Las Vegas, NV
- Represents: All entertainers

Seattle Entertainment Group

- Website: https://www.seattletalentbuying.com
- Location: Seattle, WA
- Represents: All entertainers

Suman Entertainment Group

- Website: https://sumanent.com
- Location: Miami, FL
- Represents: All entertainers

TAD Management

- Website: https://tadmgmt.com
- Location: Phoenix, AZ
- Represents: All entertainers

Warshaw Entertainment

- Website: https://www.warshawentertainment.com
- Location: Tamarac, FL
- Represents: All entertainers

Zoë Tyler International

- Website: https://www.zoetylerinternational.com
- Location: Celebration, FL
- Represents: Guest entertainers

Appendix D: Suggested Resources

Cruise Industry and Ship-Tracking Tools

- **MarineTraffic**—https://www.marinetraffic.com
  Real-time global ship tracking app.
- **CruiseMapper**—https://www.cruisemapper.com
  Interactive cruise ship tracker.
- **Cruise Critic**—https://www.cruisecritic.com
  Passenger reviews, ship details, and active forums.
- **Crew Center**—http://www.crew-center.com
  Site run by former crew members offering tools for life onboard.
- **SHIPLIFE**—https://shiplife.org
  Online hub about working and living on ships.

Performance Materials and Show Resources

- **Sheet Music Plus**—https://www.sheetmusicplus.com
  Vast online sheet-music library.
- **Show Band Charts**—https://www.showbandcharts.com
  Professional sheet-music catalog with downloadable charts.
- **Musicnotes**—https://www.musicnotes.com
  Digital and transposable downloads of sheet music.
- **MuseScore**—https://www.musescore.org
  Open-source music notation program and library of user-uploaded scores.
- **Scribd**—https://www.scribd.com
  A digital library subscription service.
- **forScore**—https://www.forscore.co
  Leading iOS sheet-music reader app for performers.
- **Karaoke Version**—https://www.karaoke-version.com
  Customizable backing tracks with click options.

- **Motion Array**—https://www.motionarray.com
  Video background loops, animations, and stock footage.
- **Storyblocks**—https://www.storyblocks.com
  Stock-media platform offering unlimited downloads of royalty-free video.
- **Canva**—https://www.canva.com
  User-friendly online design platform.
- **Adobe Creative Cloud**—https://www.adobe.com/creativecloud
  Suite of professional creative software.
- **QLab**—https://www.figure53.com/qlab
  Industry-standard show control software for Mac.
- **Easy Song Licensing**—https://www.easysonglicensing.com
  Service to legally obtain mechanical, synchronization, and master-use licenses.
- **Songfile** (Harry Fox Agency)—https://www.harryfox.com/songfile
  Online tool to obtain mechanical licenses to legally distribute cover songs.

Training and Certifications

- **STCW.online**—https://www.stcw.online
  Online training platform offering STCW-compliant courses.
- **STCW Direct**—https://www.stcwdirect.com
  Search and compare maritime training providers worldwide.
- **Seven Seas Preparatory Academy**—https://www.sevenseasprep.com
  Offers blended programs combining online theory with in-person training.
- **Northeast Maritime Online**—https://northeastmaritimeonline.com
  Provides STCW theory modules online followed by in-person assessments.
- **VIRSEC**—https://www.virsec.org
  UK-based provider offering approved STCW courses online.

Audition and Casting Resources

- **Backstage**—https://www.backstage.com
  Cruise ship casting calls and general entertainment jobs.
- **Casting Networks**—https://www.castingnetworks.com
  Global casting site for stage, screen, and cruise ship opportunities.

- **Playbill Jobs**—https://www.playbill.com/jobs
  Theater and cruise entertainment listings.
- **Actors Access**—https://www.actorsaccess.com
  Online casting platform where performers can find and register for auditions.
- **Spotlight**—https://www.spotlight.com
  UK-based casting platform used for stage, screen, and cruise auditions.
- **YAP Tracker**—https://www.yaptracker.com
  Online platform listing opera and classical music opportunities worldwide.

Miscellaneous Helpful Tools

- **Dropbox**—https://www.dropbox.com
  Cloud storage for large-file sharing.
- **WhatsApp**—https://www.whatsapp.com
  Messaging app widely used by crew, often available without charge on crew Wi-Fi networks.
- **Flighty**—https://www.flighty.com
  Flight-tracking app with real-time updates and seamless calendar integration.
- **GPSmyCity**—https://www.gpsmycity.com
  Travel app offering self-guided walking tours and offline maps.

BIBLIOGRAPHY

Applefeld Olson, Cathy. "Live Music's Tale of Two Recoveries: Indie Venues Still Struggle Despite 'Golden' Return of Touring." *Forbes*, March 18, 2024. https://www.forbes.com/sites/cathyolson/2024/03/18/live-musics-tale-of-two-recoveries-indie-venues-still-struggle-despite-golden-return-of-touring.

Carnival Entertainment. "Why Carnival?" Accessed August 15, 2025. https://www.carnivalentertainment.com/about/why-carnival.

Chang, Brittany. "I've Sailed on Royal Caribbean, Carnival, and Norwegian Ships. Here's Which Was My Favorite—and How to Choose the Right Cruise for You." *Business Insider*, November 16, 2024. https://www.businessinsider.com/royal-caribbean-vs-carnival-norwegian-cruises-compared-review-2024-11.

Church, Eve. "Women in Maritime: The Stats You Need to Know." *Martide*, accessed August 15, 2025. https://www.martide.com/en/blog/women-in-maritime-stats-to-know.

Cohen, Randy. "NEA Budget Losses." Americans for the Arts, accessed February 22, 2025. https://www.americansforthearts.org/sites/default/files/5.%202018%20NEA%20Discretionary%20Spending.pdf.

Cooper, Michael. "New York City Opera Files for Bankruptcy." *New York Times*, October 3, 2013. https://www.nytimes.com/2013/10/04/arts/music/new-york-city-opera-files-for-bankruptcy.html?smid=nytcore-ios-share&referringSource=articleShare.

Crockett, Zachary. "The Economics of Cruise Ships." *Hustle*, updated June 24, 2024. https://thehustle.co/the-economics-of-cruise-ships.

Cruise Lines International Association. "2022 Global Market Report." Accessed August 15, 2025. https://cruising.org/sites/default/files/2025-03/2022%201R%20CLIA%20001%20Overview%20Global%20FINAL.pdf.

Cruise Lines International Association. "State of the Cruise Industry Report." April 9, 2024. https://cruising.org/sites/default/files/2025-03/2024%20State%20of%20the%20Cruise%20Industry%20Report_updated%20050824_Web.pdf.

Cruise Lines International Association. "State of the Cruise Industry Report 2025." May 22, 2025. https://cruising.org/sites/default/files/2025-07/State%20of%20the%20Cruise%20Industry%20Report%202025.pdf.

Cullinan, Charlotte. "Must-Watch Cruise Ship Shows: The Best Live Acts This Year." *Love Exploring*, July 10, 2022. https://www.loveexploring.com/galleries/amp/141637/mustwatch-cruise-ship-shows-the-best-live-acts-this-year.

Gibson, Rebecca. "Millennials Leading the Charge for Luxury Cruising, Says CLIA." *Cruise & Ferry*, January 29, 2018. https://www.cruiseandferry.net/articles/millennials-leading-the-charge-for-luxury-cruising-says-clia.

Grisler, Alissa. "Best Luxury Cruise Lines." *U.S. News & World Report*, updated November 18, 2024. https://travel.usnews.com/cruises/best-cruise-lines.

Hardingham-Gill, Tamara. "'The Love Boat': How a TV Show Transformed the Cruise Industry." *CNN*, February 14, 2025. https://edition.cnn.com/travel/the-love-boat-how-a-tv-show-transformed-cruise-industry/index.html.

Hernández, Javier C. "Met Opera Taps Its Endowment Again to Weather Downturn." *New York Times*, January 25, 2024. https://www.nytimes.com/2024/01/25/arts/music/met-opera-endowment-finances.html?smid=nytcore-ios-share&referringSource=articleShare.

Paulson, Michael. "A Crisis in America's Theaters Leaves Prestigious Stages Dark." *New York Times*, updated July 25, 2023. https://www.nytimes.com/2023/07/23/theater/regional-theater-crisis.html?smid=nytcore-ios-share&referringSource=articleShare.

Sayles, Jill. "Discover the World's Most Beautiful Cruise Ships That Rival Five-Star Hotels." *MSN*, accessed February 21, 2025. https://www.msn.com/en-us/travel/tripideas/discover-the-world-s-most-beautiful-cruise-ships-that-rival-five-star-hotels/ss-AA1oK8Xy.

Walsh, David. "Syracuse Opera Files for Bankruptcy, One of Numerous Smaller Companies in the US in Trouble or Simply Closing Down." *World Socialist Web Site*, December 26, 2024. https://www.wsws.org/en/articles/2024/12/27/rqfc-d27.html.

Warshaw Entertainment. "Top 5 Reasons to Work on a Cruise Ship as a Musician, Vocalist or Performer." Accessed February 22, 2025. https://www.warshawentertainment.com/blog/top-5-reasons-to-work-on-a-cruise-ship-as-a-musician-vocalist-or-performer.

INDEX